Annals of Life Insurance Medicine

Volume 4

Editorial Committee:
R. D. C. Brackenridge, London
B. A. Bradlow, Johannesburg
J. E. Clarke, Melbourne
Eugene V. Higgins, New York
J. C. Sinclair, Toronto
E. Tanner, Zurich
Harry E. Ungerleider, New York

Editor:
Swiss Reinsurance Company Zurich

With 26 Figures

Springer-Verlag
Berlin · Heidelberg · New York 1969

ISBN-13: 978-3-642-85622-8 e-ISBN-13: 978-3-642-85620-4

DOI: 10.1007/978-3-642-85620-4

Softcover reprint of the hardcover 1st edition 1969

Contents

An investigation into the validity of the multiple table hypothesis as a basis for the underwriting of substandard risks in life assurance

H. W. Kreis

1. Introduction

It might seem surprising at first glance that one should wish to add a further publication to those which have already appeared on the subject of the multiple table hypothesis. However, on closer inspection of the literature available it soon becomes clear that this hypothesis is an ever recurrent topic for discussion, especially after the appearance of statistical studies in this respect. JECKLIN in particular has recently written in support of the application of this method in a series of studies [1, 2, 3, 4]. In reply to an article by SACHS [5] and his colleagues, he states at one point [6]:

"The whole problem of selection is therefore clearly more complex than one would naturally assume. Nevertheless we are far from advocating the multiple table hypothesis simply for reasons of convenience as the only proper underwriting basis. If the results of statistical studies should show that a more dynamic method of assessing extra mortality is required, then practice would have to adapt itself accordingly, not so much for the sake of premium computation but rather because of the effects this would have on policy reserves. There should be few special technical difficulties involved since the technical handling of substandard risks is very adaptable, as the author has already had occasion to show [1]."

In his study "Betrachtungen zum Sterblichkeitsverlauf erhöhter Risiken" [4], edited in 1961, Jecklin refers to the studies made by H. v. Denffer, G. Berger and J. Gugumus [7] who reach the common conclusion that the multiple table hypothesis is quite consistent with the actual mortality experience of substandard risks, at least during the first ten years of assurance. He furthermore examines the *Impairment Study 1951* of the Society of Actuaries, a work which includes comprehensive and detailed tables on the mortality experience of substandard risks with years of entry 1935—1949. In this paper he calls repeatedly for further statistical studies [8], as he believes that new statistical evidence of this kind is necessary before more dynamic methods for the assessment of substandard mortality can be adopted.

The present study is based on just such a statistical investigation, carried out on the basis of observation data collected at the Swiss Reinsurance Company in Zurich. We have departed from the above-mentioned statistics in so far as we have calculated two-dimensional tables by means of a computer, grouped on the one hand according to policy years and on the other hand according to the attained age. In his last-named study Jecklin already refers to the possibility of producing such tables, but expresses the fear that in practice there would be too few figures for statistical significance in the individual sub-groups [9]. Despite these considerations we have ventured into the task and are already in a position to assert that the results have justified our efforts.

2. Description of the observation data

2.1. Data collection

The Life Department of the Swiss Reinsurance Company in Zurich compiles mortality statistics which include each risk for which the following conditions are fulfilled:

a) The reassurance covers the death risk.

b) A medical examination was carried out in connection with the inspection of the proposal, a report of which was handed over by the ceding company to the reassurer.

c) The proposed duration of the reassurance is at least one year.

2.2. Scope of the observation data

In order to obtain a certain homogeneity in a mortality investigation, general conditions have to be adopted which the risks to be evaluated must satisfy. Unfortunately the amount of experience data available is thus further reduced. In the present study we have examined only those risks which meet the following conditions:

a) Sex: male
b) Race: Caucasian
c) Domicile: Europe
d) Age at entry: more than 19 and less than 70
e) Issue year of assurance: between 1946 and 1964

The years 1946—1965 were taken as the period of observation. In contrast to the study by Gugumus and Berger [7], we chose a relatively long period because we wished to examine the validity of the multiple table hypothesis beyond the tenth year of assurance. In order to eliminate as far as possible the distorting effects of the Second World War, we have only included risks assured as from the beginning of 1946. We were unable to extend our period of observation beyond the 31st December, 1965, as at the time of processing, reports on cancellations and claims for the year 1966 were still outstanding. Furthermore, we only investigated risks up to 69 years of age. The observation material so chosen comprises the following:

number of cessions	50,765
number of life-years observed	315,183.5
number of deaths	2,402
average period of observation	6.2 years

The authors of the *Impairment Study 1951* point out in their comments various provisos which must be borne in mind in the interpretation of the results achieved [10]. Unfortunately these provisos apply in essence to all extra mortality statistics. Nevertheless, by means of the aforementioned restriction of observation data we were able to obtain certain improvements as — in contrast with the *Impairment Study* — we analysed only records which had been coded by the same team and which did not include female risks.

However this improvement in the homogeneity of the observation data proved costly since scarcely 60% of the cessions effected during the years 1946 to 1964 were covered by our investigation, i. e. 60% of those risks for which punched cards had been prepared in accordance with the above guide-lines.

2.3. Construction of the tables and breakdown of the observation data

Our investigation was particularly directed towards answering the question of how well the empirical results agree with the multiple table hypothesis. For this purpose we drew up two-dimensional tables — on the one hand according to policy years and on the other according to attained age. For the individual sections of the table, we calculated the actual number of deaths and the number of expected deaths on the basis of normal mortality as well as the mortality ratio, i. e. the relationship between the actual number and the expected number of deaths. The first table of this kind appears under sub-section 3.1. "Comparative mortality".

For the i-th section of the table, which covers the duration a_i to e_i and the attained ages α_i to ε_i, the number of expected deaths assuming normal mortality is calculated as follows:

$$\text{Number of expected deaths} = \sum_{j=1}^{z} \sum_{t=a_i}^{e_i} f_{j,t} \quad r_{j,t} \quad q_{x_{j,t}}(k_{j,t}),$$

where

$$f_{j,t} = \begin{cases} 1, \text{ when } \alpha_i \leqq x_j + t - 1 \leqq \varepsilon_i \\ 0, \text{ when } x_j + t - 1 < \alpha_i \text{ or } x_j + t - 1 > \varepsilon_i, \end{cases}$$

$k_{j,t}$ = calendar year during which the t-th assurance year of the risk j began (As stated in the explanations under point 3.1., our comparative mortality is also dependent on the calendar year.),

$q_{x_{j,t}}(k_{j,t})$ = normal probability of death of the risk j at age $x_j + t - 1$ in calendar year $k_{j,t}$,

$r_{j,t}$ = period of observation of risk j in calendar year $k_{j,t}$ with $0 \leqq r_{j,t} \leqq 1$,

x_j = age at entry of risk j in year $k_{j,1}$, rounded off to the nearer year,

z = number of risks entered in the corresponding table, i. e. the number of the last risk if these are numbered consecutively 1, 2, 3, ... z.

As JECKLIN and SACHS both rightly emphasize [11], certain arbitrary factors enter inevitably into all studies of mortality. This is particularly true of studies such as ours, where sub-division of the observation data is unavoidable. We tried to maintain equal and statistically significant sub-sections in this division. Thus we classified our risks according to either the estimated extra mortality only or the medical characteristics only. A division according to classes of mortality and at the same time according to impairments would hardly have produced a sufficiently broad empirical basis of case figures in the tables.

2.4. Statistical testing methods

In order to investigate whether the deviations from the multiple table hypothesis found in our study are to be considered as significant we systematically applied two well-proven testing methods.

2.4.1. χ^2-test

The first method we chose was the χ^2-test. We applied it to the tables in section 3. "Mortality Experience" and also to a limited extent to the tables in section 4.

"Investigation into the validity of the multiple table hypothesis". According to the particular question involved, we included only the individual figures without totals in the χ^2-calculation or then only the corresponding totals.

The formula for this calculation is:

$$\chi^2 = \sum_{i=1}^{n} \frac{(f_i - r_i T)^2}{r_i T}$$

with

$$r_i = \frac{\varphi_i}{\Theta} \text{ and } T = \sum_{i=1}^{n} f_i \text{ and } \Theta = \sum_{i=1}^{n} \varphi_i.$$

where

i = table section number
n = number of table sections considered
f_i = actual number of deaths in table section i
φ_i = number of expected deaths according to normal mortality in table section i.

The number of degrees of freedom for the assessment of the value of χ^2 emerged as the value $(n-1)$ with this method in each single test.

2.4.2. *Positive and negative deviations test*

In section 4. "Investigation into the validity of the multiple table hypothesis", we have carried out as a second testing method, a positive and negative deviations test. Explanations and corresponding definitions may be found at the beginning of that section.

2.4.3. *Coordination of testing methods*

The χ^2-test gives indications of the absolute amount of the deviations, but not of their direction. The deviations test, on the other hand, shows the direction but not the extent. In order to facilitate more complete control and comprehensive assessment we applied both testing methods. The application of both of these methods did not, however, lead to the same conclusions as to the justification of the multiple table hypothesis for all observation data. In order to obtain definite confirmation of one or the other, further investigation would be necessary. Such additional investigation goes beyond the scope of this work and must be dealt with in later studies.

2.4.4. *Conditions of significance*

The tests, which are intended to show whether the deviation of an actual figure from the hypothetical, expected figure, should be regarded as significant, are based on threshold values corresponding to a probability of error of 1% (resp. 5%). This means that a deviation may be called significant if the probability of its arising by chance is smaller than 1%, or random when the same probability is more than 5%. We consider the area between 1% and 5% as a kind of "no-man's land" from which no positive conclusions can be drawn.

2.5. Mortality by number of policies and lives assured

The data collection method previously described is based on the principle of mortality according to the number of policies, as the drawing up of statistics by lives assured would involve too much administrative work. However, wherever necessary, and particularly in the investigations into the causes of death, we have counted not only the number of policies but also the number of deaths involved. We would expressly point out that our results are therefore coloured by the difference between mortality by the number of policies and mortality by lives assured.

3. Mortality experience

3.1. Comparative mortality

At regular intervals the Swiss Reinsurance Company draws up for various geographical regions statistical records of the mortality experience in respect of risks reinsured at standard conditions. For the comparative mortality we drew on the tables for Europe covering the period of observation. The years observed thus came under the influence of the secular improvement in mortality. As Ederer, Axtell and Cutler [12] have already pointed out, inaccurate results ensue if this improvement is not taken into consideration in the test groups of medical/statistical investigations. For the sake of simplicity we made such allowance by means of a linear interpolation, justification for which was found *inter alia* in a study by Wettenschwiler [13].

The probability of death upon which the calculation of the number of expected deaths in our tables is based depends therefore as far as the individual risk is concerned not only on the attained age but also on the calendar year.

First of all we examined the suitability of the comparative mortality chosen for our study material. We refer in this connection to the explanations given under 2.1. As indicated, the present study deals only with risks examined medically at entry. The above-mentioned mortality tables are based, however, on the total of standard risks, i. e. also on those underwritten by the ceding company and for which no medical papers were submitted.

The risks accepted at standard conditions and examined in the present study thus represent a portion of those which form in their totality the calculation material for the mortality tables mentioned. Obviously the next step was to determine the suitability of our comparative mortality by applying it to this portion of risks. This table produced the following picture:

Table I. *Standard risks*

Number of risks: 20,128

Attained age		Policy years					
		1—2 yrs	3—5 yrs	6—10 yrs	11—15 yrs	16—20 yrs	1—20 yrs
20—29	Actual deaths	6	3	—	—	—	9
	Expected deaths	4.67	3.45	0.72	0.01	—	8.85
	Mortality ratio	128%	87%	0%	0%	—	102%
30—39	Actual deaths	25	21	12	1	1	60
	Expected deaths	21.29	24.84	13.15	2.93	0.12	62.33
	Mortality ratio	117%	85%	91%	34%	833%	96%
40—49	Actual deaths	34	54	42	20	3	153
	Expected deaths	33.17	51.81	45.25	16.86	3.13	150.22
	Mortality ratio	103%	104%	93%	119%	96%	102%
50—59	Actual deaths	25	51	76	43	18	213
	Expected deaths	26.62	51.91	67.96	43.52	14.28	204.29
	Mortality ratio	94%	98%	112%	99%	126%	104%
60—69	Actual deaths	1	24	51	30	15	121
	Expected deaths	8.23	20.96	39.00	36.04	13.72	117.95
	Mortality ratio	12%	115%	131%	83%	109%	103%
20—69	Actual deaths	91	153	181	94	37	556
	Expected deaths	93.98	152.97	166.08	99.36	31.25	543.64
	Mortality ratio	97%	100%	109%	95%	118%	102%

a) *Mortality ratio in the totals column 'policy years 1—20'*. For the whole period of observation of the individual risks the mortality ratio lies very near to 100%.

b) *Mortality ratio in the totals line 'attained age 20—69'*. For all attained ages together, the mortality ratio for each group of policy years is in the region of 100%. It is a remarkable fact that there are no signs in the first two years of the selection which otherwise usually affects all assured risks. In contrast with other studies of substandard risks [14], we have used aggregate tables for our comparative mortality because select tables were only available for a part of the observation period. Thus in the first two years of assurance a mortality ratio of significantly less than 100% may be expected. The scope of this study did not allow the investigation of the absence of selection; we were only able to ascertain that in cases of death the ratio of policies to persons was 1.31 for the first two years and 1.11 for the remaining years (also calculated for all ages). We believe that the difference between the corresponding ratios for the business in force would not be as great as this. Therefore we assume that persons dying with several policies would in fact partially obscure the effects of selection in the first two years.

c) *Mortality ratio in the inner sections of the table.* The deviation of the mortality ratio is of course greater in the inner table sections than in the totals sections. With one exception (Attained age 60—69, policy years 1—2), which nevertheless falls within the selection period, the extreme deviations of more than one third, i. e. a mortality ratio of below 67% or above 133%, are to be found in the sections with less than five expected deaths. When the number of expected deaths is this small, an actual death more or less makes a difference of 21% — 10,000% (!).

As testing by means of the χ^2-test with Yates' correction revealed, there is in fact no significant discrepancy between our mortality experience with standard risks and our comparative mortality. We are therefore justified in using this comparative mortality as the standard mortality for our study.

3.2. Total observation data

The following table II shows the mortality experience for the total observation data without further sub-division. As already mentioned, the study material consists of a mixture of standard and substandard risks. The portion of standard risks showed the trend indicated in table I under point 3.1. The total study material appears therefore as follows:

Table II. *All risks*
Number of risks: 50,765

Attained age		Policy years					
		1—2 yrs	3—5 yrs	6—10 yrs	11—15 yrs	16—20 yrs	1—20 yrs
20—29	Actual deaths	16	12	3	—	—	31
	Expected deaths	11.25	8.65	1.81	0.01	—	21.72
	Mortality ratio	142%	139%	166%	0%	—	143%
30—39	Actual deaths	59	62	58	9	1	189
	Expected deaths	49.10	60.58	37.06	7.84	0.51	155.09
	Mortality ratio	120%	102%	157%	115%	196%	122%
40—49	Actual deaths	118	207	168	49	16	558
	Expected deaths	86.52	135.65	127.50	47.75	10.77	408.19
	Mortality ratio	136%	153%	132%	103%	149%	137%
50—59	Actual deaths	118	280	349	228	69	1,044
	Expected deaths	94.18	178.62	226.01	127.79	43.73	670.33
	Mortality ratio	125%	157%	154%	178%	158%	156%
60—69	Actual deaths	30	124	232	136	58	580
	Expected deaths	33.85	85.35	153.36	112.62	40.33	425.51
	Mortality ratio	89%	145%	151%	121%	144%	136%
20—69	Actual deaths	341	685	810	422	144	2,402
	Expected deaths	274.90	468.85	545.74	296.01	95.34	1,680.84
	Mortality ratio	124%	146%	148%	143%	151%	143%

a) *Mortality ratio in the totals column 'policy years 1—20'.* The mortality ratio for the individual age groups varies between 122% and 156%, where deviations from the average value of 143% are to be regarded as significant.

b) *Mortality ratio in the totals line 'attained age 20—69'.* Here we observe values of 124% for the first two years and of 143% to 151% for the remaining years. The hypothesis that selection is present in the first two years and that the value for the remaining duration is constant survives the χ^2-test and cannot be rejected.

c) *Mortality ratio in the inner sections of the table.* The relative fluctuations compared with the average values in the totals sections again appear here. It is remarkable that no selection is present during the first two years for the age groups 20—29, 30—39 and 40—49. The same phenomenon has already been observed with the standard risks described under point 3.1 and which form part of the table in question. Here too we found a preponderance of the ratio of policies to persons for the groups not affected by selection. We examined the hypothesis that the mortality ratio as from the third year is constant within one age group and found that this is in fact the case for all age groups.

3.3. Substandard risks

3.3.1. All risks

Table II revealed the development of the total observation data chosen for the study; the standard risks therein were dealt with in table I. The mortality experience of substandard risks which represent the difference between this one part and the whole will be shown in table III.

a) *Mortality ratio in the totals column 'policy years 1—20'.* The mortality ratio for the individual age groups fluctuates considerably and the deviations from the average value of 162% are statistically significant.

b) *Mortality ratio in the totals line 'attained age 20—69'.* Here we perceive statistically significant selection at the beginning and then a surprisingly constant value as from the third year of assurance.

c) *Mortality ratio in the inner sections of the table.* The selection in the first two years affects all but the age group 40—49. For the remaining groups we again tested the hypothesis that the mortality ratio within one age group is constant as from the third year. The fluctuations in the age group 40—49 are no longer random because of the column 'policy years 11—15'.

Of course the special features of tables I and III appear more or less conspicuously in table II, since the latter is a combination of the other two.

Before proceeding to the tables with sub-division by medical impairments, we shall deal in the next section with the mortality experience by extra mortality class.

Table III. *Substandard risks*
Number of risks: 30,637

Attained age		Policy years 1—2 yrs	3—5 yrs	6—10 yrs	11—15 yrs	16—20 yrs	1—20 yrs
20—29	Actual deaths	10	9	3	—	—	22
	Expected deaths	6.58	5.20	1.09	—	—	12.87
	Mortality ratio	152%	173%	275%	—	—	171%
30—39	Actual deaths	34	41	46	8	—	129
	Expected deaths	27.81	35.74	23.91	4.91	0.39	92.76
	Mortality ratio	122%	115%	192%	163%	0%	139%
40—49	Actual deaths	84	153	126	29	13	405
	Expected deaths	53.35	83.84	82.25	30.89	7.64	257.97
	Mortality ratio	157%	182%	153%	94%	170%	157%
50—59	Actual deaths	93	229	273	185	51	831
	Expected deaths	67.56	126.71	158.05	84.27	29.45	466.04
	Mortality ratio	138%	181%	173%	220%	173%	178%
60—69	Actual deaths	29	100	181	106	43	459
	Expected deaths	25.62	64.39	114.36	76.58	26.61	307.56
	Mortality ratio	113%	155%	158%	138%	162%	149%
20—69	Actual deaths	250	532	629	328	107	1,846
	Expected deaths	180.92	315.88	379.66	196.65	64.09	1,137.20
	Mortality ratio	138%	168%	166%	167%	167%	162%

3.3.2. Substandard risks of classes 1—8

3.3.2.1. Introductory remarks

The multiple table method expresses the mortality of enhanced risks by increasing the mortality for standard risks by a constant percentage throughout the duration of the assurance. The sign α has become generally adopted for the extra mortality rate, and consequently we obtain q_x' for the probability of death of the substandard risks, expressing that for standard risks as q_x, as

$$q_x' = (1 + \alpha)\, q_x .$$

In practice the extra mortality ratio α is not allowed to vary continuously, but its range of values is divided into fixed classes, each being characterized by an average α. The division is as follows:

Extra mortality class	Extra mortality rate	Extra mortality class	Extra mortality rate
1	25%	7	250%
2	50%	8	300%
3	75%	9	400%
4	100%	10	500%
5	150 %	11	600% and more
6	200%		

Separate tables of l_x and related commutation figures are calculated for the individual extra mortality classes. With the calculating machines now at our disposal the amount of work involved is insignificant, so that the approximation formulae used in previous years, particularly by JECKLIN [2], have lost some of their practical value.

3.3.2.2. Division according to extra mortality classes

A total of 30,637 substandard risks fell within our observation data. These were divided up into individual extra mortality classes as follows:

Class	No. of risks	Years of observation	No. of deaths
1	7,726	56,004.0	412
2	8,782	58,007.0	468
3	4,982	32,303.5	312
4	4,253	26,471.0	303
5—8	3,538	20,389.5	288
Remainder	1,356	7,464.5	63
	30,637	200,639.5	1,846

Classes 5—8 were grouped together because they were so limited in size compared with classes 1—4 and the table sections were thus so sparsely filled that the figures would hardly have been representative. The group described as 'Remainder' contains the few risks falling under classes 9—11 as well as those which were not placed in an extra mortality class when rated. They are therefore substandard by virtue of single or temporary extra premiums, liens or exclusion clauses. These allowances for increased risks are partially combined or are applied in addition to the grouping into an extra mortality class. The proportion of the group 'Remainder' is small; with regard to the number of risks, years of observation and number of deaths it lies between 2.4% and 2.7% measured against the total observation data, and between 3.4% and 4.4% measured against the substandard risks.

3.3.2.3. Mortality experience

Detailed figures for each of the six groups mentioned in the foregoing paragraph are shown in tables IV—IX.

Owing to its non-homogeneous constitution table IX has not been taken into consideration in the following remarks:

a) Mortality ratio in the totals column 'policy years 1—20'. As in tables II and III, we observe considerable fluctuations in the individual age groups. A χ^2-test revealed however that they are only significant in table V of extra mortality class 2. In the totals line for all ages we obtain a value in tables IV—VII which lies very near to the average value for the corresponding class. This fact would seem to confirm the multiple table hypothesis, the balance which is repeat-

Table IV. *Risks falling under the extra mortality class 1*
Number of risks: 7,726

Attained age		Policy years 1—2 yrs	3—5 yrs	6—10 yrs	11—15 yrs	16—20 yrs	1—20 yrs
20—29	Actual deaths	2	—	—	—	—	2
	Expected deaths	1.19	0.96	0.23	—	—	2.38
	Mortality ratio	168%	0%	0%	—	—	84%
30—39	Actual deaths	7	10	6	—	—	23
	Expected deaths	6.90	8.98	6.03	1.28	0.10	23.29
	Mortality ratio	101%	111%	100%	0%	0%	99%
40—49	Actual deaths	17	25	28	7	2	79
	Expected deaths	14.85	23.82	24.61	9.44	2.46	75.18
	Mortality ratio	114%	105%	114%	74%	81%	105%
50—59	Actual deaths	24	57	54	50	15	200
	Expected deaths	19.47	37.90	48.50	28.06	9.78	143.71
	Mortality ratio	123%	150%	111%	178%	153%	139%
60—69	Actual deaths	5	20	49	22	12	108
	Expected deaths	7.83	19.36	35.54	27.69	11.19	101.61
	Mortality ratio	64%	103%	138%	79%	107%	106%
20—69	Actual deaths	55	112	137	79	29	412
	Expected deaths	50.24	91.02	114.91	66.47	23.53	346.17
	Mortality ratio	109%	123%	119%	119%	123%	119%

Table V. *Risks falling under the extra mortality class 2*
Number of risks: 8,782

Attained age		Policy years 1—2 yrs	3—5 yrs	6—10 yrs	11—15 yrs	16—20 yrs	1—20 yrs
20—29	Actual deaths	2	2	—	—	—	4
	Expected deaths	2.11	1.66	0.34	—	—	4.11
	Mortality ratio	95%	120%	0%	—	—	97%
30—39	Actual deaths	9	11	12	2	—	34
	Expected deaths	8.47	10.87	7.37	1.69	0.15	28.55
	Mortality ratio	106%	101%	163%	118%	0%	119%
40—49	Actual deaths	24	29	31	12	4	100
	Expected deaths	14.84	24.03	24.88	9.37	2.36	75.48
	Mortality ratio	162%	121%	125%	128%	169%	132%
50—59	Actual deaths	22	57	83	47	15	224
	Expected deaths	16.97	32.88	41.44	23.94	9.15	124.38
	Mortality ratio	130%	173%	200%	196%	164%	180%
60—69	Actual deaths	4	26	39	23	14	106
	Expected deaths	6.08	16.70	30.71	19.93	7.53	80.95
	Mortality ratio	66%	156%	127%	115%	186%	131%
20—69	Actual deaths	61	125	165	84	33	468
	Expected deaths	48.47	86.14	104.74	54.93	19.19	313.47
	Mortality ratio	126%	145%	158%	153%	172%	149%

Table VI. *Risks falling under the extra mortality class 3*
Number of risks: 4,982

Attained age		Policy years 1—2 yrs	3—5 yrs	6—10 yrs	11—15 yrs	16—20 yrs	1—20 yrs
20—29	Actual deaths	1	3	1	—	—	5
	Expected deaths	1.21	0.93	0.18	—	—	2.32
	Mortality ratio	83%	323%	556%	—	—	216%
30—39	Actual deaths	5	3	9	2	—	19
	Expected deaths	4.72	6.01	3.93	0.73	0.04	15.43
	Mortality ratio	106%	50%	229%	274%	0%	123%
40—49	Actual deaths	18	31	23	5	4	81
	Expected deaths	8.16	13.27	13.37	5.14	1.25	41.19
	Mortality ratio	221%	234%	172%	97%	320%	197%
50—59	Actual deaths	15	32	36	35	6	124
	Expected deaths	10.23	19.09	23.98	13.91	5.16	72.37
	Mortality ratio	147%	168%	150%	252%	116%	171%
60—69	Actual deaths	5	14	33	28	3	83
	Expected deaths	3.63	9.20	18.18	12.28	3.72	47.01
	Mortality ratio	138%	152%	182%	228%	81%	177%
20—69	Actual deaths	44	83	102	70	13	312
	Expected deaths	27.95	48.50	59.64	32.06	10.17	178.32
	Mortality ratio	157%	171%	171%	218%	128%	175%

Table VII. *Risks falling under the extra mortality class 4*
Number of risks: 4,253

Attained age		Policy years 1—2 yrs	3—5 yrs	6—10 yrs	11—15 yrs	16—20 yrs	1—20 yrs
20—29	Actual deaths	2	1	1	—	—	4
	Expected deaths	0.95	0.78	0.17	—	—	1.90
	Mortality ratio	211%	128%	588%	—	—	211%
30—39	Actual deaths	7	7	6	3	—	23
	Expected deaths	3.85	5.07	3.43	0.67	0.07	13.09
	Mortality ratio	182%	138%	175%	448%	0%	176%
40—49	Actual deaths	6	37	17	2	2	64
	Expected deaths	7.14	10.85	9.74	3.85	0.98	32.56
	Mortality ratio	84%	341%	175%	52%	204%	197%
50—59	Actual deaths	12	47	41	29	10	139
	Expected deaths	9.30	16.80	20.18	9.65	2.92	58.85
	Mortality ratio	129%	280%	203%	301%	342%	236%
60—69	Actual deaths	7	23	22	13	8	73
	Expected deaths	3.45	8.46	14.87	9.69	2.64	39.11
	Mortality ratio	203%	272%	148%	134%	303%	187%
20—69	Actual deaths	34	115	87	47	20	303
	Expected deaths	24.69	41.96	48.39	23.86	6.61	145.51
	Mortality ratio	138%	274%	180%	197%	303%	208%

Table VIII. *Risks falling under the extra mortality classes 5—8*
Number of risks: 3,538

Attained age		Policy years 1—2 yrs	3—5 yrs	6—10 yrs	11—15 yrs	16—20 yrs	1—20 yrs
20—29	Actual deaths	3	3	1	—	—	7
	Expected deaths	0.87	0.71	0.14	—	—	1.72
	Mortality ratio	345%	423%	714%	—	—	407%
30—39	Actual deaths	5	7	13	1	—	26
	Expected deaths	2.74	3.49	2.45	0.45	0.03	9.16
	Mortality ratio	182%	201%	531%	222%	0%	284%
40—49	Actual deaths	14	21	23	3	1	62
	Expected deaths	6.08	8.50	7.00	2.28	0.47	24.33
	Mortality ratio	230%	247%	329%	132%	213%	255%
50—59	Actual deaths	16	28	53	20	5	122
	Expected deaths	8.58	14.81	17.33	6.58	1.75	49.05
	Mortality ratio	186%	189%	306%	304%	286%	249%
60—69	Actual deaths	4	11	35	15	6	71
	Expected deaths	2.78	7.37	11.74	4.94	1.11	27.94
	Mortality ratio	144%	149%	298%	304%	541%	254%
20—69	Actual deaths	42	70	125	39	12	288
	Expected deaths	21.05	34.88	38.66	14.25	3.36	112.20
	Mortality ratio	200%	201%	323%	274%	357%	257%

Table IX. *Risks falling under the remaining extra mortality classes*
Number of risks: 1,356

Attained age		Policy years 1—2 yrs	3—5 yrs	6—10 yrs	11—15 yrs	16—20 yrs	1—20 yrs
20—29	Actual deaths	—	—	—	—	—	—
	Expected deaths	0.25	0.16	0.03	—	—	0.44
	Mortality ratio	0%	0%	0%	—	—	0%
30—39	Actual deaths	1	3	—	—	—	4
	Expected deaths	1.13	1.32	0.70	0.09	0.00	3.24
	Mortality ratio	88%	227%	0%	0%	0%	123%
40—49	Actual deaths	5	10	4	—	—	19
	Expected deaths	2.28	3.37	2.65	0.81	0.12	9.23
	Mortality ratio	219%	297%	151%	0%	0%	206%
50—59	Actual deaths	4	8	6	4	—	22
	Expected deaths	3.01	5.23	6.62	2.13	0.69	17.68
	Mortality ratio	133%	153%	91%	188%	0%	124%
60—69	Actual deaths	4	6	3	5	—	18
	Expected deaths	1.85	3.30	3.32	2.05	0.42	10.94
	Mortality ratio	216%	182%	90%	244%	0%	165%
20—69	Actual deaths	14	27	13	9	—	63
	Expected deaths	8.52	13.38	13.32	5.08	1.23	41.53
	Mortality ratio	164%	202%	98%	177%	0%	152%

edly found in sufficiently broad statistical data, and the realistic rating policy which was carried out in respect of the risks observed.

b) Mortality ratio in the totals line 'attained age 20—69'. Tables IV—VIII show in the first two years a visible if not pronounced selection which is only statistically significant in table VII of mortality class 4. Furthermore we have tested whether the hypothesis that the mortality ratio is constant as from the third year of assurance holds good; this is true of tables IV—VI and VIII, whereas in table VII the likelihood of random occurrence of fluctuations is less than 1%.

c) Mortality ratio in the inner sections of the table. We shall revert to the individual table sections, where fluctuations are considerably larger than in the totals sections owing to the smaller figures, in the section 4. "Investigation into the validity of the multiple table hypothesis".

3.4. Impairment groups

3.4.1. Preliminary remarks

As indicated in the appendix under point 2.4 our impairments code has been constructed on a decimal system. The individual impairments have been coded by means of numbers with three digits. In the following tables we have subdivided the observation data according to the first digit of this code and therefore we have nine main groups. To these nine tables we have added seven further tables showing the mortality experience of selected individual impairments. In choosing the individual impairment groups we took into consideration not only the number of risks but above all the number of deaths in order to obtain representative results.

In our individual risk record we have the possibility of coding up to four impairments at the same time (See appendix 2.4). In the observation data under discussion, a single risk carries on average 1.4 coded impairments. We have included a risk in one of the following tables only if it is coded with the respective impairment or impairment group. We did not take into account here whether it had already appeared in another table and did not take into consideration the rated extra mortality and the time difference between the emergence of the impairment and the inception of the insurance. Thus a single risk figures on average in 1.2 of the nine tables showing the mortality experience of the nine main groups mentioned. This average value of 1.2 is somewhat smaller than that of 1.4 previously mentioned because several of the impairments coded for the same risk may fall within the same main group, e. g. cardiac hypertrophy (code 361) and mitral stenosis (code 372).

In the tables of this section we tested the mortality ratio by means of the χ^2-test in order to find out whether

a) the deviations in the age groups of the totals column 'policy years 1—20' were to be regarded as random,

b) a significant selection was present in the first two years in the totals line 'attained age 20—69', and

c) the hypothesis of a constant mortality ratio as from the third year in the totals line 'attained age 20—69' was valid.

We shall deal with the inner sections of the table in detail in part 4. "Investigation into the validity of the multiple table hypothesis".

3.4.2. General impairments

The group 'General impairments' covers the codes 100—189. More than half of the risks are coded as 'Moderate abuse of nicotine' or 'Heavy abuse of nicotine'. The following tables X—XII show the mortality experience of the three risk groups mentioned. The borderline between 'Moderate abuse of nicotine' and 'Heavy abuse of nicotine' was fixed at 20 cigarettes a day.

3.4.2.1. Table X: General impairments

a) The fluctuations around the average value of 153% in the age groups of the totals column are to be regarded as significant.

Table X. *Impairment group: General impairments*

Number of risks: 10,061

Attained age		Policy years					
		1—2 yrs	3—5 yrs	6—10 yrs	11—15 yrs	16—20 yrs	1—20 yrs
20—29	Actual deaths	4	2	—	—	—	6
	Expected deaths	1.86	1.18	0.20	—	—	3.24
	Mortality ratio	215%	169%	0%	—	—	185%
30—39	Actual deaths	11	5	5	1	—	22
	Expected deaths	9.98	10.32	3.88	0.54	0.05	24.77
	Mortality ratio	110%	48%	129%	185%	0%	89%
40—49	Actual deaths	19	31	14	4	1	69
	Expected deaths	16.23	22.33	14.00	3.08	0.58	56.22
	Mortality ratio	117%	139%	100%	130%	172%	123%
50—59	Actual deaths	25	51	42	14	4	136
	Expected deaths	15.06	25.26	23.37	7.73	2.48	73.90
	Mortality ratio	166%	202%	180%	181%	161%	184%
60—69	Actual deaths	2	23	22	11	5	63
	Expected deaths	4.97	11.24	12.50	4.63	1.48	34.82
	Mortality ratio	40%	205%	176%	238%	338%	181%
20—69	Actual deaths	61	112	83	30	10	296
	Expected deaths	48.10	70.33	53.95	15.98	4.59	192.95
	Mortality ratio	127%	159%	154%	188%	218%	153%

b) The selection which is apparent in the first two years of the totals line is not statistically significant.

c) The hypothesis of a constant mortality ratio as from the third year is valid for the totals line.

3.4.2.2. Table XI: Impairment 'Moderate abuse of nicotine'

a) The fluctuations around the average value of 130% are to be regarded as significant.

b) The barely perceptible selection in the first two years of the totals line is not significant.

c) The hypothesis of a constant mortality ratio as from the third year is valid for the totals line.

3.4.2.3. Table XII: Impairment 'Heavy abuse of nicotine'

a) The fluctuations around the average value of 211% in the age groups of the totals column are to be regarded as random.

b) The pronounced selection in the first two years of the totals line is not significant because of the small number of deaths.

c) The hypothesis of a constant mortality ratio as from the third year is valid.

It is remarkable that, viewed as a whole, the mortality ratio of risks with the feature 'Heavy abuse of nicotine' is considerably higher compared with that of risks with the feature 'Moderate abuse of nicotine' and compared with all substandard risks of the 'General impairments' group.

3.4.3. Impairment group 'Diseases of the respiratory system'

The main group 'Respiratory system' includes the codes 200—294. More than half of the corresponding risks fall within the sub-groups 'Diseases of the upper respiratory tract' or 'Diseases of the lower respiratory tract'. We chose 'Bronchitis' as a single impairment within which most of the risks of the sub-group 'Diseases of the lower respiratory tract' fall.

3.4.3.1. Table XIII: Impairment group 'Diseases of the respiratory system'

a) The fluctuations around the average value of 146% in the age groups of the totals column are to be regarded as significant.

b) The noticeable selection in the first two years of the totals line is not statistically significant.

c) The hypothesis of a constant mortality ratio as from the third year is valid for the totals line.

3.4.3.2. Table XIV: Impairment 'Bronchitis' (Code 213)

a) The fluctuations around the average value of 164% in the age groups of the totals column may be regarded as random.

Table XI. *Impairment: Moderate abuse of nicotine*
Number of risks: 4,948

Attained age		Policy years					
		1—2 yrs	3—5 yrs	6—10 yrs	11—15 yrs	16—20 yrs	1—20 yrs
20—29	Actual deaths	2	2	—	—	—	4
	Expected deaths	0.91	0.46	0.02	—	—	1.39
	Mortality ratio	220%	435%	0%	—	—	288%
30—39	Actual deaths	4	2	1	—	—	7
	Expected deaths	5.16	4.84	1.08	0.03	—	11.11
	Mortality ratio	78%	41%	93%	0%	—	63%
40—49	Actual deaths	8	8	3	—	—	19
	Expected deaths	7.47	9.12	3.37	0.10	0.01	20.07
	Mortality ratio	107%	88%	89%	0%	0%	95%
50—59	Actual deaths	10	17	10	—	—	37
	Expected deaths	5.77	8.55	4.89	0.41	0.07	19.69
	Mortality ratio	173%	199%	204%	0%	0%	188%
60—69	Actual deaths	2	8	2	—	—	12
	Expected deaths	1.81	3.62	2.75	0.15	0.04	8.37
	Mortality ratio	110%	221%	73%	0%	0%	143%
20—69	Actual deaths	26	37	16	—	—	79
	Expected deaths	21.12	26.59	12.11	0.69	0.12	60.63
	Mortality ratio	123%	139%	132%	0%	0%	130%

Table XII. *Impairment: Heavy abuse of nicotine*
Number of risks: 1,279

Attained age		Policy years					
		1—2 yrs	3—5 yrs	6—10 yrs	11—15 yrs	16—20 yrs	1—20 yrs
20—29	Actual deaths	—	—	—	—	—	—
	Expected deaths	0.15	0.10	0.00	—	—	0.25
	Mortality ratio	0%	0%	0%	—	—	0%
30—39	Actual deaths	1	2	2	—	—	5
	Expected deaths	1.20	1.06	0.37	0.04	—	2.67
	Mortality ratio	83%	189%	541%	0%	—	187%
40—49	Actual deaths	3	9	3	—	—	15
	Expected deaths	2.31	3.43	2.48	0.42	0.02	8.66
	Mortality ratio	130%	262%	121%	0%	0%	173%
50—59	Actual deaths	4	6	9	7	—	26
	Expected deaths	2.22	4.23	4.58	1.58	0.19	12.80
	Mortality ratio	180%	142%	197%	443%	0%	203%
60—69	Actual deaths	—	4	10	1	—	15
	Expected deaths	0.43	0.78	1.73	1.25	0.36	4.55
	Mortality ratio	0%	513%	578%	80%	0%	330%
20—69	Actual deaths	8	21	24	8	—	61
	Expected deaths	6.31	9.60	9.16	3.29	0.57	28.93
	Mortality ratio	127%	219%	262%	243%	0%	211%

Table XIII. *Impairment group: Diseases of the respiratory system*
Number of risks: 9,294

Attained age		Policy years 1—2 yrs	3—5 yrs	6—10 yrs	11—15 yrs	16—20 yrs	1—20 yrs
20—29	Actual deaths	4	2	—	—	—	6
	Expected deaths	2.07	1.53	0.28	0.00	—	3.88
	Mortality ratio	193%	131%	0%	0%	—	155%
30—39	Actual deaths	11	12	5	—	—	28
	Expected deaths	9.63	11.76	6.36	1.06	0.10	28.91
	Mortality ratio	114%	102%	79%	0%	0%	97%
40—49	Actual deaths	12	24	28	4	1	69
	Expected deaths	14.19	23.13	20.30	6.36	1.59	65.57
	Mortality ratio	85%	104%	138%	63%	63%	105%
50—59	Actual deaths	22	55	61	23	12	173
	Expected deaths	15.54	28.54	33.95	15.45	5.35	98.83
	Mortality ratio	142%	193%	180%	149%	224%	175%
60—69	Actual deaths	6	31	36	19	11	103
	Expected deaths	6.29	15.15	22.85	14.08	4.85	63.22
	Mortality ratio	95%	205%	158%	135%	227%	163%
20—69	Actual deaths	55	124	130	46	24	379
	Expected deaths	47.72	80.11	83.74	36.95	11.89	260.41
	Mortality ratio	115%	155%	155%	124%	202%	146%

Table XIV. *Impairment: Bronchitis (Code 213)*
Number of risks: 1,738

Attained age		Policy years 1—2 yrs	3—5 yrs	6—10 yrs	11—15 yrs	16—20 yrs	1—20 yrs
20—29	Actual deaths	2	—	—	—	—	2
	Expected deaths	0.34	0.28	0.06	—	—	0.68
	Mortality ratio	588%	0%	0%	—	—	294%
30—39	Actual deaths	5	3	—	—	—	8
	Expected deaths	1.47	1.85	1.15	0.24	0.02	4.73
	Mortality ratio	340%	162%	0%	0%	0%	169%
40—49	Actual deaths	2	7	4	1	—	14
	Expected deaths	3.24	5.30	4.74	1.60	0.37	15.25
	Mortality ratio	62%	132%	84%	63%	0%	92%
50—59	Actual deaths	5	20	18	5	4	52
	Expected deaths	4.04	7.52	10.75	5.11	1.50	28.92
	Mortality ratio	124%	266%	167%	98%	267%	180%
60—69	Actual deaths	2	11	12	6	3	34
	Expected deaths	1.47	3.67	5.69	4.94	1.90	17.67
	Mortality ratio	136%	300%	211%	121%	158%	192%
20—69	Actual deaths	16	41	34	12	7	110
	Expected deaths	10.56	18.62	22.39	11.89	3.79	67.25
	Mortality ratio	152%	220%	152%	101%	185%	164%

b) The mild selection in the first two years of the totals line is not statistically significant.

c) The hypothesis of a constant mortality ratio as from the third year is valid in the totals line.

3.4.4. Impairment group 'Diseases of the circulatory system'

The main group 'Circulatory system' covers codes 300—399. The largest sub-groups are 'Diseases of the blood vessels', 'Abnormalities in cardiac rate, rhythm and conduction', as well as 'Changes and diseases of the myocardium'. We have chosen the latter sub-group as a separate impairment group, with the mortality experience shown in table XVI.

3.4.4.1. Table XV: Impairment group 'Diseases of the circulatory system'

a) As regards the deviations from the average value of 174% in the age groups of the totals column, we must take both randomness and significance into consideration in accordance with our conditions of significance (See point 2.4.4)

Table XV. *Impairment group: Diseases of the circulatory system*

Number of risks: 10,586

Attained age		Policy years					
		1—2 yrs	3—5 yrs	6—10 yrs	11—15 yrs	16—20 yrs	1—20 yrs
20—29	Actual deaths	8	3	—	—	—	11
	Expected deaths	1.83	1.34	0.26	—	—	3.43
	Mortality ratio	437%	224%	0%	—	—	321%
30—39	Actual deaths	14	18	25	3	—	60
	Expected deaths	8.73	10.44	5.94	1.01	0.09	26.21
	Mortality ratio	160%	172%	421%	297%	0%	229%
40—49	Actual deaths	23	65	33	10	3	134
	Expected deaths	18.09	26.78	21.89	6.72	1.42	74.90
	Mortality ratio	127%	243%	151%	149%	211%	179%
50—59	Actual deaths	37	74	87	41	11	250
	Expected deaths	26.63	46.30	46.03	18.73	6.51	144.20
	Mortality ratio	139%	160%	189%	219%	169%	173%
60—69	Actual deaths	11	51	66	20	8	156
	Expected deaths	12.34	28.07	39.92	16.88	4.77	101.98
	Mortality ratio	89%	182%	165%	118%	168%	153%
20—69	Actual deaths	93	211	211	74	22	611
	Expected deaths	67.62	112.93	114.04	43.34	12.79	350.72
	Mortality ratio	138%	187%	185%	171%	172%	174%

since the probability of the random appearance of deviations lies between 2% and 3%.

b) The probability of the random appearance of the pronounced selection in the first two years lies between 1% and 2%; accordingly no positive statement regarding randomness or significance can be made.

c) The hypothesis of a constant mortality ratio as from the third year appears to be clearly valid.

3.4.4.2. Table XVI: Impairment group 'Changes and diseases of the myocardium'

a) The fluctuations around the average value of 190% in the age groups of the totals column are to be regarded as fortuitous.

b) In the first two years of the totals line the mortality ratio of 201% is slightly higher than the average value for all years together of 190%; the deviation is however not statistically significant. The extra mortality in this risk group seems to be very high at first and to decrease slightly during the course of the observation period. Over against this, however, we have the fact that

c) the hypothesis of a constant mortality ratio as from the third year is valid.

Table XVI. *Impairment group: Changes and diseases of the myocardium*

Number of risks: 1,976

Attained age		Policy years 1—2 yrs	3—5 yrs	6—10 yrs	11—15 yrs	16—20 yrs	1—20 yrs
20—29	Actual deaths	1	—	—	—	—	1
	Expected deaths	0.28	0.21	0.05	—	—	0.54
	Mortality ratio	357%	0%	0%	—	—	185%
30—39	Actual deaths	3	5	5	1	—	14
	Expected deaths	1.41	1.77	1.07	0.25	0.02	4.52
	Mortality ratio	213%	282%	467%	400%	0%	310%
40—49	Actual deaths	8	13	8	2	—	31
	Expected deaths	3.58	5.46	4.93	1.58	0.31	15.86
	Mortality ratio	223%	238%	162%	127%	0%	195%
50—59	Actual deaths	13	14	26	10	4	67
	Expected deaths	5.67	10.51	11.05	5.03	1.72	33.98
	Mortality ratio	229%	133%	235%	199%	233%	197%
60—69	Actual deaths	4	16	17	4	1	42
	Expected deaths	3.49	7.46	11.09	3.85	0.93	26.82
	Mortality ratio	115%	214%	153%	104%	108%	157%
20—69	Actual deaths	29	48	56	17	5	155
	Expected deaths	14.43	25.41	28.19	10.71	2.98	81.72
	Mortality ratio	201%	189%	199%	159%	168%	190%

3.4.5. *Impairment group 'Infectious, metabolic, vitamin deficiency and allergic diseases; diseases of the bones, the blood and the endocrine system'*

This main group covers the codes 400—499. The sub-groups with the most figures are 'Tuberculosis of the respiratory system' and 'Rheumatism; diseases of the bones and joints'. We show the risks of the sub-group 'Tuberculosis of the respiratory system' as a separate impairment group in table XVIII.

Table XVII. *Impairment group: Infectious, metabolic, vitamin deficiency and allergic diseases; diseases of the bones, the blood and the endocrine system*

Number of risks: 10,393

Attained age		Policy years					
		1—2 yrs	3—5 yrs	6—10 yrs	11—15 yrs	16—20 yrs	1—20 yrs
20—29	Actual deaths	2	3	2	—	—	7
	Expected deaths	2.35	1.81	0.34	0.00	—	4.50
	Mortality ratio	85%	166%	588%	0%	—	156%
30—39	Actual deaths	12	13	20	2	—	47
	Expected deaths	10.92	13.75	8.48	1.55	0.09	34.79
	Mortality ratio	110%	95%	236%	129%	0%	135%
40—49	Actual deaths	18	50	41	12	4	125
	Expected deaths	16.53	27.15	25.92	10.00	2.58	82.18
	Mortality ratio	109%	184%	158%	120%	155%	152%
50—59	Actual deaths	15	57	61	36	8	177
	Expected deaths	17.69	33.48	40.23	21.12	7.99	120.51
	Mortality ratio	85%	170%	152%	170%	100%	147%
60—69	Actual deaths	3	19	39	17	14	92
	Expected deaths	5.87	14.90	26.64	18.63	5.87	71.91
	Mortality ratio	51%	128%	146%	91%	239%	128%
20—69	Actual deaths	50	142	163	67	26	448
	Expected deaths	53.36	91.09	101.61	51.30	16.53	313.89
	Mortality ratio	94%	156%	160%	131%	157%	143%

3.4.5.1. Table XVII: Impairment group 'Infectious, metabolic, vitamin deficiency and allergic diseases; diseases of the bones, the blood and the endocrine system'

a) The fluctuations around the average value of 143% in the age groups of the totals column are to be regarded as random.

b) Selection is clearly apparent in the first two years of the totals line and is here statistically significant.

c) The hypothesis of a constant mortality ratio as from the third year is valid in the totals line.

3.4.5.2. Table XVIII: Impairment group 'Tuberculosis of the respiratory system'

a) The fluctuations around the average value of 113% in the age groups of the totals column are to be regarded as random.

b) The noticeable selection in the first two years of the totals line is not statistically significant.

c) No firm statement can be made regarding the hypothesis of the constant mortality ratio as from the third year as the probability of the random appearance of fluctuations lies between 1% and 2%.

Table XVIII. *Impairment group: Tuberculosis of the respiratory system*

Number of risks: 3,477

Attained age		Policy years					
		1—2 yrs	3—5 yrs	6—10 yrs	11—15 yrs	16—20 yrs	1—20 yrs
20—29	Actual deaths	1	1	2	—	—	4
	Expected deaths	0.96	0.75	0.13	—	—	1.84
	Mortality ratio	104%	133%	1,538%	—	—	217%
30—39	Actual deaths	4	2	6	—	—	12
	Expected deaths	4.62	6.30	4.13	0.66	0.02	15.73
	Mortality ratio	87%	32%	145%	0%	0%	76%
40—49	Actual deaths	5	8	14	6	3	36
	Expected deaths	4.72	9.20	10.86	5.16	1.35	31.29
	Mortality ratio	106%	87%	129%	116%	222%	115%
50—59	Actual deaths	1	5	13	7	3	29
	Expected deaths	3.01	6.86	9.87	6.81	3.32	29.87
	Mortality ratio	33%	73%	132%	103%	90%	97%
60—69	Actual deaths	—	1	6	6	7	20
	Expected deaths	0.66	1.69	4.04	3.00	1.39	10.78
	Mortality ratio	0%	59%	149%	200%	504%	186%
20—69	Actual deaths	11	17	41	19	13	101
	Expected deaths	13.97	24.80	29.03	15.63	6.08	89.51
	Mortality ratio	79%	69%	141%	122%	214%	113%

3.4.6. Impairment group 'Diseases of the genito-urinary system'

This main group includes codes 500—594. The largest sub-groups are 'Pathological urinary findings; disorders of the renal function' and 'Renal and bladder stones'. Table XX shows the mortality experience of the latter sub-group as a separate impairment group.

3.4.6.1. Table XIX: Impairment group 'Diseases of the genito-urinary system'

a) Fluctuations around the average value of 144% in the age groups of the totals column are still random.

b) The slight selection in the first two years of the totals line is not statistically significant.

c) The hypothesis of a constant mortality ratio as from the third year is valid in the totals line.

Table XIX. *Impairment group: Diseases of the genito-urinary system*

Number of risks: 4,443

Attained age		Policy years					
		1—2 yrs	3—5 yrs	6—10 yrs	11—15 yrs	16—20 yrs	1—20 yrs
20—29	Actual deaths	1	—	—	—	—	1
	Expected deaths	0.78	0.57	0.13	0.00	—	1.48
	Mortality ratio	128%	0%	0%	0%	—	68%
30—39	Actual deaths	4	4	8	—	—	16
	Expected deaths	4.02	4.46	2.32	0.40	0.05	11.25
	Mortality ratio	100%	90%	345%	0%	0%	142%
40—49	Actual deaths	9	15	16	2	—	42
	Expected deaths	7.86	12.10	10.05	3.25	0.61	33.87
	Mortality ratio	115%	124%	159%	62%	0%	124%
50—59	Actual deaths	13	21	29	29	5	97
	Expected deaths	9.47	18.06	19.86	10.36	3.53	61.28
	Mortality ratio	137%	116%	146%	280%	142%	158%
60—69	Actual deaths	5	12	24	12	7	60
	Expected deaths	4.53	10.89	15.84	8.34	2.86	42.46
	Mortality ratio	110%	110%	152%	144%	245%	141%
20—69	Actual deaths	32	52	77	43	12	216
	Expected deaths	26.66	46.08	48.20	22.35	7.05	150.34
	Mortality ratio	120%	113%	160%	192%	170%	144%

3.4.6.2. Table XX: Impairment group 'Renal and bladder stones'

a) The fluctuations around the average value of 106% in the age groups of the totals column are to be regarded as random.

b) In the first two years of the totals line the mortality ratio of 143% is considerably higher than the average value for all years together of 106%; this fluctuation is not, however, statistically significant. After a decline to 86% in the third to fifth year the mortality ratio increases again in the following years. On the other hand we have the fact that

c) the hypothesis of a constant mortality ratio as from the third year is valid in the totals line. The probability of the random appearance of fluctuations lies in fact above 80%.

3.4.7. *Impairment group 'Diseases of the brain and the nervous system'*

This main group encompasses the codes 600—698. In view of the lack of figures we decided not to evaluate individual sub-groups.

Table XX. *Impairment group: Renal and bladder stones*

Number of risks: 1,686

Attained age		Policy years					
		1—2 yrs	3—5 yrs	6—10 yrs	11—15 yrs	16—20 yrs	1—20 yrs
20—29	Actual deaths	—	—	—	—	—	—
	Expected deaths	0.17	0.10	0.02	—	—	0.29
	Mortality ratio	0%	0%	0%	—	—	0%
30—39	Actual deaths	1	1	—	—	—	2
	Expected deaths	1.50	1.59	0.73	0.09	—	3.91
	Mortality ratio	67%	63%	0%	0%	—	51%
40—49	Actual deaths	7	6	4	—	—	17
	Expected deaths	3.25	4.87	3.75	1.13	0.18	13.18
	Mortality ratio	215%	123%	107%	0%	0%	129%
50—59	Actual deaths	4	4	7	4	1	20
	Expected deaths	4.10	8.11	8.63	4.04	1.14	26.02
	Mortality ratio	98%	49%	81%	99%	88%	77%
60—69	Actual deaths	3	5	9	6	2	25
	Expected deaths	1.48	4.00	7.11	3.66	0.88	17.13
	Mortality ratio	203%	125%	127%	164%	227%	146%
20—69	Actual deaths	15	16	20	10	3	64
	Expected deaths	10.50	18.67	20.24	8.92	2.20	60.53
	Mortality ratio	143%	86%	99%	112%	136%	106%

3.4.7.1. Table XXI: Impairment group 'Diseases of the brain and the nervous system'

a) The fluctuations around the average value of 175% in the age groups of the totals column do not allow any firm statement as the probability of random appearance lies between 3% and 5%.

b) As regards selection in the first two years of the totals line we are also unable to decide whether it is fortuitous or significant, as the probability of the random appearance of the figure 109% lies between 3% and 5%.

c) The hypothesis of a constant mortality ratio as from the third year is clearly valid in the totals line.

3.4.8. *Impairment group 'Diseases of the sense organs and the skin'*

This main group covers codes 700—783. Here again due to the limited data available we decided not to evaluate individual sub-groups.

Table XXI. *Impairment group: Diseases of the brain and the nervous system*
Number of risks: 2,794

Attained age		Policy years					
		1—2 yrs	3—5 yrs	6—10 yrs	11—15 yrs	16—20 yrs	1—20 yrs
20—29	Actual deaths	1	—	—	—	—	1
	Expected deaths	0.74	0.53	0.08	—	—	1.35
	Mortality ratio	135%	0%	0%	—	—	74%
30—39	Actual deaths	2	—	2	1	—	5
	Expected deaths	2.76	3.41	1.96	0.41	0.03	8.57
	Mortality ratio	72%	0%	102%	244%	0%	58%
40—49	Actual deaths	7	17	14	—	2	40
	Expected deaths	4.31	6.82	5.57	1.80	0.51	19.01
	Mortality ratio	162%	249%	251%	0%	392%	210%
50—59	Actual deaths	3	24	14	10	5	56
	Expected deaths	4.62	8.39	9.03	4.30	1.90	28.24
	Mortality ratio	65%	286%	155%	233%	263%	198%
60—69	Actual deaths	2	2	14	4	—	22
	Expected deaths	1.36	3.19	4.74	3.08	1.20	13.57
	Mortality ratio	147%	63%	295%	130%	0%	162%
20—69	Actual deaths	15	43	44	15	7	124
	Expected deaths	13.79	22.34	21.38	9.59	3.64	70.74
	Mortality ratio	109%	192%	206%	156%	192%	175%

Table XXII. *Impairment group: Diseases of the sense organs and the skin*
Number of risks: 2,425

Attained age		Policy years					
		1—2 yrs	3—5 yrs	6—10 yrs	11—15 yrs	16—20 yrs	1—20 yrs
20—29	Actual deaths	—	—	—	—	—	—
	Expected deaths	0.59	0.45	0.12	—	—	1.16
	Mortality ratio	0%	0%	0%	—	—	0%
30—39	Actual deaths	8	2	1	—	—	11
	Expected deaths	2.42	2.85	1.60	0.27	0.02	7.16
	Mortality ratio	331%	70%	63%	0%	0%	154%
40—49	Actual deaths	2	4	3	—	1	10
	Expected deaths	3.66	5.60	4.07	1.48	0.37	15.18
	Mortality ratio	55%	71%	74%	0%	270%	66%
50—59	Actual deaths	8	4	6	6	2	26
	Expected deaths	4.15	6.69	6.83	3.01	1.28	21.96
	Mortality ratio	193%	60%	88%	199%	156%	118%
60—69	Actual deaths	—	7	5	—	1	13
	Expected deaths	1.26	3.25	4.55	2.73	1.41	13.20
	Mortality ratio	0%	215%	110%	0%	71%	98%
20—69	Actual deaths	18	17	15	6	4	60
	Expected deaths	12.08	18.84	17.17	7.49	3.08	58.66
	Mortality ratio	149%	90%	87%	80%	130%	102%

3.4.8.1. Table XXII: Impairment group 'Diseases of the sense organs and the skin'

a) Fluctuations around the average value of 102% in the age groups of the totals column are to be regarded as random.

b) In the first two years of the totals line the mortality ratio of 149% lies above the average value of 102% for all years together; as with previous tables with this phenomenon the deviation is not statistically significant.

c) The hypothesis of a constant mortality ratio as from the third year is valid in the totals line.

3.4.9. Impairment group 'Diseases of the digestive system'

This main group covers codes 800—896. More than half of the risks belonging to the group fall within the sub-groups 'Diseases of stomach and duodenum' and 'Diseases of the liver'. We have chosen 'Gastric ulcer' as a single impairment from the former sub-group; the related mortality experience is shown in table XXIV.

3.4.9.1. Table XXIII: Impairment group 'Diseases of the digestive system'

a) The fluctuations around the average value of 138% in the age groups of the totals column are to be regarded as random.

Table XXIII. *Impairment group: Diseases of the digestive system*
Number of risks: 11,545

Attained age		Policy years					
		1—2 yrs	3—5 yrs	6—10 yrs	11—15 yrs	16—20 yrs	1—20 yrs
20—29	Actual deaths	2	2	1	—	—	5
	Expected deaths	1.93	1.39	0.19	—	—	3.51
	Mortality ratio	104%	144%	526%	—	—	142%
30—39	Actual deaths	10	9	9	4	—	32
	Expected deaths	10.44	12.23	6.18	0.82	0.04	29.71
	Mortality ratio	96%	74%	146%	488%	0%	108%
40—49	Actual deaths	39	45	33	5	2	124
	Expected deaths	21.32	32.01	26.73	8.04	1.50	89.60
	Mortality ratio	183%	141%	123%	62%	133%	138%
50—59	Actual deaths	27	80	84	42	18	251
	Expected deaths	23.93	45.87	56.03	27.17	8.27	161.27
	Mortality ratio	113%	174%	150%	155%	218%	156%
60—69	Actual deaths	10	27	48	30	7	122
	Expected deaths	8.92	22.07	38.16	26.32	8.22	103.69
	Mortality ratio	112%	122%	126%	114%	85%	118%
20—69	Actual deaths	88	163	175	81	27	534
	Expected deaths	66.54	113.57	127.29	62.35	18.03	387.78
	Mortality ratio	132%	144%	137%	130%	150%	138%

b) The selection in the first two years of the totals line almost disappears and is therefore not significant.

c) The hypothesis of a constant mortality ratio is clearly valid.

3.4.9.2. Table XXIV: Impairment 'Gastric ulcer'

a) The fluctuations around the average value of 179% in the age groups of the totals column may be regarded as random.

b) In the first two years of the totals line the mortality ratio of 224% is above the average of 179% for all years together; this deviation is not statistically significant however. As with the impairment group 'Renal and bladder stones' the mortality ratio decreases sharply in the 3rd—5th years and then gradually increases in the later years observed. However, on the other hand,

c) the hypothesis of a constant mortality ratio as from the third insurance year is valid in the totals line.

Table XXIV. *Impairment: Gastric ulcer*
Number of risks: 1,566

Attained age		Policy years					
		1—2 yrs	3—5 yrs	6—10 yrs	11—15 yrs	16—20 yrs	1—20 yrs
20—29	Actual deaths	1	—	—	—	—	1
	Expected deaths	0.21	0.14	0.02	—	—	0.37
	Mortality ratio	476%	0%	0%	—	—	270%
30—39	Actual deaths	1	1	3	1	—	6
	Expected deaths	1.55	1.79	1.05	0.18	0.01	4.58
	Mortality ratio	65%	56%	286%	556%	0%	131%
40—49	Actual deaths	10	8	16	3	1	38
	Expected deaths	3.22	5.18	5.35	2.19	0.45	16.39
	Mortality ratio	311%	154%	299%	137%	222%	232%
50—59	Actual deaths	7	8	15	15	7	52
	Expected deaths	3.20	6.69	9.52	6.41	2.33	28.15
	Mortality ratio	219%	120%	158%	234%	300%	185%
60—69	Actual deaths	1	3	4	10	2	20
	Expected deaths	0.75	2.37	5.92	5.05	1.74	15.83
	Mortality ratio	133%	127%	68%	198%	115%	126%
20—69	Actual deaths	20	20	38	29	10	117
	Expected deaths	8.93	16.17	21.86	13.83	4.53	65.32
	Mortality ratio	224%	124%	174%	210%	221%	179%

3.4.10. *Impairment group 'Tumours'*

This main group includes codes 900—928 and contains risks of which it was known at the inception of the assurance that a cancer was present or had been present. As such risks are only insurable under exceptionally favourable circumstances, the figures for this group are few in number. There was no point in dividing up the group into separate sub-sections, as the main group itself barely produced significant results.

3.4.10.1. Table XXV: Impairment group 'Tumours'

We did not carry out the χ^2-tests as mentioned under point 3.4.1 in respect of this table. We would in this way have contravened the basic principle that one may work with the χ^2-distribution only if none of the table sections contains less than one expected death and at most one fifth of the sections contain less than five.

Table XXV. *Impairment group: Tumours*
Number of risks: 488

Attained age		Policy years					
		1—2 yrs	3—5 yrs	6—10 yrs	11—15 yrs	16—20 yrs	1—20 yrs
20—29	Actual deaths	—	—	—	—	—	—
	Expected deaths	0.08	0.05	0.00	—	—	0.13
	Mortality ratio	0%	0%	0%	—	—	0%
30—39	Actual deaths	2	1	1	—	—	4
	Expected deaths	0.40	0.50	0.24	0.03	—	1.17
	Mortality ratio	500%	200%	417%	0%	—	342%
40—49	Actual deaths	3	4	—	—	—	7
	Expected deaths	0.88	1.11	0.76	0.14	0.04	2.93
	Mortality ratio	341%	360%	0%	0%	0%	239%
50—59	Actual deaths	3	1	1	2	—	7
	Expected deaths	1.16	2.11	2.04	0.68	0.18	6.17
	Mortality ratio	259%	47%	49%	294%	0%	113%
60—69	Actual deaths	—	2	—	—	—	2
	Expected deaths	0.50	1.22	1.34	0.29	0.06	3.41
	Mortality ratio	0%	164%	0%	0%	0%	59%
20—69	Actual deaths	8	8	2	2	—	20
	Expected deaths	3.02	4.99	4.38	1.14	0.28	13.81
	Mortality ratio	265%	160%	46%	175%	0%	145%

With regard to the mortality ratios the fact that these were made up of small figures must be taken into account as this led to large differences in the percentages (This observation also applies in part to the previous tables). Thus one actual death more or less, where the number of expected deaths is very small, makes a difference of between 7% and 769% in the totals sections and in an extreme case up to 3,333% in the inner table sections. Furthermore we discovered that the total of 20 deaths involved only 16 persons since four lives were each covered by two policies.

Without an exact and separate investigation of all aspects of this observation data such as type and treatment of cancer, time gap between diagnosis and inception of assurance, other diseases present or suffered, relation between policies and persons on risk etc., no conclusions may be drawn from the present table. Such an investigation would exceed the scope of this work and will therefore be dealt with later in a special study. The table was included for the sake of completeness since we have thus given the mortality experience with all nine main groups of our impairments code.

3.5. Distribution of causes of death

3.5.1. Introductory remarks

In this study the main emphasis has been laid on the multiple table hypothesis. For this purpose we have drawn up, in the previous sections, tables which show the mortality experience, divided according to different features. In order to complete the picture we shall now give two tables on the causes of death. We are fully aware that conclusions may only be drawn with considerable caution from statistics based on causes of death. A detailed study of these problems would be beyond the scope of this work. Suffice it to mention that the disease which was the direct cause of death can often only be determined with difficulty and that insufficient attention is paid in some countries to the establishment of the cause of death, which is of particular relevance to our study.

The causes of death were enumerated according to the number of deceased persons, the corresponding number of policies terminated by death being given in the first table only. In order to facilitate comparisons between the two tables we have used in both an order of succession which was fixed according to the frequency of the causes of death with standard risks.

3.5.2. Grouping according to standard and substandard risks

In table XXVI following we show the distribution of causes of death for three groups of lives assured, i. e. for standard, substandard and all risks together.

The frequency of causes of death for the two groups standard and substandard risks diverges strongly. The differences are statistically significant as a χ^2-test shows, for which we chose the frequency of causes of death with standard risks as the theoretical distribution. The differences apply primarily to the degree of frequency of the individual causes of death and only secondly to the order of succession. As far as the latter is concerned only diseases of the respiratory system are worthy of mention as they occupy eleventh place with standard risks and sixth place with substandard risks.

First place is taken in both groups by diseases of the circulatory system followed in both cases by tumours (cancers of all kinds). The position of circulatory impairments in the substandard risks group is remarkable, since they account for more than one third of all deaths and there is a gap of more than 20% before the next group.

Noteworthy also is the substantially higher proportion of accidents with standard risks compared with substandard. These deaths occupy only fourth place in the second group, close behind diseases of the nervous system and sense organs (principally apoplexies).

Table XXVI. *Distribution of causes of death*

No.	Causes of death by groups	Standard risks		Substandard risks		All risks	
		No. Pers.	%	No. Pers.	%	No. Pers.	%
1	Diseases of the circulatory system	129	26.9	567	34.3	696	32.6
2	Tumours	94	19.6	234	14.2	328	15.4
3	Accidents and acts of violence	80	16.7	159	9.6	239	11.2
4	Diseases of the nervous system and sense organs	51	10.6	163	9.9	214	10.0
5	Diseases of the digestive system	26	5.4	108	6.5	134	6.3
6	Suicide	21	4.4	42	2.5	63	3.0
7	Diseases of the genito-urinary system	7	1.5	55	3.3	62	2.9
8	Infectious and parasitic diseases	7	1.5	40	2.4	47	2.2
9	Diseases of the blood and blood-forming organs	6	1.2	24	1.5	30	1.4
10	Rheumatic, metabolic, nutritional diseases and diseases of the endocrine system	6	1.2	20	1.2	26	1.2
11	Diseases of the respiratory system	4	0.8	66	4.0	70	3.3
12	Other known causes of death	5	1.0	25	1.5	30	1.4
13	Unknown or inadequately defined causes of death	44	9.2	150	9.1	194	9.1
	Total	480	100.0	1,653	100.0	2,133	100.0
	Number of policies	556		1,846		2,402	

With suicides, the ratio of 'policies to persons' is substantially higher than with other causes of death, both for standard and substandard risks. For standard and substandard risks together the ratio for suicides is 1.29 whereas for the other causes of death it fluctuates marginally around an average value of 1.13 (with maximum and minimum values of 1.17 and 1.06). We assume on the basis of this fact that there is an anti-selection, in that persons contemplating suicide conclude a number of policies.

3.5.3. Classification according to impairment groups

In table XXVII following we show the distribution of the causes of death for the nine impairment groups which form the rough sub-divisions of our decimal impairments code (See appendix point 2.4.1).

Table XXVII. *Distribution of causes of death according to impairment groups*

No.	Causes of death by groups	Standard risks	Impairment groups: General impairments		Respiratory system		Circulatory system		Infectious a. metabolic diseases; dis. of bones and blood		Genito-urinary system		Brain and nervous system		Sense organs and skin		Digestive system		Tumours	
		%	Pers.	%	Pers.	%	Pers.	%	Pers.	%	Pers.	%	Pers.	%	Pers.	%	Pers.	%	Pers.	%
		(1)	(2)	(3)	(4)	(5)	(6)	(7)	(8)	(9)	(10)	(11)	(12)	(13)	(14)	(15)	(16)	(17)	(18)	(19)
1	Dis. of the circulatory system	26.9	95	36.6	109	31.4	242	44.3	107	27.7	65	36.1	42	39.6	15	29.4	123	26.2	2	12.5
2	Tumours	19.6	43	16.6	59	17.0	64	11.7	59	15.3	19	10.6	17	16.0	11	21.5	93	19.8	6	37.5
3	Accidents and acts of viol.	16.7	28	10.8	38	10.9	55	10.1	53	13.7	15	8.3	14	13.2	8	15.7	55	11.7	4	25.0
4	Diseases of the nervous system and sense organs	10.6	17	6.6	28	8.1	49	9.0	24	6.2	19	10.6	14	13.2	4	7.8	33	7.0	—	—
5	Diseases of the digestive syst.	5.4	18	6.9	17	4.9	26	4.8	26	6.7	7	3.9	3	2.8	—	—	46	9.8	—	—
6	Suicide	4.4	10	3.9	10	2.9	10	1.8	6	1.6	5	2.8	4	3.8	2	3.9	16	3.4	—	—
7	Diseases of the urogen. system	1.5	3	1.2	7	2.0	13	2.4	8	2.1	17	9.4	1	1.0	1	2.0	10	2.2	1	6.3
8	Infectious and parasitic dis.	1.5	7	2.7	12	3.5	6	1.1	16	4.1	6	3.3	1	1.0	2	3.9	15	3.2	1	6.2
9	Diseases of the blood and blood-forming organs	1.2	1	0.4	2	0.6	7	1.3	9	2.3	1	0.6	—	—	1	2.0	6	1.3	—	—
10	Rheumatic, metabolic, nutritional diseases and diseases of the endocrine system	1.2	2	0.8	2	0.6	4	0.7	11	2.9	2	1.1	—	—	—	—	6	1.3	—	—
11	Diseases of the respiratory system	0.8	9	3.5	36	10.4	20	3.7	14	3.6	6	3.3	2	1.9	1	2.0	13	2.8	2	12.5
12	Other known causes of death	1.0	6	2.3	6	1.7	11	2.0	6	1.6	2	1.1	3	2.8	1	2.0	11	2.3	—	—
13	Unknown or inadequately defined causes of death	9.2	20	7.7	21	6.0	39	7.1	47	12.2	16	8.9	5	4.7	5	9.8	42	9.0	—	—
	Total	100.0	259	100.0	347	100.0	546	100.0	386	100.0	180	100.0	106	100.0	51	100.0	469	100.0	16	100.0

The reasons for the substantial differences between the distributions for standard and substandard risks are to be found to a large extent in the causal relationship which exists in the case of the latter between the risk features at inception of the assurance and the subsequent causes of death. Unfortunately the correlation is not completely clear from the data included in the table. Special investigations which would go beyond the scope of this work would be necessary to trace this correlation completely. Nevertheless where the correlation is unmistakable we have drawn a double line around the table section in question.

As stated in our remarks under point 3.4.1, the same person can figure in more than one impairment group. Consequently we have not added a totals column, but show the shares of individual groups of causes of death for standard risks in column 1 in accordance with table XXVI.

4. Investigation into the validity of the multiple table hypothesis

4.1. Introductory remarks

We shall examine in this chapter whether the results obtained from table II to XXV in sections 3.2 to 3.4 are compatible with or contradictory to the multiple table hypothesis. In so doing we shall bear in mind the comments made by JECKLIN: "However, nowhere is it claimed that the constant multiplicative extra mortality method corresponds generally to the actual mortality of increased risks. It is a working hypothesis and should not be classified otherwise. Any argument against the hypothesis, if it is to be taken seriously, should therefore examine the question of whether the results obtained with the method coincide so little with reality that it can no longer be responsibly applied with a clear conscience" [15]. It is by no means our intention to prove that the multiple table hypothesis represents exactly the mortality experience with increased risks, but we shall attempt to answer the following question: Are our results such that on average the multiple table hypothesis is valid or are they an indication that this easy-to-apply working hypothesis should be abandoned in favour of more dynamic methods?

4.2. Deviations tests

The various χ^2-tests which we have carried out and mentioned in the comments on the tables show at times significant deviations between the actual mortality experience and that expected according to our working hypothesis, i. e. for the individual groups of attained ages the average α-values are significantly different. For the time being we shall not proceed further with the χ^2-tests but shall take a mathematically and statistically more simple approach.

In the following tables we show the mortality ratio for individual risk groups and have added extra sections containing either a + or − sign depending on whether the corresponding value of the mortality ratio is higher or lower than the average value for the whole risk group. The structure is similar to that in tables I to XXV with the following changes:

a) we have omitted the attained ages 20—29, since only 1.3% of the deaths for the whole observation data fall in this age group, thus causing correspondingly excessive differences in the mortality ratio.

b) The first two years of observation have been omitted since we wished to eliminate the diverse effects of selection and since our comparative mortality is not based on select tables as mentioned in our comments under paragraph 3.1.

c) We have combined the values for columns 'policy years 11—15' and 'policy years 16—20', because they contain substantially fewer figures than the columns for 3—5 years and 6—10 years. We now have only three columns, the latter covering almost half as many years of observation as the first two.

As a result of omitting and combining elements of the observation data in the manner described above, there are slight deviations in the mortality ratio in the following tables compared with those in the tables for the same risk groups contained in sections 3.1 to 3.4. If the mortality ratio in a given section of the table is based on less than five expected deaths according to normal mortality, we have placed the respective value and a + or − sign in brackets.

If the working hypothesis of a constant multiplicative increase in mortality is applicable, we may assume that in the signs tables the + and − signs maintain a balance and are randomly spread over the individual table sections; this may be checked by means of a binominal distribution. It is theoretically possible that the mortality ratio in a given table section may tally exactly with the average value for the risk group, i. e. there is a third possibility other than the signs + and −. However as may be easily proved the likelihood of this phenomenon is so minute that it may be disregarded.

In the following explanations we shall use certain symbols:

n = Number of table sections or groups of tables under discussion.

s^+ = Number of + signs in the table or groups of tables under discussion.

s^- = Number of − signs in the table or groups of tables under discussion.

$P_1(s^+)$ = The probability that a binominal distribution with base probability $p = 0.5$ $[B_n(0.5)]$ will produce the value expressed under s^+ in n trials.

$P_2(s^+)$ = The probability that a binominal distribution with base probability $p = 0.5$ $[B_n(0.5)]$ will produce the value expressed under s^+ or smaller value in n trials.

The following relations of course apply here:

$$s^+ + s^- = n$$

$$P_2(s^+) = \sum_{x=0}^{s^+} P_1(x)$$

4.3. Risks of the extra mortality classes 1—8

Having divided up the risks according to the extra mortality classes we first applied the above-mentioned tests to these groups. Table XXVIII, following, shows separately the mortality ratio values and the signs for the extra mortality classes 1, 2, 3, 4 and 5—8. For purposes of comparison we have added the figures for classes 1—8 and for all risks together.

4.3.1. Enumeration of signs according to tables

Enumeration of the signs from the tables of the individual extra mortality classes gives the following picture:

Class	s^+	s^-	$P_1(s^+)$	$P_2(s^+)$
1	3	9	0.054	0.073
2	5	7	0.193	0.387
3	6	6	0.226	0.613
4	5	7	0.193	0.387
5—8	6	6	0.226	0.613
	25	35	0.045	0.123

Viewed as a whole we observe a slight predominance of negative signs. However in accordance with the probabilities of error given under section 2.4.4 we can uphold the working hypothesis of constant multiplicative increase in mortality on the basis of this test. The binominal distribution taken as a base gives in fact, in the individual tables, a probability that the actual combination of signs obtained would occur of more than 5%.

In order to decide whether the results are random or significant, the accumulated values $P_2(s^+)$ must be taken into account as well as the values $P_1(s^+)$. The former show the probability with which one of the combinations of signs will appear with the number of + signs obtained or fewer. We may thus regard the ratio of 25 : 35 for all tables together as a random deviation from the ratio expected of 30 : 30.

For the sake of completeness we would mention that with 12 sections of the table only the combinations of signs 0 : 12 and 1 : 11 or 12 : 0 and 11 : 1, show individually as well as added together a probability of less than 1%. The base distribution $B_{12}(0.5)$ gives a probability of $1/2^{12} = 0.0002$ for the appearance of the combination 0 : 12 oder 12 : 0. However according to the way in which we constructed the sign tables, the probability is exactly zero, since the deviations are relative to an average value which lies between the maximum and minimum values of the mortality ratios in the individual table sections. The deviations can never therefore all be in the same direction, at least one must be in the opposite direction. We may nevertheless make allowance in our considerations for this slight incompatibility.

The two tables 'Classes 1—8' and 'All risks' show sign combinations of 5 : 7 and 6 : 6 and give therefore from this point of view no cause to reject our working hypothesis of constant multiplicative extra mortality.

Finally we shall show the results obtained by applying the χ^2-test to the deviations of the mortality ratio from the average value in the individual table sections, in fact for the grouping in table XXVIII:

Class 1:	No positive indication, since the probability of the random occurrence of deviations lies between 1% and 5%.
Class 2:	The deviations are to be regarded as random.
Class 3:	The deviations are to be regarded as random.
Class 4:	The deviations are to be regarded as significant.
Classes 5—8:	No positive indication, since the probability of the random occurrence of deviations lies between 1% and 5%.
Classes 1—8:	The deviations are to be regarded as significant.
All risks:	The deviations are to be regarded as significant.

4.3.2. Enumeration of signs according to policy years

One single column in a sign table can scarcely give any positive indications, since with the binominal distribution which we have taken as a basis, the probability of the occurrence of four similar signs is 0.063. In accordance with our conditions of significance (See section 2.4.4), we can never determine a significant deviation in a single column. We have therefore added together the signs for the five tables 'Class 1' to 'Classes 5—8' and have obtained the following picture:

Policy years	s^+	s^-	$P_1(s^+)$	$P_2(s^+)$
3—5	7	13	0.074	0.132
6—10	9	11	0.160	0.412
11—20	9	11	0.160	0.412
	25	35	0.045	0.123

Overall we see once again the slight predominance of negative signs. The values in the individual lines do not deviate significantly compared with our working hypothesis of a constant multiplicative increase in mortality. The noticeable predominance of negative signs in the group 3—5 years may be explained by the selection which extends beyond the second year of observation.

In particular the above figures do not coincide with the conclusion drawn by Sachs and his colleagues in their theoretical studies [5] that a decreasing mortality is of greater significance than a constant or increasing mortality. This would of course reveal itself in a tangible predominance of negative signs in the columns 6—10 years and 11—20 years.

Table XXVIII. *Risks of the extra mortality classes 1—8. Table of mortality ratios, i. e. actual deaths as percentages of expected deaths according to normal mortality, and table of signs showing deviations from the average value per risk group*

Attained age	Class 1				Class 2				Class 3				Class 4				Classes 5—8				Classes 1—8				All risks			
	Policy years				Policy years				Policy years				Policy years				Policy years				Policy years				Policy years			
	3-5	6-10	11-20	3-20	3-5	6-10	11-20	3-20	3-5	6-10	11-20	3-20	3-5	6-10	11-20	3-20	3-5	6-10	11-20	3-20	3-5	6-10	11-20	3-20	3-5	6-10	11-20	3-20
30-39	111	100	(0)	98	101	163	(109)	125	50	(229)	(260)	131	138	(175)	(405)	173	(201)	(531)	(208)	327	110	198	154	146	102	157	120	123
40-49	105	114	76	103	121	125	136	125	234	172	141	191	341	175	(83)	228	247	329	(145)	263	178	153	112	155	153	132	111	137
50-59	150	111	172	142	173	200	187	188	168	150	215	175	280	203	310	256	189	306	300	262	182	176	209	188	157	154	173	161
60-69	103	138	87	110	156	127	135	136	152	182	194	180	272	148	170	185	149	298	347	266	154	160	143	152	145	151	127	140
30-69	124	119	120	121	146	158	158	154	168	170	197	177	277	178	220	223	196	322	290	268	167	168	167	167	146	148	145	147
30-39	—	—	(—)		—	+	(—)		—	(+)	(+)		—	(—)	(+)		(—)	(+)	(—)		—	+	—		—	+	—	
40-49	—	—	—		—	—	—		+	—	—		+	—	(—)		—	+	(—)		+	—	—		+	—	—	
50-59	+	—	+		+	+	+		—	—	+		+	—	+		—	+	+		+	+	+		+	+	+	
60-69	—	+	—		+	—	—		—	+	+		+	—	—		—	+	+		—	—	—		—	+	—	

4.3.3. Enumeration of signs according to attained ages

As in the previous section a single line of age groups can give no positive indication, since the probability of the occurrence of three similar signs is as high as 0.125. We therefore combined the signs for the five tables 'Class 1' to 'Classes 5—8' giving us the following distribution:

Attained age	s^+	s^-	$P_1(s^+)$	$P_2(s^+)$
30—39	5	10	0.092	0.151
40—49	3	12	0.014	0.018
50—59	10	5	0.092	0.941
60—69	7	8	0.196	0.500
	25	35	0.045	0.123

Viewed as a whole we still have a slight predominance of the negative signs. The first three lines show a very one-sided ratio of signs whereas the age group 60—69 shows equal values. In contrast with the enumeration according to policy years, where the slight predominance of negative signs was present in all groups, we observe here a marked predominance of negative signs in the age groups 30 to 49 and of positive signs in the age group 50—59. According to our conditions of significance we must in fact regard the extreme ratios in group 30—39 and 50—59 as fortuitous deviations and make no firm statement in respect of the group 40—49. Despite the lack of statistical significance our results seem to indicate that the extra mortality is not primarily a function of the years of observation elapsed but of the attained age. Classes 1, 2 and 4, which include 70% of the years of observation in respect of substandard risks, show in fact substantially higher mortality ratios in the age group 50—59 than in the other age groups.

Within the scope of this study we cannot examine more closely the interrelationship of increasing duration and increasing age. We must therefore content ourselves with pointing out certain empirically established signs of this correlation.

4.4. Risks from impairment groups

The grouping of our impairment code according to the first number gives nine main groups. For six of these main groups we have drawn up tables as described under point 4.2. In making our choice we applied the condition that for at least six of the twelve table sections the mortality ratio was based on at least five or more expected deaths according to normal mortality. The sample thus obtained is presented in table XXIX following.

Table XXIX. *Risks of the different impairment groups. Table of the mortality ratios, i. e. actual deaths as percentages of expected deaths according to normal mortality, and table of signs showing deviations from the average value per risk group*

Attained age	General impairments				Respiratory system				Circulatory system				Infectious, metabolic and allergic diseases; diseases of the bones, the blood and the endocrine system				Genito-urinary system				Digestive system			
	Policy years				Policy years				Policy years				Policy years				Policy years				Policy years			
	3-5	6-10	11-20	3-20	3-5	6-10	11-20	3-20	3-5	6-10	11-20	3-20	3-5	6-10	11-20	3-20	3-5	6-10	11-20	3-20	3-5	6-10	11-20	3-20
30-39	48	(129)	(169)	74	102	79	(0)	88	172	421	(273)	263	95	236	(122)	147	(90)	(345)	(0)	166	74	146	(465)	114
40-49	139	100	(137)	125	104	138	63	111	243	151	160	195	184	158	127	163	124	159	(52)	127	141	123	73	124
50-59	202	180	176	189	193	180	168	181	160	189	206	181	170	152	151	158	116	146	245	162	174	150	169	163
60-69	205	176	262	204	205	158	158	170	182	165	129	162	128	146	127	135	110	152	170	145	122	126	107	118
30-69	159	154	194	162	155	156	143	153	186	185	171	183	156	159	137	152	114	160	187	150	144	137	134	139
30-39	—	(—)	(+)		—	—	(—)		—	+	(+)		—	+	(—)		(—)	(+)	(—)		—	+	(+)	
40-49	—	—	(—)		—	—	—		+	—	—		+	+	—		—	+	(—)		+	—	—	
50-59	+	+	+		+	+	+		—	+	+		+	—	—		—	—	+		+	+	+	
60-69	+	+	+		+	+	+		—	—	—		—	—	—		—	+	+		—	—	—	

4.4.1. Enumeration of signs according to tables

Enumeration of the signs from the table for the six impairment groups gives the following picture:

Impairment group	s^+	s^-	$P_1(s^+)$	$P_2(s^+)$
General impairments	7	5	0.193	0.806
Respiratory system	6	6	0.226	0.613
Circulatory system	5	7	0.193	0.387
Infectious, metabolic, vitamin deficiency and allergic diseases; diseases of the bones, the blood and the endocrine system	4	8	0.121	0.194
Genito-urinary system	5	7	0.193	0.387
Digestive system	6	6	0.226	0.613
	33	39	0.073	0.278

Viewed as a whole the negative signs again predominate here, but the ratios in the individual lines are more balanced. There is nothing in these figures which would lead us to reject the working hypothesis of constant multiplicative extra mortality.

For the above impairment groups contained in table XXIX we shall show the results obtained by applying the χ^2-test to the deviations from the average value of the mortality ratio in the individual table sections.

General Impairments:

No positive indication because the probability of the random occurrence of deviations lies between 1% and 5%.

Respiratory System:

The deviations are to be regarded as significant.

Circulatory System:

The deviations are to be regarded as significant.

Infectious, Metabolic, Vitamin Deficiency and Allergic Diseases; Diseases of the Bones, the Blood and the Endocrine System:

The deviations are to be regarded as random.

Genito-urinary System:

No positive indication, since the probability of the random occurrence of deviations lies between 1% and 5%.

Digestive System:

No positive indication, since the probability of the random occurrence of deviations lies between 1% and 5%.

4.4.2. Enumeration of signs according to policy years

The comments made under point 4.3.2 also apply here. We have therefore counted the signs for the six tables of the impairment groups chosen and thus obtained the following picture:

Policy years	s^+	s^-	$P_1(s^+)$	$P_2(s^+)$
3—5	9	15	0.078	0.154
6—10	13	11	0.149	0.729
11—20	11	13	0.149	0.419
	33	39	0.073	0.278

We receive a similar picture as in the corresponding table divided up according to extra mortality classes, i. e. a noticeable albeit not statistically significant predominance of the negative signs in the group '3—5 years' and balanced ratios for the other two groups. This global examination is therefore in line with the working hypothesis of constant multiplicative extra mortality.

4.4.3. Enumeration of signs according to attained ages

We have added the signs for the six impairment groups of table XXIX and obtained the following distribution:

Attained age	s^+	s^-	$P_1(s^+)$	$P_2(s^+)$
30—39	7	11	0.121	0.240
40—49	5	13	0.033	0.048
50—59	13	5	0.033	0.985
60—69	8	10	0.167	0.407
	33	39	0.073	0.278

Viewed as a whole, the slight predominance of the negative signs again appears. The age group 60—69 shows a balanced result whereas the other lines reveal one-sided sign ratios. According to our conditions of significance the sign ratio in the age group 30—39 is still a random deviation whereas we can make no positive statements in respect of the age groups 40—49 and 50—59. As with the grouping according to extra mortality classes it would seem correct to assume that the extra mortality is a function of attained age rather than of the policy year.

5. Transition to more dynamic methods for the assessment of the mortality of substandard risks

Our investigation has revealed that the overall picture of the individual extra mortality classes coincides fairly well with the hypothesis of constant multiplicative extra mortality, although large fluctuations occur in the table sections, particularly in the age groups. This result is in accord with the following comments made by JECKLIN in his study 'Betrachtungen zum Sterblichkeitsverlauf erhöhter Risiken': "Even if therefore the working hypothesis of constant multiplicative extra mortality represents for the time being a thoroughly useful method, there are indications that it could be replaced in time by more dynamic methods" [16]. Within the scope of this work we can only discuss to a limited extent these methods as well as the risk groups suitable for this purpose.

5.1. Choice of risk groups and introduction of more dynamic methods

For the choice of risk groups, in respect of which a transition to more dynamic methods for the assessment of extra mortality would seem necessary and for the formation of new working hypotheses the internal statistical records of assurance companies would no longer be adequate. This even applies for the professional reinsurers who combine the small portions of substandard risks issued by direct companies into portfolios of considerable size. In order to determine the mortality experience with individual impairments, life assurers must also draw on external material, particularly that of medical institutions. The assurance company is however repeatedly faced with the problem of converting the survival rates in hospital records into death rates. MARX has developed a comparatively simple method of conversion [17].

5.2. Simple administrative application

One of the greatest advantages of the multiple table hypothesis for the assessment of substandard risks is its simple administrative application. This advantage should be given due consideration before a transition to more dynamic methods is undertaken, since even in an age of automation all efforts for administrative simplicity are justified. Contrary to a widespread misconception, computers do not simplify complex problems, but require every detail in order to provide a solution in involved cases; this may in certain circumstances call for excessive work in programming.

6. Summary and final remarks

The working hypothesis of a constant multiplicative increase in mortality for the assessment of substandard risks in life assurance has been repeatedly criticised for not doing justice to the actual mortality experience. On the basis of observation data on substandard risks collected at the Swiss Reinsurance Company in Zurich the validity of this working hypothesis was examined. An innovation compared with previous similar studies was the use of two-dimensional tables produced by a computer, divided according to attained age and policy years. The observation material was divided on the one hand according to the estimated extra mortality and on the other hand according to medical features. We drew up two-dimensional tables for each sub-group. In order to round off the results we touched briefly on the distribution of the causes of death.

Our study has revealed that the overall picture of the individual substandard groups coincides fairly well with the working hypothesis examined, however in the individual table sections and above all in the individual age groups severe fluctuations appeared. Our results seem to indicate that the extra mortality is not primarily a function of the year of observation but rather of the attained age.

It was not and could not be the aim of our study to deal comprehensively and conclusively with the problem of the constant multiplicative increase in mortality for the assessment of substandard risks. We hope, however, that our efforts, which were in the main restricted to the gathering and interpretation of experience data, will give rise to further discussion on the subject of substandard risks.

7. References

VSVM = Vereinigung schweizerischer Versicherungsmathematiker (Association of Swiss Actuaries)

1. Jecklin, H.: Beitrag zur technischen Behandlung anormaler Risiken in der Lebensversicherung. Mitteilungen VSVM, Vol. 53, April 1953.
2. — in W. Saxer: Versicherungsmathematik, Part II. Annex: Grundlagen und Technik der Behandlung erhöhter Risiken in der Lebensversicherung. Berlin: Springer 1958.
3. — Beitrag zum Problem der sinkenden Übersterblichkeit. Mitteilungen VSVM, Vol. 58, October 1958.
4. — Betrachtungen zum Sterblichkeitsverlauf erhöhter Risiken. Mitteilungen VSVM, Vol. 61, April 1961.
5. Sachs, W., J. Staniszewsky, and G. Röper: Vom Wesen der Auslese. Mitteilungen VSVM, Vol. 54, April 1954.
6. See pp. 198/99 of the work mentioned under [3].
7. Denffer, H. v.: Zur Hypothese der gleichbleibenden Übersterblichkeit erhöhter Risiken. Septième conférence internationale concernant l'assurance sur la vie des risques aggravés. Aix-les-Bains 1955.

   Berger, G.: Zur Frage des Verlaufs der Übersterblichkeit erhöhter Risiken. Blätter of the German Actuarial Society, Vol. III, 1956.

   Gugumus, J., and G. Berger: Sterblichkeitsbeobachtung 48/56 am Bestand erhöhter Risiken der Kölnischen Rückversicherungsgesellschaft. Huitième conférence internationale concernant l'assurance sur la vie des risques aggravés. Helsinki 1958.
8. Cf. the work mentioned under [4], p. 133, 137, 140, 145.
9. Cf. the work mentioned under [4], p. 141.
10. Society of Actuaries: Impairment Study 1951. New York: Peter F. Mallon, Inc., April 1954, p. 12.
11. Cf. the work mentioned under [4], p. 141.
12. Ederer, F., L. M. Axtell, and S. J. Cutler: The relative survival rate; a statistical methodology. National Cancer Institute, Monograph No. 6, Washington, 1961, p. 108.
13. Wettenschwiler, K.: Über den Zusammenhang zwischen Perioden- und Generationstafeln auf der Sterbefläche. Blätter of the German Actuarial Society, Vol. VII, 1965.

14. See Impairment Study 1951 mentioned under [10], p. 4—5, and A. M. Lyle: Coronary disease as an underwriting problem. Transactions. Society of Actuaries, 1963, Part 1, p. 325.
15. See the work mentioned under [4], p. 133.
16. See the work mentioned under [4], p. 145.
17. Marx, A.: A life insurer's interpretation of survival rates. Annals of Life Insurance Medicine, Vol. III. Berlin: Springer 1967.

Other literature used

Croxton, F. E.: *Elementary Statistics with Applications in Medicine and the Biological Sciences.* New York: Dover Publications, Inc. 1953.
Documenta Geigy: *Scientific Tables,* 6th Edition. Basel 1960.
Hill, A. B.: *Principles of Medical Statistics,* 7th Edition. London 1961.
Pfanzagl, J.: *Allgemeine Methodenlehre der Statistik II.* Sammlung Göschen, Vol. 747/747 a. Berlin 1966.
Reich, Th.: *Idee und Praxis der medizinischen Statistik.* Bern und Stuttgart: Hans Huber 1964.
Spiegel, M. R.: *Theory and Problems of Statistics.* New York: Schaum Publishing Company 1961.
Van der Waerden, B. L.: *Mathematische Statistik.* Berlin: Springer 1957.

Appendix

1. Lay-out of punched cards for recording risks

Col.	1— 7	Reassurance number
"	8—11	Ceding company
"	12—14	Country in which life assured is domiciled
"	15	Race and sex
"	16—17	Type of policy
"	18	Rating office
"	19—20	Extra mortality class
"	21—22	Year of birth
"	23—24	Year of modification
"	25—26	Year of entry
"	27—28	Expiry of assurance
"	29—31	Profession
"	32	Reason for exit
"	33—35	Cause of death
"	36—37	Year of exit
"	38—40	Height in cm
"	41—43	Weight in kg
"	44—46	Circumference of thorax in cm (at inspiration)
"	47—49	Circumference of thorax in cm (at expiration)
"	50—52	Circumference of abdomen in cm
"	53—55	Systolic blood pressure in mm Hg

Col.	56—58	Diastolic blood pressure in mm Hg
"	59	Heredity
"	60—63	1st impairment
"	64—67	2nd impairment
"	68—71	3rd impairment
"	72—75	4th impairment
"	76—80	Further identifying features and spare positions

2. Coding of data

For sections of the punched card in which absolute values cannot be entered the data are coded. With one exception, the multi-digit codes are all of a decimal structure. In the following we shall make some explanatory comments on the individual sections of the table:

2.1. Race and sex

These two features are combined in one column, with an X punch mark in addition to the code designating female sex.

2.2. Year of entry and year of modification

Under year of entry the date of commencement of the direct assurance is entered. If the date of commencement of the reassurance is not the same, this appears under the section year of modification. The same section is also used for other exceptional cases, which cannot be discussed in detail here.

2.3. Blood pressure values

The entry is made in millimetres (mm Hg). Abnormal blood pressures, which affect the rating and are more closely defined, are recorded in the sections for the impairments by means of the respective numbers.

2.4. Impairments

An impairment means any deviation in the present condition (status praesens) of the life assured, his previous diseases (anamnesis) or his family history (heredity) from the norm. Each impairment is designated primarily by three numbers according to the code described under 2.4.1, the final number 0 is only used if the impairment cannot be more precisely described. Furthermore a fourth number records the time of the impairment. With an X punch above this last number it is shown whether the malady has been treated or not, or whether or not an operation has been performed.

2.4.1. Impairments code

General impairments 100

10 0 *Doubts concerning appearance*
1 Abnormal growth (dwarfism/gigantism)
3 Puffy appearance
4 Congested appearance
5 Cyanosed appearance
6 Yellowish or pigmented appearance
7 Sickly, weak, pale appearance
8 Overweight w. f. i.
9 Underweight w. f. i.

11 0 *Special signs and symptoms of disease*
1 Increased erythrocyte sedimentation rate
2 Other special laboratory findings (not separately listed below), regarding blood, circulation, respiration, digestion, urine, cerebrospinal fluid
3 Oedemas of unknown origin
4 Difficult respiration
5 Glandular swellings
6 Haemoptysis of unknown aetiology
7 Sleeplessness
8 Pollakisuria
9 Clubbed fingers

12 0 *Intemperance; addiction*
1 Abuse of nicotine, moderate
2 Abuse of nicotine, heavy
3 Abuse of alcohol, moderate
4 Abuse of alcohol, heavy
5 Opium, cannabis (hashish, marihuana) and heroin addiction
6 Morphinism
7 Cocainism
8 Abuse of medicaments

13 0 *Doubts concerning occupation, environment or character*
1 Unhealthy or dangerous occupation
2 Heavy professional stress (managerial type)
3 Unhealthy living conditions
4 Unfavourable environment or family conditions
5 Residence in unfavourable climate (not permanent)
6 Bad reputation or character
7 Bad financial circumstances
8 Suspicion that assurance is speculative
9 Hazardous avocations

14 0 *Deformities of skeleton; malformations (e. g. flat feet, fallen arch)*
1 Funnel chest or pigeon breast
2 Kyphosis/scoliosis without pronounced displacement of internal organs
3 Kyphosis/scoliosis with displaced internal organs

4 Coxa vara, dislocation of hip
5 Lordosis

15 0 *Amputation*
1 Amputation caused by accident, injury (incl. war injury)
2 Amputation caused by diabetes, gangrene and peripheral vascular diseases
3 Amputation caused by unspecified local infections
4 Amputation due to other causes

16 0 *Gunshot wounds*
1 Head, bullet not present
2 Head, bullet present
3 Lung, bullet not present
4 Lung, bullet present
5 Heart
6 Abdomen, bullet not present
7 Abdomen, bullet present
8 Spinal column, bullet not present
9 Spinal column, bullet present

17 0 *Aftereffects of accident*
1 Head injury (without fracture of the skull)
2 Head injury with concussion or cerebral contusion, fractured skull
3 Lung injury
4 Heart injury
5 Injury of abdominal or pelvic organs
6 Spinal injury
7 Fractures of the upper and lower limbs
8 Pathological displacement of bones (without fracture)
9 Sprains and strains of joints and adjacent muscles

18 0 *Damage by thermal or chemical action as well as by radiation*
1 Frostbite
2 Burn
3 Damage through X-rays or radioactive substances
4 Poisoning by derivatives of opium, barbituric acid, salicylic acid, belladonna, bromine, by pain killing and sleeping tablets w. f. i.
5 Poisoning by sulfonamides, strychnine, deadly nightshade, tainted food
6 Poisoning by petroleum by-products
7 Poisoning by lead, mercury, arsenic, antimony and their derivatives, by fluorides, acids, lyes, industrial solvents w. f. i.
8 Poisoning by illuminating gas, exhaust gas and other gases or fumes
9 Other poisoning

Diseases of the respiratory system 200

20 0 *Diseases of the upper respiratory tract*
1 Diseases of the nasopharynx
2 Tonsillectomy
3 Diseases of the paranasal sinuses (sinusitis)
4 Diseases of the larynx and the true vocal cords (laryngitis)

21 0 *Diseases of the lower respiratory tract*
1 Bronchial asthma
2 Bronchial asthma with emphysema
3 Bronchitis
4 Bronchitis with emphysema
5 Bronchiectasis (dilatation of the lung), congenital
6 Bronchiectasis, acquired
7 Bronchiectasis with emphysema
8 Bronchostenosis
9 Emphysema of the lung

22 0 *Diseases and abnormalities of the lungs (excl. tuberculosis)*
1 Pneumonia
2 Transient lung shadows, eosinophilic lung infiltration
3 Abscess of the lung
4 Gangrene of the lung
5 Cystic and honeycomb lung
6 Atelectasis
7 Fibrosis of lung (e. g. Hamman's syndrome), collagenosis, pulmonary sclerosis
8 Pulmonary embolism, thrombosis, infarction

23 0 *Diseases of the pleura*
1 Dry pleurisy
2 Exudative pleurisy
3 Pleural thickening, pachypleuritis
4 Empyema or history of empyema
5 History of empyema with marked thorax deformation

24 0 *Pneumoconiosis*
1 Silicosis, 1st stage
2 Silicosis, 2nd stage
3 Silicosis, 3rd stage
4 Asbestosis
5 Anthracosis

25 0 *Pathological lung conditions*
1 Changed percussion sound of the lungs
2 Mobility of the lung borders restricted or absent
3 Changed respiratory sound of the lung
4 Spontaneous pneumothorax
5 Residues after pulmonary tuberculosis, circumscribed
6 Residues after pulmonary tuberculosis, extensive

27 0 *Changes of the hilus* (except if caused by tuberculosis)
1 Enlargement of the hilus caused by pneumonia
2 Enlargement of the hilus caused by heart disease
3 Enlargement of the hilus caused by blood disease
4 Enlargement of the hilus caused by tumour
9 Changes of the hilus caused by other diseases

28 0 *Therapeutic interventions in lung diseases*
1 Pneumothorax, artificial
2 Extrapleural pneumothorax

3 Oleothorax
4 Thoracoplasty
5 Segmental resection
6 Lobectomy
7 Pneumonectomy
8 Phrenic crush (phreniclasis), exeresis
9 Decortication

29 0 *Other diseases of the respiratory system; special symptoms*
1 Shortness of breath (Respiratory rate: more than 20 per minute)
2 Chronic cough
3 Nosebleed
4 Barrel-shaped thorax, rigid thorax

Diseases of the circulatory system 300

30 0 *Diseases of the blood vessels*
1 Varicose veins, ulcus cruris, haemorrhoids
2 Thrombophlebitis, thrombosis
3 Arteriosclerosis, atheromatosis, atherosclerosis
4 Sclerosis of the aorta
5 Arteritis (Buerger's disease etc.)
6 Gangrene
7 Aneurysm of the arteries
8 Aneurysm of the aorta
9 Impaired peripheral vascular circulation of undetermined origin

31 0 *Elevated blood pressure (hypertension) w. f. i.*
1 Hypertension, not renal in origin w. f. i.
2 Essential benign hypertension (red hypertension)
3 Renal hypertension (white hypertension)

32 0 *Hypotension w. f. i.*
1 Constitutional hypotension
2 Circulatory hypotension
3 Endocrine hypotension

34 0 *Functional heart disorders; diseases of the coronary arteries*
1 Functional heart disorders, cardiac neurosis
2 Coronary insufficiency, diseases of the coronary arteries
3 Angina pectoris vasomotorica
4 Angina pectoris vera
5 Myocardial infarction
9 Delayed return of pulse after exercise (more than 2 min.)

35 0 *Abnormalities in cardiac rate, rhythm and conduction*
1 Tachycardia, 88—100 per minute
2 Tachycardia, 101 and more per minute
3 Bradycardia, 55 and less per minute
4 Paroxysmal tachycardia

5 Irregular pulse, respiratory arrhythmia, extrasystoles, sinus arrhythmia
6 Arrhythmia absoluta, atrial (auricular) flutter, atrial (auricular) fibrillation
7 Disturbances in conduction, atrioventricular (A-V) block, bundle-branch block, arborization block, Wilson block, interventricular block
8 Nodal rhythm
9 Disturbed repolarisation

36 0 *Changes and diseases of the myocardium*
1 Cardiac hypertrophy
2 Cardiac dilatation
3 Myocardial damage
4 Cardiac failure with signs of congestion in kidney, liver or lungs; oedema of the lungs, cardiac oedema etc.

37 0 *Valvular defects*
1 Mitral insufficiency
2 Mitral stenosis
3 Combined mitral valvular defect
4 Aortic insufficiency
5 Aortic stenosis
6 Combined aortic valvular defect
7 Tricuspid valvular defect, pulmonary valvular defect
8 Other combined valvular defects
9 Congenital valvular defect (e. g. persistent ductus arteriosus)

38 0 *Combined heart diseases; decompensated heart disease*
1 Cardiac defect not specified, with or without myocardial damage
2 Mitral valvular defect and myocardial damage
3 Aortic valvular defect and myocardial damage
4 Tricuspid valvular defect and myocardial damage, pulmonary valvular defect and myocardial damage
5 Congenital cardiac defect and myocardial damage
6 Mitral valvular defect, not completely compensated
7 Aortic valvular defect, not completely compensated
8 Myocardial damage, not completely compensated
9 Cardiac defect, not completely compensated

39 0 *Other diseases of the circulatory system*
1 Endocarditis
2 Myocarditis
3 Pericarditis
4 Pancarditis
5 Endocarditis lenta
6 Myocardial insufficiency
7 Circulatory insufficiency, collapse, fainting
8 Displacement of the heart (lateral, transverse, situs inversus)
9 Accidental heart murmur (functional murmur)

Infectious, metabolic, vitamin deficiency and allergic diseases; diseases of the bones, the blood and the endocrine system 400

40 0 *Tuberculosis of the respiratory system*
1 Tuberculosis of the upper respiratory system (mouth, pharynx, tonsils, larynx, trachea, bronchus)
2 Hilar gland and primary tuberculosis

3 Non bacillary, unilateral lung tuberculosis
4 Non bacillary, bilateral lung tuberculosis
5 Bacillary, unilateral lung tuberculosis (incl. cavities)
6 Bacillary, bilateral lung tuberculosis (incl. cavities)
9 Miliary tuberculosis

41 0 *Non-pulmonary tuberculosis*
1 Tuberculosis of the digestive system
2 Tuberculosis of the genito-urinary system
3 Tuberculosis of the glands (except hilar gland tuberculosis)
4 Tuberculosis of bones and joints
5 Tuberculosis of the skin (lupus vulgaris)
6 Meningitis tuberculosa
7 Peritonitis tuberculosa
8 Tuberculosis of the sense organs

42 0 *Venereal diseases*
1 Gonorrhoea
2 Syphilis, thoroughly treated
3 Syphilis, not thoroughly treated
4 Congenital syphilis
5 Serological tests for syphilis in blood negative
6 Serological tests for syphilis in blood positive
7 Serological tests for syphilis in spinal fluid negative
8 Serological tests for syphilis in spinal fluid positive
9 Serological tests for syphilis in blood and spinal fluid positive

43 0 *Other infectious and parasitic diseases*
1 Diphtheria
2 Scarlet fever
3 Dysentery (all forms)
4 Typhus abdominalis, paratyphoid fever, other salmonella infections
5 Malaria
6 Other tropical diseases (cholera etc.)
7 Actinomycosis
8 Brucellosis
9 Sepsis, all forms

44 0 *Rheumatism; diseases of bones and joints*
1 Muscular rheumatism
2 Articular rheumatism, monarticular
3 Articular rheumatism, polyarticular; rheumatic fever
4 Arthrosis deformans
5 Degenerative and rheumatic diseases of the spinal column incl. Bechterew's disease, Scheuermann's disease
6 Prolapse of intervertebral disc, lesion of meniscus, herniated intervertebral disc
7 Osteomyelitis and periostitis
8 Osteochondrosis, osteochondritis
9 Ankylosis of joint

45 0 *Metabolic diseases*
1 Pentosuria, levulosuria
2 Glycosuria, without diabetes mellitus

3 Ketonuria, acetone or acetoacetic acid in the urine
4 Hypoglycaemia
5 Hyperglycaemia
6 Diabetes mellitus, no history of coma up to now
7 Diabetes with history of coma
9 Gout, uratic diathesis (uratic arthritis)

46 0 *Diseases of the endocrine system*
1 Goiter, simple
2 Goiter, retrosternal or with clinical signs of obstruction
3 Hyperthyroidism, Graves' disease
4 Hyperthyroidism, myxoedema
5 Tetany, other diseases of the parathyroid gland
6 Diseases of pituitary gland, incl. diabetes insipidus
7 Diseases of thymus gland
8 Diseases of adrenal glands (Addison's disease)
9 Testicular or ovarian dysfunction

47 0 *Vitamin deficiency diseases, dystrophy, allergy*
1 Rickets
2 Beriberi
3 Scurvy
4 Other vitamin deficiency diseases
5 Dystrophy w. f. i.
6 Allergy w. f. i.
7 Allergy of the skin (eczema)
8 Allergy of the digestive organs
9 Medicamentous/chemical allergy

48 0 *Diseases of the blood and the blood-forming organs*
1 Anaemia w. f. i.
2 Hypoferric and other hypochromic anaemias
3 Pernicious and other hyperchromic anaemias
4 Hemolytic anaemias
5 Panmyelopathy
6 Polycythaemia vera
7 Leukaemias, also aleukemic forms
8 Haemophilia and other haemorrhagic diatheses

49 0 *Diseases of the spleen and the lymph nodes (glands)*
1 Splenic enlargement
2 Splenectomy
3 Lymphogranulomatosis (Hodgkin's disease)
4 Boeck's disease
6 Lymphoblastoma
9 Enlargement of lymph nodes (glands), lymphadenitis

Diseases of the genito-urinary system 500

50 0 *Pathological urinary findings; disorders of the renal function*
1 Albuminuria
2 Haematuria

3 Pyuria
4 Cylindruria
5 Limited ability to urinate; ability of concentration or dilution reduced
6 Increased nonprotein nitrogen
7 Pathological clearance values

51 0 *Diseases of the urinary tract*
1 Pyelitis, cystopyelitis
2 Diseases of the ureter
3 Stricture of the ureter
4 Cystitis, diverticulum of the bladder
5 Urethritis
6 Urethral stricture

52 0 *Diseases of the kidney*
1 Nephritis, also combined forms (glomerulo-tubular diseases)
2 Nephrosis
3 Granular kidney, primary (nephrosclerosis)
4 Granular kidney, secondary
5 Uraemia
6 Paranephritic abscess, renal carbuncle

53 0 *Renal and bladder stones*
1 Renal colic without positive indication of stones
2 Renal sand, renal gravel
3 Renal stones
4 Calculi of ureter
5 Bladder stones

54 0 *Malformations of the urogenital organs*
1 Hydronephrosis
2 Cystic kidney
3 Horseshoe kidney
4 Hypospadias

55 0 *Nephrectomy*
1 Nephrectomy because of trauma
2 Nephrectomy because of stone disease
3 Nephrectomy because of tuberculosis
4 Nephrectomy because of malignant tumours
5 Nephrectomy because of pyohydronephrosis

56 0 *Diseases of the male genital organs*
1 Prostatitis
2 Hypertrophy of the prostate, benign tumours of the prostate
3 Orchitis and epididymitis

57 0 *Diseases of the female genital organs*
1 Diseases of the breasts (except tumour)
2 Diseases of the ovaries and fallopian tubes

3 Diseases of uterus, vagina and vulva
4 Displacement of uterus (e. g. prolapsed uterus)
5 Disorders of menstruation
6 Menopausal troubles

58 0 *Pregnancy w. f. i.*
1 Pregnancy, normal
2 Extra-uterine pregnancy
3 Premature birth or miscarriage
4 Difficult labour
5 Caesarean section
6 Eclampsia

59 0 *Other diseases of the urogenital organs* (nephrotosis, floating kidney)
1 Hydrocele, varicocele, cystocele
2 Cryptorchidism
3 Sterilisation, vasectomy
4 Castration

Diseases of the brain and the nervous system 600

60 0 *Diseases of the peripheral nerves*
1 Neuralgia
2 Neuritis, polyneuritis, sciatica
3 Peripheral paralysis and muscular atrophy, Bell's palsy
4 Herpes zoster (shingles)

61 0 *Diseases of the spinal cord; myopathies*
1 Localized or systemic diseases of the spinal cord (except multiple sclerosis)
2 Multiple sclerosis (disseminated sclerosis)
3 Tabes dorsalis
4 Poliomyelitis anterior (Heine-Medin disease)
5 Thomsen's disease
6 Dermatomyositis
9 Myopathies

63 0 *Circulatory diseases of the brain*
1 Cerebral haemorrhage
2 Cerebral embolism
3 Cerebral thrombosis
4 Subarachnoid haemorrhage
5 Central paralysis (e. g. of sclerotic nature)

64 0 *Other diseases of the brain and the meninges*
1 Meningitis, meningococcus sepsis, meningism caused by virus diseases, etc.
2 Encephalitis
3 Cerebral abscess

65 0 *Syphilitic diseases of the brain*
1 Lues cerebri
2 Progressive paralysis

66 0 *Epilepsy*
1 Absence (temporary loss of consciousness), narcolepsy (petit mal, acquired or idiopathic)
2 Epilepsy, acquired
3 Epilepsy, idiopathic

67 0 *Diseases of the extrapyramidal system*
1 Paralysis agitans, Parkinson's disease
2 Chorea minor
3 Huntington's chorea

68 0 *Nervous and psychic diseases*
1 Neurosis without organic findings, nervousness, hysteria, melancholia
2 Depressions
3 Neurasthenia, nervous breakdown, psychoneurosis, anxiety neurosis
4 Psychopathy
5 Psychosis w. f. i.
6 Manic-depressive psychosis
7 Schizophrenia (dementia praecox)
8 Mental weakness
9 Attempted suicide

69 0 *Other diseases of the peripheral or central nervous system, particular symptoms*
1 Absence of the patellar or Achilles tendon reflex without detectable disease of the central nervous system
2 Pupillary abnormalities or abnormal pupillary reaction without detectable disease of the central nervous system (Adie's syndrome, etc.)
3 Tremor
4 Headaches, migraine
5 Vertigo, vestibular damage, etc.
6 Menière's disease
7 Sunstroke, heatstroke
8 Neurovegetative dystonia

Diseases of the sense organs and the skin 700

70 0 *Marked vision impairment*
1 Blindness, unilateral
2 Blindness, bilateral

71 0 *Inflammatory diseases of the eye*
1 Conjunctivitis
2 Iritis
3 Chorioiditis
4 Retinitis

72 0 *Diseases of the optic nerves*
1 Optic neuritis
2 Optic atrophy

73 0 *Cataract, glaucoma*
1 Cataract
2 Glaucoma

74 0 *Other diseases of the eye*
1 Papilloedema
2 Detached retina
3 Extreme myopia (over +5 diopters)
9 Eyeground changes as a result of hypertension

75 0 *Hearing disorders*
1 Otosclerosis
2 Hard of hearing (inner ear)
3 Deafness, one ear
4 Deafness, both ears
5 Deaf-mutism
6 Acoustic trauma

76 0 *Ear diseases*
1 Otitis media, mild
2 Otitis media, severe, with bone involvement

77 0 *Diseases of skin and mucous membranes (except syphilis and tuberculosis)*
1 Chronic eczema (if not allergic in origin)
2 Psoriasis
3 Erythema nodosum
4 Neurofibromatosis, Recklinghausen's disease

78 0 *Abscess, phlegmon, fistula*
1 Furuncle, carbuncle, abscess
2 Phlegmon
3 Fistula

Diseases of the digestive system 800

80 0 *Diseases of mouth cavity*
1 Bad denture
2 Alveolar pyorrhoea and other diseases of teeth and gum
3 Tonsillitis
4 Peritonsillar abscess
5 Parotitis

81 0 *Diseases of oesophagus*
1 Oesophageal spasms
2 Oesophageal stricture
3 Oesophageal diverticulum
4 Oesophageal varicose veins

82 0 *Diseases of stomach and duodenum*
1 Nervous stomach troubles
2 Gastritis, duodenitis
3 Hyperacidity
4 Subacidity, hypochlorhydria, anacidity, achylia
5 Stomach bleeding without detectable cause
6 Gastric ulcer, peptic ulcer
7 Duodenal ulcer
8 Stricture of pylorus, duodenal stenosis, cicatricial bulb
9 Gastric diverticulum, duodenal diverticulum

83 0 *Diseases of small and large intestine*
1 Intestinal pains of nervous origin
2 Enteritis, colitis
3 Terminal ileitis
4 Intestinal haemorrhages
5 Intestinal diverticulum
6 Rectal ulcer
7 Rectal stricture
8 Anal prolapse
9 Periproctic abscess

84 0 *Diseases of the liver*
1 Liver function tests: pathological findings
2 Urobilinogen increased
3 Icterus, hepatitis
4 Damage of liver parenchyma
5 Liver cirrhosis
6 Hepatic insufficiency (hepatargia)
7 Liver abscess
8 Enlarged liver if not cardiac in origin
9 Liver parasites, bilharziosis

85 0 *Diseases of the gall bladder and the bile-ducts*
1 Dyskinesia of the gall bladder and the bile-ducts
2 Cholecystitis
3 Cholelithiasis
4 Cholangitis
5 Empyema of the gall bladder
6 Congenital anomalies of the gall bladder and the bile-ducts

86 0 *Diseases of the pancreas*
1 Disorders of the pancreatic function, pancreatic achylia
2 Pancreatitis
3 Pancreatic necrosis (cured)

87 0 *Appendicitis*
1 Appendicitis, without perforation
2 Appendicitis, with perforation

88 0 *Hernia w. f. i.*
1 Hernia, reducible
2 Hernia, not reducible

3 Hernia, strangulated
4 Diaphragmatic hernia, hiatus hernia
5 Inguinal hernia
6 Umbilical hernia
7 Incisional hernia
8 Femoral hernia

89 0 *Other diseases of the digestive system and the peritoneum*
1 Meteorism
2 Ascites of unknown origin
3 Abdominal adhesions
4 Ileus, volvulus
5 Peritonitis
6 Arteriomesenteric occlusion

Tumours 900

90 0 *Benign tumours*
1 Benign tumours of the brain and the spinal cord
2 Benign tumours of the respiratory organs
3 Benign tumours of the digestive organs
4 Benign tumours of the urinary organs
5 Benign tumours of the genital organs (except prostate 562)
6 Benign tumours of the mamma
7 Benign tumours of the skin
8 Benign tumours of the bones
9 Benign tumours of the mediastinum

92 0 *Malignant tumours, treated*
1 Malignant tumours of the brain and the spinal cord
2 Malignant tumours of the respiratory organs
3 Malignant tumours of the digestive organs
4 Malignant tumours of the urinary organs
5 Malignant tumours of the genital organs (incl. prostate)
6 Malignant tumours of the mamma
7 Malignant tumours of the skin
8 Malignant tumours of the bones

The electrocardiogram in insurance medicine *

HARRY E. UNGERLEIDER, M.D. · EUGENE V. HIGGINS, M.D.

The electrocardiograph was originally a research device. It gradually became a major instrument in the cardiologist's study of the heart in health and disease. From this somewhat limited area of medical application, its use has progressed until today, it is found in the offices of practically all internists and many general practitioners. This development resulted from the facts that morbidity and mortality due to heart disease have shown a steady increase and the widespread study of electrocardiography has produced reliable interpretation criteria of diagnostic and prognostic value.

The same reasons made the electrocardiogram an increasingly important medical underwriting aid. It became particularly valuable because of the ever greater number of definite and suspected cardiovascular risks requiring medical mortality and morbidity classification. In the occasional case, it also was an effective guard against antiselection.

The obvious value of the electrocardiogram in insurance medicine made it a subject of study and report by medical directors of insurance companies. Life insurance actuaries and well backgrounded underwriting executives have also taken a keen interest in this specialized field of risk evaluation — particularly since the electrocardiogram became an automatic requirement in large amount cases, even though the applicant had no significant medical history and presented a satisfactory medical examination. Some of what is written here is directed to these sizable lay groups in an effort to assist their understanding of the medical underwriting application of electrocardiography. Listed at the end of this presentation are some of the sources, life insurance medical and actuarial, as well as clinical, which provided valuable foundation material adapted and applied for life insurance medicine use as our own experience and judgment directed. We realize many of the conclusions expressed and rating actions advised here are debatable — this is the normal basis for progress in both clinical and insurance medicine. Results will be studied as time passes and, with increasing experience in applying these extra mortality ratings, judgments will be made as to the need for and nature of their revision.

---

* This material was originally prepared for and is used in the Life Underwriting Manual of the North American Reassurance Company. It was revised and slightly enlarged for presentation in this chapter of the Annals. As it now stands, it corresponds substantially with the Electrocardiogram sections of both the North American Reassurance Company's Manual and that of the Swiss Reinsurance Company.

We stress that training and skill in the fields of cardiology and electrocardiography are necessary for the best possible application of this material to the problems involved in so technical an area of medical underwriting.

It is so evident as hardly to need stating but, to eliminate any questioning, we repeat that this consideration of the electrocardiogram in medical underwriting is not an application of extra mortality ratings to single electrocardiographic abnormalities. The electrocardiogram is a laboratory study which can reflect an aspect of cardiac condition and it is the variation of the heart from normal that receives rating recognition. We are concerned with the patterns of the electrocardiogram rather than with a single aberration. In this respect, electrocardiographic abnormalities are basically similar to heart murmurs or pulse irregularities noted clinically. In the latter case, pulse irregularity, the electrocardiogram can not only confirm the presence of the arrhythmia, it can also show details as to its place of origin in the conduction system or myocardium and the possibility of its cause being serious heart disease.

Throughout this presentation, we emphasize the need for correlating all underwriting data with the electrocardiographic evidence of normal or abnormal cardiac status. In considering practically any of the electrocardiographic patterns reviewed here, the importance of a stable pattern which has persisted unchanged for a period of years must, of course, be contrasted with a similar pattern which has developed suddenly or has transient recurrences. The significance of such factors will always require, not merely a table of extra mortality ratings, but a skillful individual case evaluation of an over-all picture by the Medical Director.

1. General considerations

1.1. Definition
1.2. Conduction in heart contraction
1.3. Electrocardiographic reflection of conduction and contraction
1.4. Time measurement in the electrocardiogram
1.5. Mechanics of the electrocardiogram
1.6. What the electrocardiogram shows
1.7. The current 12 lead electrocardiogram
1.8. Technical errors and artifacts
1.9. Factors in interpretation of electrocardiograms and x-rays
1.10. Electrocardiographic changes — normal or abnormal?
1.11. Extra mortality rating of electrocardiographic patterns

2. Electrocardiogram and x-ray requirements

3. Waves, patterns and segments

3.1. P wave
3.2. QRS pattern

3.3. Q wave
3.4. QS pattern
3.5. ST segment
3.6. T wave
Syndrome of the "suspended heart"
Minor and Major T wave changes
3.7. U wave

4. Axis deviation and hypertrophy

4.1. Right axis deviation
Intrinsicoid deflection
Ventricular activation time (V.A.T.)
4.2. Right ventricular hypertrophy
4.3. Left axis deviation
4.4. Left ventricular hypertrophy

5. Heart rate, rhythm and conduction

5.1. Heart rate and sinus rhythms
- 5.1.1. Heart rate shown by the electrocardiogram
- 5.1.2. Sinus rhythm
- 5.1.3. Sinus arrhythmia
- 5.1.4. Sinus tachycardia
- 5.1.5. Sinus bradycardia
- 5.1.6. Electrical alternans

5.2. Premature beats, premature systoles, premature contractions, ectopic beats, extra systoles, irregular pulse
- 5.2.1. Supraventricular premature beats
  Atrial premature beats
  Nodal premature beats
- 5.2.2. Ventricular premature beats
- 5.2.3. Multifocal premature beats

5.3. Paroxysmal tachycardia
- 5.3.1. Supraventricular paroxysmal tachycardia
  Atrial paroxysmal tachycardia
  Nodal paroxysmal tachycardia
- 5.3.2. Ventricular paroxysmal tachycardia

5.4. Block patterns
- 5.4.1. Sinoatrial (SA) block
- 5.4.2. Atrioventricular (AV) nodal escape
- 5.4.3. Ventricular escape
  Idioventricular rhythm
- 5.4.4. Wandering pacemaker

1. General considerations

1.1. **Definition.** Essentially, the electrocardiogram is a graphic record of the electrical activity of the heart. It provides information about the heart muscle (myocardium), and also about the conduction through the heart of the stimuli which cause the atria (auricles) and ventricles to contract.

1.2. **Conduction in heart contraction.** The heart contraction impulse originates in the sinus (sinoatrial, SA) node located at the upper border of the atria, and it spreads rapidly through the atrial myocardium. The impulse continues through the atrioventricular (AV) node, located at the junction of the atrial and ventricular septa, and then through the atrioventricular bundle (bundle of His) which divides into right and left bundle branches passing through the right and left sides of the ventricular septum. These branches further subdivide into the terminal Purkinje fibers which spread through the subendocardium and into the thick wall of the ventricular myocardium.

1.3. **Electrocardiographic reflection of conduction and contraction.** The passage of this impulse and the activity it arouses are shown in the electrocardiographic recording of a single heart beat as:

(a) The P wave — reflecting the initiation of the stimulus in the SA node and the depolarization, contraction, of the atria.

(b) The PR interval — the time during which the impulse travels from the SA node to the AV node.

(c) The QRS complex — the spread of the stimulus from the AV node, through the bundle of His, the right and left bundle branches, the Purkinje fibers and the ventricular myocardium, the beginning of ventricular depolarization, contraction.

(d) The RS-T segment — the end of ventricular depolarization, contraction.

(e) The T wave — reflecting the process of ventricular repolarization.

1.4. **Time measurement in the electrocardiogram.** Obviously, and it is mentioned only to stress the fine judgments made in interpreting the electrocardiogram, when the heart rate is 60 per minute, all the above takes place in one second. Hence, the time durations of the various electrocardiographic components of a complete contraction-relaxation (systole-diastole) cycle are measured in tenths and hundredths of a second.

In routine electrocardiography the time-marked tracing paper moves under the recording stylus at a speed of 2.5 cm (25 mm) per sec. For better study of the complexes, most machines also permit a speed of 5 cm (50 mm) per sec. In research electrocardiography speeds of 10 cm (100 mm) per sec. and even 20 cm (200 mm) per sec. (4 and 8 × the usual speed) are used and the component waves, intervals and segments of each PQRST complex are prolonged so as to be measurable not only in tenths and hundredths, but even in thousandths of a second (milleseconds).

1.5. **Mechanics of the electrocardiogram.** All muscle tissue produces electrical energy when it contracts in response to a stimulus. The tiny electrical currents produced by the activity of the heart are picked up by electrodes attached to the right and left arms, the left leg and the chest (in various combinations which produce the usual twelve lead electrocardiogram). Amplification of these currents by the electrocardiograph causes the quartz string of the measuring galvanometer to deflect in a series of up and down movements. The deflections are recorded photographically on a moving strip of sensitized paper in the photoelectrocardiograph. This machine gives excellent results, but has the disadvantage of not permitting immediate inspection of the tracing as it is being made, i. e., the recording must be developed and dried just as any photograph requires. In the direct-writing electrocardiograph the addition of another device converts the string deflections into mechanical energy which causes a pen or stylus to record them on a moving strip of paper ready for immediate inspection.

1.6. **What the electrocardiogram shows.** The electrocardiogram reveals abnormalities of rate and rhythm, i. e., of the origin and distribution of the contraction impulses. It also shows changes associated with active inflammatory processes of the endocardium, myocardium and pericardium and the residuals which persist after recovery. It can also reveal muscle wall enlargement, right and/or left cardiac hypertrophy.

It is particularly valuable in indicating the presence of coronary insufficiency, acute coronary occlusion, myocardial infarction, and the residual changes which often continue to be present long after an acute coronary episode.

1.7. **The current 12 lead electrocardiogram.** An electrocardiogram submitted for insurance evaluation should include the date and the applicant's signature for identification purposes. Currently a complete electrocardiogram consist of a properly standardized series of twelve leads —

(a) The three standard bipolar limb leads: 1, 2, and 3; these may be referred to as leads S1, S2 and S3; also as leads I, II and III.

(b) The three augmented unipolar limb leads, the aV leads: aVL, aVR and aVF.

(c) The six precordial V leads: V1 to V6.

1.8. **Technical errors and artifacts.** If there is any question of technical errors or artifacts in the electrocardiogram, it will help to recall —

(a) Lead 1 and aVL are similar.
(b) Lead 2 is shown as its mirror image in aVR.
(c) Lead 3 and aVF are similar.
(d) Lead 1 equals aVL minus aVR.
(e) Lead 2 equals aVF minus aVR.
(f) Lead 3 equals aVF minus aVL.
(g) Lead 1 plus lead 3 equals lead 2.
(h) Transposed leads, i. e. arm and leg leads incorrectly applied, show readily identified changes. This error usually occurs only when the technician is inexperienced or in a great hurry.

(h.1.) Right arm and left arm leads reversed. The error is identified and the electrocardiogram may be read by remembering:

Lead 1 is actually lead 1 inverted.

Lead 2 is actually lead 3.

Lead 3 is actually lead 2.

aVR is actually aVL.

aVL is actually aVR.

aVF is actually aVF.

(h.2.) Left arm and left leg leads reversed. The error is identified and the electrocardiogram may be read by remembering:

Lead 1 is actually lead 2.
Lead 2 is actually lead 1.
Lead 3 is actually lead 3 inverted.
aVR is actually aVR.
aVL is actually aVF.
aVF is actually aVL.

(h.3.) Right arm and left leg leads reversed. The error is identified and the electrocardiogram may be read by remembering:

Lead 1 is actually lead 3 inverted.
Lead 2 is actually lead 2 inverted.
Lead 3 is actually lead 1 inverted.
aVR is actually aVF.
aVL is actually aVL.
aVF is actually aVR.

(i) Inadequate or poor standardization. Properly standardized electrocardiograms show an artificially induced standardization wave, or square wave, which results from the momentary application of 1 mv (millevolt) of current, from a small replaceable dry cell battery, to the galvanometer string. This causes the string to deflect and record a square wave ten small or two large paper divisions in amplitude — on regular electrocardiographic paper these divisions measure 1 cm (10 mm).

The recorded standardization wave should have straight up and down deflections and sharply angled corners. Slurring of the ascending and descending lines with rounding of the corners of the 1 mv standardizing impulse occurs if the galvanometer is not correctly energized. The appearance of overshooting in the standardizing wave is described as underdamping. The appearance of curved sides and rounded corners in what should be a square wave is described as overdamping. These technical faults or artifacts can cause abnormal appearing changes in the PQRST complexes which may be interpreted as conduction or myocardial impairments. They may be due to inadequate skin preparation with the electrode jelly, or loose electrode connections, or carelessly applied electrodes.

(j) High voltage. The standardization in each electrocardiogram should be noted as it may show more than a 1 mv (10 small or 2 large paper divisions) deflection. This may mean careless adjustment of the string tension when it is tested with the standardizing 1 mv impulse. It may also mean the small battery which supplies the current for the standardization test has lost some of its normal voltage and can produce a 1 cm deflection only if the string is very loose. This results in all waves having abnormally high voltage because of the loose string. It may also cause abnormal appearing QRS complexes and/or ST deflections.

(k) Low voltage. The standardization may show less than a 1 mv deflection. This may mean careless adjustment of the string tension when it is tested with the standardizing 1 mv impulse. All waves will be low due to the tight string.

(l) In the case of the V leads, proper insulation of each precordial electrode contact point (V1 to V6) is necessary. This is accomplished by applying the electrode jelly to each, isolated V lead position on the chest wall. If it is applied as a wide, continuous band from V1 to V6, the pick-up of the heart's activity by the electrode may show an abnormal lack of change and an uncertain transition point.

1.9. **Factors in interpretation of electrocardiograms and x-rays.** Original electrocardiograms and x-rays should be seen whenever possible. If electrocardiogram copies must be used, they should be actual size, clear, and show the time lines so important to good interpretation. Photo copies of x-rays are seldom of any value and, if used for reinsurance purposes, should be accompanied by a satisfactory interpretation of the original film.

All electrocardiograms and x-rays must be referred to the Medical Director for his specialized mortality evaluation. However, all interpretations of electrocardiograms and x-rays, whether submitted by the physician doing the study, by a consultant, or by an attending physician, should be included as part of the reinsurance application file.

1.10. **Electrocardiographic changes — normal or abnormal?** The extra mortality ratings presented here for consideration with various electrocardiographic patterns attempt to recognize the fact that many pattern variants are associated with serious heart disease, but may also occur as physiologic deviations from normal in some individuals entirely free of heart disease. This dilemma is approached cautiously by thoughtful consideration of the medical history, medical examination, laboratory studies, family history, the existence of past normal electrocardiograms, the stable duration of the questionable pattern (i. e., do old grams show a similar variant?), the degree of gram deviation from normal (i. e., is it a small rr′ only or a complete right bundle branch block?), the age and sex of the applicant (with all else favorable, usually the younger ages and women receive more favorable consideration, except for those changes which may be regarded as compatible with the aging process and hence less significant after age 55 or 60 than before) and, finally, the exercise electrocardiogram may furnish the evidence needed to best assess the problem.

1.11. **Extramortality significance of electrocardiographic changes.** It is not possible to provide underwriting evaluation for every electrocardiographic variant or combination of deviations from normal. Consequently, the following material considers only the mortality assessment of the electrocardiographic variations from normal usually associated with the more commonly encountered cardiac impairments.

In applying these guides, it is important to realize that every electrocardiographic change must be reviewed and evaluated in the light of all the particulars of the case, notably the configuration of the other complexes in the electrocardiogram, comparison with previous and/or subsequent tracings, the applicant's age and sex, possible effects of medication, the clinical history, and other current findings.

2. Electrocardiogram and x-ray requirements

An electrocardiogram and x-ray should be furnished when a large amount of insurance is applied for. Since the incidence of cardiac disease rises with advancing age, consideration must be given to the need for requesting such studies for decreasingly sizable amounts as age increases. The exact amount level requiring special studies is a variable which depends on a combination of factors which must be evaluated by both ceding companies and reassurers.

This requirement may be waived if such studies have been completed within six months of the current application, are available for review and the interval history is satisfactory. When the amount applied for, or the total amount in force is substantial, particular consideration should be given to the possible need for, and the underwriting value of, special studies such as the exercise electrocardiogram, additional x-rays (chest, intestinal, renal, etc.), blood examinations and other diagnostic procedures (proctoscopy, prostate examination, etc.).

3. Waves, patterns and segments

3.1. **P wave.** This wave reflects atrial electrical activity, the initiation of the stimulus in the SA node and the depolarization, contraction, of the atria.

The normal P wave is upright in 1 and 2; it may be upright, flat, or even inverted in 3; it is usually upright in aVL and aVF; always inverted in aVR; usually inverted in V1; may be inverted, flat or upright in V2 and V3; usually upright in V4 to V6.

The normal P wave is less than 0.10 sec. wide and less than 3 mm tall; it is usually smooth, without notching or slurring.

P waves of abnormal appearance but with normal rate and rhythm indicate atrial muscle abnormality — hypertrophy, congenital defect, arteriosclerosis, etc.

P waves of normal appearance with an abnormal rate and/or rhythm indicate an arrhythmia originating in the SA node.

P waves of abnormal appearance with an abnormal rate and/or rhythm indicate an arrhythmia of atrial, AV nodal or ventricular origin. In some cases the P wave may seem absent as it disappears due to being superimposed on other waves of the electrocardiogram.

Leads 1, 2 and aVL showing notched and slurred P waves more than 0.12 sec long indicate left atrial abnormality, the "P mitrale" of mitral stenosis or of congenital heart disease. Increased height of the P wave is usually associated with atrial hypertrophy.

Leads 2, 3 and aVF showing tall, peaked, abnormally shaped P waves, indicate right atrial abnormality, usually hypertrophy, the "P pulmonale" of chronic cor pulmonale; they may also be associated with myocardial infarction or arteriosclerotic heart disease.

Inverted P waves in 1, 2, and 3 and upright in aVR indicate retrograde excitation, i. e. the stimulus originates in or below the region of the AV node and travels into the atria opposite to the normal direction, e. g., as in sinoatrial block.

Abnormal P waves are very often associated with abnormal rhythms, e. g., atrial premature contractions, atrial tachycardia, atrial flutter and atrial fibrillation.

P wave changes are not ratable per se, the underlying abnormality (the clinical impairment) is to be identified and then evaluated for rating action. See Section 5 for particular examples, and details concerning the above arrhythmias.

3.2 **QRS pattern.** The intraventricular conduction system is made up of the AV node and the bundle of His with its right and left bundle branches. The QRS pattern represents the spread of the stimulus through this conduction system and the ventricular muscle. Its normal form can and does vary considerably.

Slurring, notching or splintering. Slurring may be normal if it occurs near the baseline, otherwise it has the same significance as notching. Notching or splintering may be normal if they occur in low amplitude QRS complexes with duration less than 0.10 sec.

Where there is doubt about the meaning of the QRS splintering, the following considerations usually indicate normality —

a) No heart murmurs or abnormally split sounds.

b) P waves normal.

c) A QRS pattern of rSr′ or rSr′S′ contour with r′ equal to, or smaller than r (rsR′ suggests abnormality and requires further study).

d) A negative exercise electrocardiogram.

When "M" or "W" shaped QRS complexes are found in lead 1 and/or 2, study for any other evidence of previous ischemic episode; also, for possible intraventricular (IV) block.

When "M" or "W" shaped QRS complexes are found in lead V1 (and/or V2, V3) with a wide, slurred S in V4 (and/or V5, V6) study for right bundle branch block.

When "M" or "W" shaped QRS complexes are found in lead V4 (and/or V5, V6), with a wide, slurred S in V1 (and/or V2, V3), study for left bundle branch block.

Duration. The normal QRS duration is less than 0.10 sec. Prolonged duration, i. e., 0.12 sec. up, indicates intraventricular conduction defect and may be seen as intraventricular block (IV block), left bundle branch block, right bundle branch block, false bundle branch block, and peri-infarction block (see Section 5). It may be associated with left ventricular hypertrophy or right ventricular hypertrophy (see Section 4), quinidine toxicity, coronary sclerosis, myocardial ischemia or infarction, arteriosclerotic heart disease, hyperpotassemia, etc.

Amplitude. Abnormal amplitude of the QRS complex suggests abnormality of the ventricular musculature — hypertrophy, congenital defect, arteriosclerosis, etc.

Low amplitude, low voltage. When the total amplitude of the QRS complex (above and below the isoelectric line) is 5 mm or less in all three standard leads, myocardial damage must be suspected. It is not a specific finding, for in addition to occurring with diffuse myocardial damage, it may also be found in association with pericardial or pleural effusion, emphysema, hypothyroidism (myxedema), obesity and debilitating conditions. Look for possible confirmation of these suspicions in the voltage of the aV and V leads also, as well as for other evidence of abnormality to explain the finding.

High amplitude, high voltage. The maximum normal amplitude in any V lead is 30 mm. Amplitudes greater than this may mean thickening of the left ventricular muscle wall. However, such high voltage may be found normally in people under age 30, or those with thin chest walls or hyperdynamic hearts. See Section 4 for discussion of electrocardiographic evidence of cardiac hypertrophy.

3.3. **Q wave.** It is often difficult to distinguish between pathological and physiological Q waves. Abnormal Q waves usually mean previous myocardial infarction. Generally speaking, normal Q waves should not be wider than 0.03 sec., not deeper than 25% of the amplitude of the succeeding R wave, and not slurred or notched. Q waves are ordinarily absent or quite tiny, but deep Q waves may appear and be due to benign causes such as cardiac rotation or position. The prominence of the Q wave may be markedly influenced by respiration and also by position, i. e., standing or sitting. The benign Q wave in 3 and aVF may decrease or disappear on deep inspiration or in standing or sitting position. Unfortunately, the abnormal Q may show similar changes but, in combination with other considerations, this alteration may be helpful in evaluating the borderline Q wave.

Deep Q in Lead 1 to be considered abnormal must be more than 15% of the tallest R in the three standard leads.

Deep Q in Lead 2 to be considered abnormal must be more than 20% of the tallest R in the three standard leads.

Deep Q in Lead 3. The significance of this possible residual of a posterior infarction is further evaluated by inspecting the electrocardiogram for confirmatory evidence of abnormality:

a) A Q in aVF. If the Q in aVF is greater than 25% of the R in aVF (QR ratio: with Q 4 mm and R 8 mm; $4 \div 8 = 50\%$ and abnormal) the odds are two to one the pattern is a result of prior myocardial infarction. Naturally, if the Q pattern and abnormal QR ratio are seen in a current gram and there are prior grams without these features, the odds for coronary artery disease become much greater than two to one and rating as coronary occlusion is advisable.

b) An absent S in 1.

c) Q in 2 more than 2 mm deep.

d) QRS notching and slurring in 2, 3, and aVF.

e) T in 2 less than 2 mm tall; less than 1 mm even more significant.

f) T inversion in 3 deeper than 2.5 mm.

g) T inversion in aVF.

h) Q in 3 wide, 0.04 sec. or more from onset of Q3 to peak of R3.

The Q wave, particularly, must be underwritten as part of the whole picture.

A. Normal — small, short duration, clearly positional if large, not meeting any of the criteria for abnormality: Usually disregard.

B. Abnormal — meeting many or all of the criteria for abnormality, presumably the result of myocardial infarction: Classify as coronary occlusion, "Silent" Coronary.

C. Non-specific, indeterminate, borderline — not falling into either of the above two groups: +50 to +100 up.[1]

3.4. **QS pattern.** This is an entirely negative QRS complex, i. e., the initial deflection is downward and there is no deflection above the isoelectric baseline. In the V1 to V3 leads as small r wave is normally followed by a larger S, i. e., rS. It may happen normally that the r wave is not recorded and a QS then appears. Many QS patterns in V1 to V3 are not due to infarction and these show quick transition to rS, RS or qR patterns in V4 to V6. The QS in V1 to V3 is abnormal, and usually due to infarction, if followed by convex upward ST segments and negative T waves, or if abnormal QR complexes appear in V4 to V6.

When a small r in V1 to V3 is preceded by a Q, no matter how small, myocardial damage is the most likely explanation.

Serial electrocardiogram changes, clinical and laboratory evidence, and the exercise electrocardiogram may all be needed for the best evaluation of these patterns.

3.5. **ST segment.** This component of the electrocardiogram is normally isoelectric, but elevation is usually a normal variant, i. e., 1 to 2 mm in the standard and 2 to 3 mm in the V leads. Elevation may occur pathologically with acute pericarditis, early acute myocardial infarction and with myocardial aneurysm (review x-ray carefully). Depression below the isoelectric line is nearly always indicative of coronary insufficiency, particularly when the ST segment is horizontal, or sags downward, is prolonged and forms a sharp angle with the

[1] All figures in this text which are preceded by a+, e. g. +50, represent the extra mortality in percent to be expected for the particular impairment. Where a range is shown, such as in this case "+50 to 100 up", the specific extra mortality may be set at any figure within the stipulated range as judged by the merits of the risk.

proximal limb of the succeeding T wave. The ST pattern is also affected by digitalis, quinidine, nicotine and electrolytic imbalance involving potassium and calcium.

Minimal, suggestive ST lowering in the resting electrocardiogram is good reason for requesting an exercise electrocardiogram.

Significant, ischemic type of ST segment lowering in the resting electrocardiogram, with all else normal, should warrant rating according to the degree of ST depression —

Degree I, mild	0.1 to 0.9 mm	+200 to +300
Degree II, moderate	1.0 to 1.9 mm	+300 to +400
Degree III, severe	2.0 mm and more	Decline

With Degree I and II give serious consideration to requesting an exercise electrocardiogram, done preferably by the applicant's own personal physician, for such a gram will give a much better rating basis than the resting pattern alone. If the exercise test is to be done, stress the need for technically good electrocardiograms as described in Section 6.2. If the personal physician refuses to do the exercise test, the case is best declined. See the electrocardiogram exercise test, Section 6., for further discussion of the ST segment, particularly in reference to its cause and relation to sex and age.

3.6. **T wave.** The RST segment and T wave represent ventricular contraction and recovery. The T waves are unstable and the transition between normal and abnormal may be so gradual that great caution is required in evaluating their significance.

The T wave, clearly, is the most labile and non-specific component of the electrocardiogram. It is subject to change due to a great variety of normal and abnormal conditions as well as medications.

When T wave changes are accompanied by typical ST alterations, the diagnosis of subendocardial infarction can be made with fair certainty, but a specific diagnosis of myocardial infarction calls for the presence of abnormal Q waves together with the T and ST deviations. Clinical judgment and other laboratory studies such as sedimentation rate, white cell count, blood enzyme and lipid levels, etc., will always be essential diagnostic elements.

The occurrence of benign, non-specific, physiologic T wave changes is well recognized but, particularly in insurance medicine, the fact that similar T changes may be associated with serious heart disease must not be minimized. However, when the history is definitely negative for any signs or symptoms of cardiac disease it seems reasonably safe to accept changes such as those listed below as non-specific and benign. The problem here is, as always, complicated by the contrast between insurance medicine history and clinical medicine history — they are not infrequently found, after necessary investigation, to be widely (wildly!) at variance.

Non-specific and **probably** benign T wave changes include —

a) Low T waves in all 12 leads; often associated with obesity; accept as benign with caution.

b) Low T waves in the standard and aV leads with normal T waves in the V leads.

c) Low to flat T waves in the standard, and aV and V leads; accept as benign with caution.

d) Inverted T waves in V1, V2 and V3 may be the "persistent juvenile pattern".

e) Low or minimal T wave inversion occurring in a single lead as compared to occurrence in multiple leads; accept as benign with caution.

f) Low or inverted T waves associated with body position, i. e., negative T waves in leads 1 and 2 in sitting position which become positive in supine position. This is especially likely to occur in slender, long-chested individuals.

g) Syndrome of the "suspended heart". The chest x-ray shows a heart shadow suspended between the vascular pedicle above and the inferior vena cava below, i. e., the heart seems lifted off the diaphragm in deep inspiration. This anatomic configuration may be associated with abnormality of the ST segments (depression) and the T waves (inverted), strongly suggestive of myocardial disease. This finding is also seen in some slender, long-chested individuals. In these cases, marked ST and T changes can be produced by recording the electrocardiogram in both standing (abnormal waves) and recumbent (normal waves) position.

The T changes listed in a) to g), above, may have various etiologic mechanisms including physical position (supine, sitting, standing erect), suspended heart, obesity, exercise, tachycardia, hyperventilation, breath holding, food ingestion, drinking cold liquids, cooling, smoking, anxiety, fear, neurocirculatory asthenia, neurosis, electrolytic imbalance (potassium ion), metabolic disorders, infections, diffuse muscular diseases, medications, etc.

Additional T wave changes are the result of conditions such as bundle branch block and left ventricular hypertrophy where abnormal depolarization is followed by abnormal repolarization, producing an upright QRS and an inverted T wave (especially in the left V leads).

In evaluating these T waves "non-specific" does not mean "benign" in every case; nor does "variability" or "lability" of the T wave patterns indicate an innocuous origin. One particular fact demonstrates this very well — the increased incidence of non-specific T wave changes with advancing age. This suggests the possible serious significance of the non-specific T wave abnormalities, i. e., they may be associated with the increasing amount of heart impairment occurring as age advances.

T wave changes may, therefore, be benign or they may be serious residuals of prior coronary impairment, they may indicate the presence of left ventricular hypertrophy, or they may suggest latent coronary artery disease or even an incipient coronary episode. There is no rule for isolating simple, non-specific

T wave changes of benign origin from those caused by disease. Exact evaluation is impossible at this time, but the group of applicants with T wave changes does show an increased mortality rate and, therefore, an extra premium is required on each of them individually. Study of all possible data concerning the applicant is the only basis for underwriting action and almost identical electrocardiogram patterns can end being placed in widely different rating classes ranging from standard to declination. Judgment based on experience, knowledge and a "feel" for these problems and decisions will remain the basis for underwriting action until such time as more detailed statistical guidance is available.

Direction. The T wave is normally upright in leads 1 and 2 and in the V leads over the left side; it is normally inverted in aVR; in all other leads it is variable, often being inverted in lead 3 and in V1, less often in V2, and if inverted as far left as V3 and V4, it is probably abnormal in adults.

When the T wave points in the direction opposite to the expected direction, it is regarded as abnormal. This is referred to as a "Major" T wave abnormality and very often occurs in association with heart disease. It must be regarded seriously unless careful study tends to minimize its significance.

Shape. The T wave is normally slightly rounded and slightly asymmetrical. T waves which are sharply pointed, definitely notched or very symmetrical may be indicative of underlying heart disease.

The **ischemic or coronary T wave** has a symmetrical, deeply inverted contour; it may exist without accompanying alteration in the ST segment or the QRS complex, i. e., the infarct is limited, subendocardial, and does not extend through the entire thickness of the ventricle wall.

The **hypertrophy T wave** is asymmetric, i. e., it has the descending limb of the inverted T wave longer than the more steeply rising ascending limb, it has both limbs convex upward, and it has an associated ST lowering present.

Height. The maximum normal height of the T wave in the standard leads is 5 mm and in the V leads 10 mm. T waves of unusually low voltage are frequent and while they may be benign they may sometimes be due to heart disease, and careful consideration of the causative factors outlined above is necessary. Where there is a negative history and normal physical examination but low, flat, diphasic or inverted T waves in the electrocardiogram, it would be advisable to secure a recheck examination with inquiry concerning chest pain history, a chest x-ray, loan of old electrocardiograms for comparison, and an exercise electrocardiogram, so that the best possible evaluation of the problem can be made.

Since rotation and electrical position of the heart can affect both Q and T waves, the following notation is made before listing the advised ratings for Minor and Major T wave changes —

Vertical heart : aVF similar to V6, aVL similar to V1;
Horizontal heart : aVF similar to V1, aVL similar to V6;
Intermediate heart : aVF and aVL similar to V6.

Minor and Major T wave changes. Changes may be identified and classed according to these conditions:

A. With a normal but tall QRS pattern in leads 1, 2, V2 to V6, aVL in a horizontal heart, and aVF in a vertical heart:
Minor T changes — low, flat, notched T waves.
Major T changes — diphasic or inverted T waves.

B. With a normal but moderate to small QRS pattern in leads 1, 2, V2 to V6, aVL in a horizontal heart, and aVF in a vertical heart:
Minor T changes — low, flat, notched, slightly inverted T waves.
Major T changes — deeply inverted.

Before rating on T wave changes alone, remember that Major T changes with no other evidence of cardiac abnormality are rare; also, that recently developed changes could be much more significant than a stable pattern present for some years; and, an exercise electrocardiogram could contribute most helpfully to a sound underwriting decision.

Minor T wave changes	+ 50 to + 0
Borderline changes	+100 to +50
Major T wave changes	
Inversion less than 3 mm	+100 up
Inversion more than 3 mm	+200 up

3.7. **U wave.** This is a small wave which follows the T wave. Its exact origin is not understood. It is usually upright but may be inverted in leads where T is negative as in 3 and aVR. Large U waves are abnormal and may occur with left ventricular hypertrophy, with digitalis and quinidine medication, and in hypotassemia. Abnormal negative U waves are seen with myocardial ischemia and infarction and with hyperpotassemia.

4. Axis deviation and hypertrophy

4.1. **Right axis deviation.** In this instance, the bulk of the myocardial mass is to the right and the electrocardiogram shows a prominent S in 1 and a prominent R in 3, i. e., the major deflection of lead 1 is down and of lead 3 is up. This may be normal in young people or those with long, thin chests and vertical hearts.

The phrase "intrinsicoid deflection" used in the evaluation of both right and left ventricular hypertrophy is, as the suffix "-oid" suggests, a necessarily inexact measurement of the true intrinsic deflection (i. e., V.A.T., ventricular activation time). It is expressed as the time interval from the onset of the QRS complex to the peak of the R wave. Hence, the phrase "early R wave" or "late R wave" is also used to describe it. When it is longer than 0.05 sec it is prolonged and abnormal.

4.2. **Right ventricular hypertrophy.** This is indicated when the following conditions are present —

a) Marked right axis deviation.

b) Tall R waves in V1 and V2 with smaller or absent S waves; this may be shown more definitely in right lead RV3; the R/S ratio in these leads is more than 1.

c) There is delayed (or late) intrinsicoid deflection, i. e., greater than 0.05 sec, in the right V leads and V2.

d) Negative T waves in V1 and V2 are not specific as they may be present normally, but they also occur in association with infarction or right bundle branch block.

e) Deep S waves in V5 and V6.

f) Tall R waves in aVR, over 5 mm.

4.3. **Left axis deviation.** In this instance, the bulk of the myocardium is to the left and the electrocardiogram shows a prominent R in lead 1 and a prominent S in lead 3, i. e., the major deflection of lead 1 is up and of lead 3 is down. This may be normal in a stocky, broad-chested individual with a horizontal heart.

4.4. **Left ventricular hypertrophy.** This is indicated when the following conditions are present —

a) Marked left axis deviation.

b) R in lead 1 exceeds 15 mm; this is almost 80% specific.

c) R1 plus S3 exceeds 25 mm.

d) R in aVL exceeds 11 mm.

e) SV2 plus RV5 exceeds 35 mm.

f) RV5 and/or RV6 exceeds 25 mm and shows delayed (or late) intrinsicoid deflection, i. e. greater than 0.05 sec.

g) ST in lead 1 depressed 0.5 mm or more.

h) T in lead 1 less than 1 mm.

i) T in lead 1 inverted is more definite evidence than h).

j) Absent S in lead 1.

k) Deep S in the right V leads with high R waves in lead 1, aVL and V6.

l) ST depression and/or low to inverted T waves of the asymmetric hypertrophy type in the left V leads. For hypertrophy T waves, see T wave, Section 3.6.

m) QRS prolonged 0.10 to 0.12.

The presence of only one or two of the criteria for hypertrophy does not necessarily indicate enlargement or strain. In general, the more of these criteria present, the more likely the diagnosis is to be correct.

In rating both right and left ventricular hypertrophy, when indicated in the electrocardiogram, action will depend on the degree, an evaluation of the cause, comparison of old and current electrocardiograms and chest x-rays, medical examination and history. Definite evidence of left ventricular hypertrophy in the electrocardiogram is a serious prognostic sign.

Rating can range from:

1. +50 up, for minimal possible evidence, to
2. Rate for cause plus an extra for hypertrophy, to
3. Decline.

5. Heart rate, rhythm and conduction

5.1. Heart rate and sinus rhythms

5.1.1. Heart rate shown by the electrocardiogram. The electrocardiogram is marked by vertical time lines. The time interval between any two fine vertical lines is 0.04 sec, two heavy vertical lines is 0.20 sec (i. e., there are five spaces between two heavy lines, $5 \times .04 = .20$). The heart rate per minute can be read from the electrocardiogram by counting the number of fine time lines between the same waves in consecutive complexes and consulting a conversion table, as below:

Fine lines	Heart rate	Fine lines	Heart rate	Fine lines	Heart rate
5	— 300	17	— 88	29	— 52
6	— 250	18	— 84	30	— 50
7	— 214	19	— 79	31	— 48
8	— 188	20	— 75	32	— 47
9	— 167	21	— 72	33	— 45
10	— 150	22	— 68	34	— 44
11	— 136	23	— 65	35	— 43
12	— 125	24	— 63	36	— 42
13	— 115	25	— 60	37	— 41
14	— 107	26	— 58	38	— 40
15	— 100	27	— 56	39	— 39
16	— 94	28	— 54	40	— 38

5.1.2. **Sinus rhythm.** Rate normal and rhythm regular.

5.1.3. **Sinus arrhythmia.** Rate normal and rhythm irregular. This pattern shows a slight change in the rhythm of the heart's contractions. The atria and ventricles participate equally and there is no change in the wave complexes of the electrocardiogram. There is only a gradually varying time interval between successive normal complexes. The sinus node (SA node) forms impulses irregularly, but conduction to the ventricles is normal so that a fluctuating lengthening and shortening of diastole, the TP interval, occurs. This is often associated with respiration, i. e., the heart rate quickens on inspiration and slows on expiration.

It is usually not significant, but in older people (sixty +), it may be associated with arteriosclerosis or myocardial ischemia.

Under age 60	Usually +0
Over age 60	Evaluate with caution

5.1.4. **Sinus tachycardia.** Rate rapid and rhythm regular +100 to +160 per min. It does not mean heart disease per se; it occurs in hyperthyroidism, fever, emotional disturbances, after exercise, etc. The tachycardia may be simply the result of examination nervousness, or a temporary infection (rhinitis, bronchitis, cystitis, etc.), and temperature elevation may help identify the cause.

90 to 100 per min.	+ 0 to + 30
101 to 110 per min.	+35 to + 75
111 to 120 per min.	+80 to +200
over 120 per min.	Usually decline.

If the electrocardiogram is entirely normal, history negative and medical examination otherwise satisfactory, consider reducing these ratings by 25%.

The nervous reaction associated with the recording of an electrocardiogram may produce a simple tachycardia. If there is no history, medical examination or heart chart evidence of prior significant tachycardia, and the electrocardiogram is otherwise normal, this may be disregarded.

5.1.5. **Sinus bradycardia.** Rate slow and rhythm regular; 30 to 50 per min; it does not mean heart disease per se. However, it may be due to heart disease involving myocardial failure, heart block, hypothyroidism, and medication for high blood pressure. It may be a normal finding in a well-conditioned athlete. In the applicant over age 50 it may have serious significance. The examination exercise test with a good rate increase, a regular pulse and a prompt return to resting rate, is a helpful underwriting guide. Where age and amount warrant it, the exercise electrocardiogram should be requested. Rating, obviously, cannot be assessed simply on the slow rate of the heart.

5.1.6. **Electrical alternans or alternation.** This pattern shows regular sinus rhythm with the QRS complexes having regularly alternating changes of high to low amplitude with every other heart contraction. The T waves may also show such alternation of amplitude. If it occurs with paroxysmal tachycardia it is usually of no significance. Under any other circumstance it is abnormal and probably associated with arteriosclerotic heart disease and/or hypertensive cardiovascular disease. This electrocardiogram change has not been demonstrated to be associated with clinical pulsus alternans.

Rating cannot be assessed on this pattern alone. It requires careful correlation with all other features of the case and would be well investigated by means of a chest x-ray and exercise electrocardiogram.

5.2. Premature beats, premature systoles, premature contractions, ectopic beats, extrasystoles, irregular pulse

5.2.1. **Supraventricular premature beats.** These irregularities are usually benign. They may originate in the atria (atrial premature beats), or in the AV node (nodal premature beats). They may be difficult to distinguish, but both are rated in terms of frequency and response to exercise if the electrocardiogram presents no other abnormal features. See ventricular premature beats, below.

5.2.2. **Ventricular premature beats.** These generally have more significance than supraventricular. Careful examination of the configuration of the premature beat will help to distinguish those which are benign from those which have a serious cause.

Heart disease is more likely when —

a) The premature beats occur in runs of three or more.

b) They occur for the first time after age 50.

c) They occur for the first time after exercise.

d) The width of the premature beat QRS is 0.18 sec or more.

e) The premature beat falls on the T wave.

f) The time between the premature beat and the sinus beat varies, i. e., the coupling interval varies.

g) The beat after the premature beat (the postextrasystolic beat) shows ischemic ST depression or T inversion.

h) Bigeminy or trigeminy is present (bigeminy or coupling occurs when each normal beat is followed by a premature beat; trigeminy occurs when every two normal beats are followed by a premature beat or when each normal beat is followed by two premature beats).

i) The premature beats have a multifocal origin (see below, section 5.2.3.).

j) Ventricular premature beats may have value in the diagnosis of myocardial infarction. When a ventricular premature beat in the standard leads, in aVF (*not* aVR or aVL), or in the V leads has a qR or a QR wave contour, it is strongly indicative of myocardial infarction. This finding is particularly helpful in evaluating electrocardiograms where left bundle branch block masks other evidence of myocardial infarction. The QS pattern in ventricular premature beats does *not* have this significance. This "**myocardial infarction ventricular premature beat**" is diagnostic in about 90% of instances.

An irregular pulse found on medical examination or in an electrocardiogram should be studied by observing the effect of exercise. If this was not done at the time of the original medical examination, request a heart recheck examination with an exercise test. If this cannot be secured, rate as in C., below. Give careful consideration to the need for, and the help to be derived from, an exercise electrocardiogram; request it if the amount and the problem at all justify it.

A. The irregularities remain unchanged, decrease or disappear immediately after exercise:

Irregularities at rest	Under age 50	Over age 50
1 to 10 per min.	+ 0 to +20	+ 0 to + 25
11 to 30 per min.	+25 to +75	+30 to +100
Over 30 per min.	Usually decline.	

B. The irregularities persist and show a relative[2] increase in frequency immediately after exercise. Increase the ratings in A. by the following debits:

[2] Relative increase: The number of irregularities increase in proportion to the increase in pulse rate; e. g., at rest 80 with 8, after exercise a relative increase (25% in each) would be +20 and +2, or a pulse rate of 100 with 10 irregularities.

Irregularities after exercise	Under age 50	Over age 50
1 to 10 per min.	+ 0	+ 0
11 to 20 per min.	+15	+30
21 to 30 per min.	+20	+40

C. The irregularities persist and show a real[3] increase in frequency immediately after exercise. These ratings are also used when the irregularity develops immediately after exercise. Increase the ratings in A. by the following debits:

Irregularities after exercise	Under age 50	Over age 50
1 to 10 per min.	+ 50	+100
11 to 20 per min.	+100	+150
21 to 30 per min.	+150	+200

D. Possible modifications of A., B. and C., above.

(a) These ratings, A., B. and C., apply only if the heart rate after exercise returns to substantially the resting rate in two or three minutes. Where this does not occur the rating assessed should be increased by +25 up, depending on the heart rate, the degree of abnormality in rhythm and in failure to return to the resting rate, and on the overall evaluation of the case.

(b) If the electrocardiogram (or grams) is entirely favorable, showing none of the above listed indications of possible serious significance, and there is no evidence in the history or examination of cardiovascular-renal impairment, these ratings for pulse irregularity may be reduced by 25% to 50%.

(c) If the electrocardiogram (or grams) shows the above listed indications of possible serious significance, these ratings will be inadequate and must be increased, depending on the degree of abnormality, by +50 to +100 and even to decline.

5.2.3. **Multifocal premature beats.** When both ventricular and supraventricular premature beats are recorded in the same electrocardiogram or the shapes of the individual premature beat complexes vary considerably, indicating different origins, heart impairment is frequently present. Rating will depend on the complete evaluation of cardiac status and can range from increasing the rating for pulse irregularity by +50 to +100, and even to decline. An exercise electrocardiogram could help secure the best rating.

5.3. Paroxysmal tachycardia

5.3.1. **Supraventricular (atrial or nodal) paroxysmal tachycardia.** This occurs when a supraventricular focus originates a rapid succession of regular heart impulses, usually in a 160 to 240 per min range, continuing for seconds, minutes,

[3] Real increase: The number of irregularities show a greater percent increase than the percent increase in the pulse rate; e. g., at rest 80 with 8, after exercise a real increase would be +20 (25%) and +4 (50%), or a pulse rate of 100 with 12 irregularities.

hours or days. If the attack does not terminate, spontaneously or by treatment, congestive heart failure and death can ensue. See Section 5.5.4., Cardioversion, below.

The onset and termination of the attacks are usually sudden and are generally recognized by the individual. They tend to be of short duration, recurrent, annoying but not disabling and are classed as of functional origin if no other evidence of heart disease is demonstrable. Rate according to age, the number of attacks, time since the last one, the nature of the symptoms and the amount of care needed.

A. If a mild attack of only a few minutes to a few hours duration and occurring not more than four times a year:

	Under age 50	Over age 50
Single attack	+ 0	+ 0
2 to 4 attacks a year		
Within 2 years	+60 to +30	+100 to +50
3rd to 5th year	+25 to + 0	+ 35 to + 0

B. If a severe attack lasting more than a day and/or occurring more than four times a year:

	Under age 50	Over age 50
Within 2 years	+200 to +100	+300 to +150
3rd to 5th year	+ 75 to + 30	+100 to + 50
6th year on	+ 25 to + 0	+ 50 to + 0

5.3.2. **Ventricular paroxysmal tachycardia.** This is a serious impairment and an applicant with a history of such episodes will usually be declined. In a particularly favorable, well worked-up and studied case, with a history of a single attack, consider offering:

Within 2 years	Postpone
3rd year on	+200 up

5.4. Block patterns

5.4.1. **Sinoatrial (SA) block.** A lesion in or adjacent to the SA node prevents or delays impulses from leaving it normally. The degree will vary with the cause and extent of the block. It may be due to a variety of causes — arteriosclerosis, infarction, rheumatic heart disease, digitalis, quinidine, vagal stimulation, carotid sinus compression, etc.

5.4.2. **Atrioventricular (AV) nodal escape.** When the SA node fails to initiate the cardiac contraction impulse, the AV node, which has its own property of rhythmicity, usually escapes the block and begins to initiate the heart beat. This results in *AV nodal rhythm* which continues until the SA node resumes its function. Ordinarily the AV node is prompt to take on the pacemaker function and maintains a slow and regular rhythm. However, any delay in this transition can cause prolonged sinus pauses, cardiac standstill, which can produce dizziness, fainting attacks and even death in sinus arrest.

5.4.3. **Ventricular escape.** At times the SA block is followed by the initiation of the contraction impulse from some focus in the ventricular musculature rather than from the AV node. This is called ventricular escape and if the heart continues to derive its stimulus to contract from such a focus, it is said to show idioventricular rhythm.

5.4.4. **Wandering pacemaker.** This describes the shift in the origin of the contraction stimulus between the sinoatrial (SA) node and the atrioventricular (AV) node or the ventricular wall focus and is recorded on the electrocardiogram by changes in the P waves and in the PR interval.

Persistent AV nodal rhythm is usually a sign of myocardial impairment, particularly when in the electrocardiogram the P and QRS waves have no fixed relationship, i. e., the activation wave rises in the upper, middle and/or lower parts of the AV node in a succession of beats so that the P wave, which is changeably notched or inverted, precedes, is superimposed on, or follows, the QRS. With so many variables of degree and duration involved, rating action must depend on over-all evaluation of the applicant's cardiac status and could range from +0 to Decline.

5.4.5. **Atrioventricular (AV) block.** AV heart block is classed as incomplete (or partial) and complete. It begins when the AV conduction time, the PR interval, exceeds 0.20 seconds. As the degree of block increases, the AV conduction time becomes longer until dropped beats occur, i. e., the ventricles fail to respond to some atrial beats. Degrees of increasing block are shown by the number of atrial beats for each ventricular beat, i. e., 2 to 1, 4 to 1, or even higher proportions. As the block further increases the ventricles fail to respond to any atrial impulses, with the result that these chambers beat independently of each other and complete AV heart block exists.

AV heart block is most often found in association with coronary artery disease, arteriosclerotic heart disease and hypertensive heart disease. It may also result from rheumatic heart disease, digitalis toxicity, congenital causes and heart surgery.

5.4.6. **Stokes-Adams syndrome.** Adams, Adams-Stokes or Stokes-Adams disease or syndrome results from intermittent or permanent AV dissociation (block) causing episodes of unconsciousness due to cardiac arrest (standstill or asystole) or ventricular arrhythmia with impairment of cerebral circulation. A history of this syndrome will usually classify an applicant as not acceptable.

5.4.7. **Incomplete AV block, 1st degree,** i. e., no dropped beats.

A. Under age 40

	PR Interval	
Pulse Rate	**0.21 to 0.25**	**0.26 to 0.30**
Under 66	+ 0	+ 25 to + 75
66 to 80	+ 0 to +25	+ 75 to +100
81 to 90	+25 to +50	+100 to +150
Over 90	+50 to Decline	+150 to Decline

B. When the PR interval is over 0.30, usually decline. A favorable case may warrant an offer at the above range plus 50 up.

C. Age 40 to 50.
Increase the above ratings by +25 up.

D. Over age 50.
Increase the above ratings by +50 up.

E. Possible modifications of A., B., C., and D. above.
When the PR interval:

(a) becomes normal after exercise and the exercise test is otherwise satisfactory; or,

(b) becomes normal on changing from the supine to the sitting (or standing) position; or,

(c) has presented essentially the same pattern for over five, or better ten, years; and when the case is favorable in all other aspects —

Consider reducing the above ratings by 25% to 50%.

(d) in serial electrocardiograms shows the AV block is of recent development or that definite progressive PR lengthening has occurred —

Consider increasing the above ratings by +100 up to decline.

5.4.8. **Incomplete AV block, 2nd degree,** i. e., with dropped beats. Advancing degrees of block are shown by the number of atrial beats for each ventricular beat, i. e., 2 to 1, 3 to 1, 4 to 1, etc. Periodic block, e. g., 6 to 5, is regarded as less serious than constant block, e. g. 2 to 1, etc.

Rate as incomplete block, 1st degree, with PR 0.26 to 0.30, but increase those ratings by +50 for periodic block up to decline for serious constant block.

5.4.9. **Wenckebach phenomenon.** This type of block is included with the 2nd degree block group; in it the PR interval gets progressively longer from beat to beat until one ventricular contraction is missed and the cycle starts over.

Rate as incomplete block, 1st degree, with PR 0.26 to 0.30, but increase those ratings by +50 up to decline.

5.4.10. **Complete AV block, 3rd degree.** The SA node sets the rate of the atria and an independent focus in the ventricles sets a slower rate for the ventricles.

Congenital — serial electrocardiograms since childhood show essentially the same pattern; current exercise electrocardiogram negative +50 to +100.

Acquired — usually decline; a well-studied, particularly favorable case may warrant an offer at +300 up.

5.4.11. **Intraventricular (IV) block, bundle branch block (B.B.B.).** In this type of block the stimulus rising in the SA node passes normally to the AV node and after going through the bifurcation is then slowed or blocked in either one or both of the right or left bundle branches. It may indicate myocardial damage due to arteriosclerosis, rheumatic myocarditis, infarction, syphilis, etc. It may be congenital. It may be due to medication with digitalis or quinidine. It may be seen in electrolyte imbalance, as with hyperpotassemia (hyperkalemia). Hence, under these latter conditions of medication or electrolytic change, it may be a transient finding. However, transient bundle branch block can be associated with serious organic disease, so this feature does not necessarily minimize its significance. Where cardiac symptoms are reported or a history of cardiac disease exists, or where cardiac abnormalities are found clinically (e. g., hypertrophy, hypertension, angina pectoris, etc.), or the block pattern has been a sudden and recent development, it must be regarded seriously and underwritten with caution.

Bundle branch block can be demonstrated conclusively only by the electrocardiogram. Its prognostic significance is based entirely on its cause. Left bundle branch block is regarded more seriously than right, for the left bundle serves a larger mass of myocardium and when it is blocked can successfully disguise the electrocardiographic evidence of other cardiac impairment. In the case of right bundle branch block it is worth remembering that in one large study the most common cause of incomplete right bundle branch block was the incorrect placement of the precordial electrode for recording V1 and V2 in the 3rd intercostal space instead of the correct 4th space.

When the electrocardiographic pattern of bundle branch block is present, it may hide or mask the pattern of myocardial infarction. This is particularly true in the case of left bundle branch block, but an R′ or a notched R in aVF may be a clue to a posterior infarction, while a Q in 1, aVL or the lateral Vs with abnormal progression of R in the Vs may indicate anterior infarction. In right bundle branch block an infarction pattern may be more readily identified, i. e., the QT pattern of posterior infarct in 3 and aVF; and low to flat Ts in 1 and aVL with deep Qs and abnormal Ts in the Vs may indicate anterior infarction.

5.4.12. **Incomplete and complete bundle branch block.** Classification depends on the duration of the QRS complex:

a) Incomplete — 0.09 to 0.11 sec;
b) Complete — 0.12 sec or more.

5.4.13. **Right bundle branch block.** The main deflection of QRS in Lead 1 is negative; main deflection implies greatest duration not necessarily greatest amplitude.

A. Incomplete. All else satisfactory: +50 to +0.

B. Complete. Rate according to age and duration.

Known present	To age 40	40 to 55	Over age 55
Recent onset	PP[a] 1 year	PP 1 year	PP 1 year
1 to 5 years	+50 to +0	+100 to +50	Decline to +200
5 to 10 years	+25 to +0	+ 75 to +25	Decline to +100
Over 10 years	+ 0	+ 25 to + 0	+100 to + 50

[a] PP = postpone.

5.4.14. **Left bundle branch block.** The main deflection of QRS in Lead 1 is positive; main deflection implies greatest duration not necessarily greatest amplitude.

Incomplete and Complete.

Recent onset PP 1 year

Otherwise, rate as Complete right bundle branch block in 5.4.13., above, BUT increase that rating by +100 up in practically all cases.

5.4.15. **False bundle branch block, the Wolff-Parkinson-White (W-P-W) pattern.** The W-P-W pattern of accelerated conduction shows a widened QRS because of a shortened PR interval; it has a "delta wave" formed by a notching or slurring of the initial deflection of the QRS complex. This abnormal process of ventricular depolarization is referred to as the preexcitation syndrome. It is often associated with a history of episodes of paroxysmal tachycardia — the combination is the **W-P-W Syndrome.** In these cases, consider the frequency, duration and severity of the attacks.

A. Asymptomatic and no history of paroxysmal tachycardia.

Under age 40	+50 to +25
Over age 40	+50 up

B. With history of paroxysmal tachycardia, see Section 5.3., and increase that rating by +50 up.

5.4.16. **Peri-infarction block, parietal block.** This apparently results from delay in conduction in the small, terminal Purkinje fibers of the bundle branches. QRS is prolonged and may show slurring and notching. Abnormal Q waves may be present. There is left axis deviation with a mainly negative QRS in Lead 2.

According to degree, rate as Left or Right Bundle Branch Block.

5.5. Flutter and fibrillation

5.5.1. **Circus movement.** Circus movement is the phrase usually used to describe the origin of stimuli in an atrial focus which result in very rapid atrial beating but, due to block, a slower ventricular rate is present. It occurs in atrial flutter and atrial fibrillation.

5.5.2. **Atrial flutter.** The very rapid atrial beating, about 200 to 400 a minute, is accompanied by AV block so that the ventricles respond regularly only to each second, third, etc., atrial stimulus.

Rate as Atrial fibrillation.

5.5.3. **Atrial fibrillation.** The atrial stimuli occur so rapidly, 300 to 500 per minute, that the response of the atria is irregular and only occasional stimuli get through to the ventricles so that the ventricular contractions are irregular and the pulse is described clinically as totally irregular. With no history of cardiovascular-renal disease and with no other evidence of cardiovascular-renal impairment present, the condition may be ratable.

Atrial fibrillation occurs most frequently in association with rheumatic heart disease which has caused mitral stenosis, with coronary artery heart disease, and with hyperthyroidism. However, it also occurs with a negative history, no prior symptoms and an apparently normal heart. In these cases the arrhythmia may have been precipitated by extreme fatigue, severe physical or psychic stress, an acute gastro-intestinal disturbance, alcohol over-indulgence, tobacco excess, or immoderate living. With these conditions as etiologic agents, the episodes are usually paroxysmal and of brief duration.

A. Recurrent, frequent (more than four a year), prolonged episodes	Decline.
B. Present on examination	Usually postpone, investigate for possible group C. consideration.

C. Chronic, persistent, stable pattern present over three years, all factors in family history, medical history and examination favorable, no medication (except possibly digitalis alone) +300 up.

D. History of not more than four paroxysmal episodes a year —

Last episode	To age 30	30 to 49	Over age 50
Within 2 years	+75 up	+100 up	+300 up
3rd to 5th year	+50 to +0	+ 75 to +50	+200 to +100
6th to 10th year	+ 0	+ 50 to + 0	+100 to + 50
11th year on	+ 0	+ 0	+ 50 to + 0

E. Possible modifications of D., above —

(a) With a history of rheumatic fever or endocarditis or past or present serious murmur:

Consider increasing the above ratings by + 50 up.

(b) With only one episode in the past the above ratings may be reduced to:

Last episode	To age 30	30 to 49	Over age 50
Within 2 years	+30 up	+50 up	+150 up

(c) If, in addition to only a single episode, a current chest x-ray and exercise electrocardiogram are normal, the above ratings may be further reduced to:

Last episode	To age 30	30 to 49	Over age 50
Within 2 years	+0	+25 up	+100 up

(d) Obviously, similar proportional reductions will apply to the above ratings for the 3rd year on.

5.5.4. **Cardioversion.** This term describes the restoration to normal sinus rhythm of a heart in fibrillation or in paroxysmal tachycardia. The means used to effect this conversion, i. e., to convert an arrythmia to sinus rhythm, may be such oral medication as quinidine alone or quinidine with procainamide (pronestyl), or an electric shock with direct current applied over the precordium. The device for administering the shock is known as a cardioverter or cardiac defibrillator. The restoration to sinus rhythm must be maintained in most cases by daily use of quinidine, for a high percentage of shock-restored sinus rhythm reverts to fibrillation.

A particularly valuable use for this shock therapy is in the operating room to restore the heart beat when cardiac arrest due to ventricular fibrillation occurs during any general surgical procedure. In the case of cardiac arrest during surgery, with treatment effecting prompt restoration of sinus rhythm and with no evidence of significant sequelae, it could be safe to disregard the history of such a serious but short episode.

When cardioversion involves treatment of a persistent or recurrent damaging cardiac arrhythmia, the problem of underwriting is much more difficult and the case will usually prove unacceptable.

5.5.5. **Cardiac pacemaking — artificial pacing of the heart.** This consisted originally of the application of an electric direct current shock over the precordium in an effort to restore the heart beat after progressive bradycardia and heart block due to a variety of causes (acute myocardial infarction, electric shock, drug effects, vagotonia, electrolyte alterations such as hyperpotassemia) had ended in ventricular asystole (cardiac arrest). This was effective therapy and restored heart action in many cases. The method is deficient in that it cannot be used prophylactically.

In recent years cardiac electrical pacing effects have been achieved by using a transvenous endocardial electrode and an external power source. This method was made more readily usable by the development of permanently implanted pacing units with the electrodes attached to the epicardium and connected by durable, flexible wires to a battery pack inserted under the skin over the pectoral muscle or in the axilla. The procedure has resulted in prolonged useful lives, but it has serious hazards, is early in its development, and, for the present, applicants under such treatment should be classed as not acceptable.

6. The exercise or stress test electrocardiogram

6.1. **Purpose, rationale, types.** This test is helpful in determining the presence of early, or latent, coronary artery disease. It is not absolutely accurate but, subject to realization of the many variables involved, it does give reliable and valid evidence of the presence of coronary insufficiency usually due to atherosclerosis. It has accepted practical use in establishing the diagnosis, evaluating the effectiveness of treatment, controlling advice concerning activity and, of particular importance in insurance medicine, basing a prognosis for coronary artery disease.

Latent coronary insufficiency may cause no, or minimal, symptoms and effect no change in the resting electrocardiogram. The use of stress, a measured amount of work effort, quickens the heart rate, alters the myocardial electrolyte balance by a marked efflux of intracellular potassium (K) ions to extracellular areas, and increases the need for additional coronary blood flow. Subsequent to these changes, it is postulated that when the coronary arteries are not normally patent, the blood flow through them is insufficient for the needs of the heart muscle and myocardial ischemia results with, usually, symptoms, signs and significant electrocardiogram changes.

There are a number of stress tests. Some use various methods of physical exercise, others, medications, and still others control the amount of oxygen inhaled. Probably the test most frequently used is the Double Standard Two-step Exercise Test devised by Dr. A. M. Master of New York City. The amount of exercise to be done is determined by an age, sex and weight controlled number of trips over a standard two-step stairs in a fixed period of time. The Single Standard Two-step Exercise Test requires x number of trips in one and one-half minutes; the Double Standard Two-step Exercise Test requires 2x number of trips in three minutes. For our purposes, the Double Standard Test is routinely requested.

Tables listing the number of trips for men and women were published by Doctors Master, Friedman and Dack in the American Heart Journal of December, 1942; they were also presented and discussed in the journal Circulation of February, 1964. Adaptations of these tables are reproduced below.

6.2. Method of conducting the Double Standard Two-Step Electrocardiogram Exercise Test.

A. General instructions

1. The procedures must be completed exactly as described.
2. The test is to be done only under the control of an experienced physician.
3. The test must not be done within one hour of smoking, or eating or drinking cold liquids.

4. The test must not be done within one week of an infection (upper respiratory infection, bronchitis, cystitis, etc.).

5. The test must not be done within twelve hours of medication with peritrate or other coronary vasodilators. Inquire concerning this and report positive answers.

Tables. *Electrocardiogram exercise test for men double standard two-step. Number of trips over the standard two-step stairs*

Weight		Men — Age in years									
Lb.	Kg.	20 24	25 29	30 34	35 39	40 44	45 49	50 54	55 59	60 64	65 69
100—109	45— 49	56	56	54	52	50	50	48	46	44	44
110—119	50— 54	54	54	52	50	50	48	46	46	44	42
120—129	54— 59	52	54	52	50	48	46	46	44	42	40
130—139	59— 63	50	52	50	48	46	46	44	42	40	40
140—149	64— 68	48	50	48	48	46	44	42	40	40	38
150—159	68— 72	48	50	48	46	44	42	40	40	38	36
160—169	73— 77	46	48	46	44	44	42	40	38	36	36
170—179	77— 81	44	46	46	44	42	40	38	36	36	34
180—189	82— 86	42	46	44	42	40	38	38	36	34	32
190—199	86— 90	40	44	42	42	40	38	36	34	32	30
200—209	91— 95	38	42	42	40	38	36	34	32	32	30
210—219	95— 99	36	42	40	38	36	34	34	32	30	28
220—229	100—104	34	40	40	38	36	34	32	30	28	26

Electrocardiogram exercise test for women double standard two-step. Number of trips over the standard two-step stairs

Weight		Women — Age in years									
Lb.	Kg.	20 24	25 29	30 34	35 39	40 44	45 49	50 54	55 59	60 64	65 69
100—109	45— 49	52	52	50	48	46	44	42	40	38	36
110—119	50— 54	50	50	48	46	44	42	40	38	36	36
120—129	54— 59	48	48	46	44	42	40	38	38	36	34
130—139	59— 63	46	46	44	42	40	38	38	36	34	32
140—149	64— 68	44	44	42	40	38	38	36	34	32	32
150—159	68— 72	42	40	40	38	38	36	34	32	32	30
160—169	73— 77	40	40	38	36	36	34	32	32	30	28
170—179	77— 81	38	36	36	34	34	32	32	30	28	26
180—189	82— 86	36	34	34	34	32	32	30	28	28	26
190—199	86— 90	34	32	32	32	30	30	28	26	26	24
200—209	91— 95	32	30	30	30	28	28	26	26	24	22
210—219	95— 99	30	28	28	28	26	26	26	24	22	22
220—229	100—104	28	26	26	26	26	24	24	22	22	20

Tables adapted from reports by Dr. Arthur J. Master, et al., N. Y. C.

6. The test must not be done within three weeks of medication with digitalis. Inquire concerning this and report positive answers.

7. The test must not be done if the resting electrocardiogram shows acute coronary insufficiency or recent myocardial infarction.

8. The exercise must be stopped at once if serious symptoms such as chest pain or troublesome distress develop. Dyspnea and leg fatigue of reasonable

degree are not infrequent and do not require termination of the test. If the exercise has to be stopped, have the subject lie down and, if practical, record the electrocardiogram as outlined below. The nature of the signs and symptoms, the changed amount of exercise, and the subject's condition when permitted to leave the office, must be reported.

B. Equipment

1. Standard two-step stairs.
2. Direct writing electrocardiograph producing technically good electrocardiograms.
3. A watch or clock with a second hand (or a stop watch) for timing the exercise ascents and the intervals between electrocardiogram recordings.
4. Tables for determining the number of ascents for the Double Standard Test.

C. Procedure

1. Good records will be assured by preliminary care that electrical contacts are clean and tight, and by vigorous application of the electrode jelly to the skin.
2. Locate and mark on the chest wall the precordial V1 to V6 positions. Apply the electrode jelly to each V position separately, i. e. *not* in a broad band across the whole chest.
3. Record a complete 12 lead resting electrocardiogram, showing string standardization, with the subject in supine position. This is needed to detect any evidence of acute coronary insufficiency or recent myocardial infarction; also, as a reference to which the post-exercise electrocardiogram will be compared.
4. Exercise the subject by having him complete the required number of trips over the two-step stairs in exactly three minutes. This exercise will normally produce a fifteen to thirty per min increase in the heart rate. To be technically satisfactory the tracing recorded immediately after exercise should show this rate increase. See A.8. above.
5. Have the subject resume the supine position immediately and relax completely. Avoid base-line wandering by having the subject breathe lightly or even hold his breath momentarily while each short strip of electrocardiogram is recorded. Encourage physical relaxation, i. e., do not permit fist clenching or toe pointing.
6. Record the post-exercise electrocardiograms by timed intervals: Immediately, 2 min, 4 min, 6 min and 10 min after exercise; and, when indicated, at 5 min intervals thereafter until the electrocardiogram has returned to its resting state or is obviously not going to do so.
7. Record at each of the above time intervals, in the sequence here listed, a strip showing five or six complexes of: V6, V5, V4, Lead 1, Lead 2, aVL and

aVF. Use this same lead sequence in recording the electrocardiogram at each stated time interval.

6.3. **Interpretation of the electrocardiogram exercise test.** The changes produced in the post-exercise electrocardiograms are classed as "Negative" when no evidence of coronary insufficiency is present, and "Positive" when ischemic alterations are evident. Unfortunately, these are not always sharply definable patterns, for there are many post-exercise changes which do not have their significance well classified as yet.

The guide for evaluation of the exercise electrocardiogram outlined here uses currently acceptable classifications in which changes in the ST segments are the main points of reference.

A. Negative. No significant ST segment changes develop.

B. Borderline — Questionable. Major T wave inversions, significant arrhythmias and block patterns develop.

C. Borderline — Questionable. ST segment changes of the junction, "J" type, develop. These may be present as —

a) Transitory "J" lowering of the ST segments with a steep, concave ascent of the ST segment to T. This is frequently seen as a result of post-exercise tachycardia.

b) Prolonged "J" lowering with a less steep ascent of the ST segment persisting after the rate begins to slow down.

c) "J" lowering with a "U" shaped ST segment.

d) Near ischemic "J" lowering with an almost horizontal segment but an identifiable upward slope.

D. Positive. Ischemic ST segment depressions develop. The degree of ST segment depression below the PQ or PR segment is measured at the beginning of the ST segment, not at its lowest point, whether the ST segment is straight and horizontal or sags down with some convexity upward. The measurement for each lead is best made in the complex showing the maximum change.

Functional (non-specific or benign) ST segment changes tend to be maximal in the immediate post-exercise tracing and ischemic ST segment changes in the 2 min and 4 min post-exercise electrocardiograms.

Ischemic ST segment depression, a positive exercise test, is classed and rated as:

Degree I, mild	0.1 mm to 0.9 mm	+100 to +200
Degree II, moderate	1.0 mm to 1.9 mm	+200 to +400
Degree III, severe	2.0 mm and more	Decline

When an exercise response as described in B., above, is the only isolated finding, it will be advisable to consider rating for the degree and duration of the change shown, i. e., see ratings for Major and Minor T wave changes (Section 3.6.) and for the arrhythmias (Section 5).

When an exercise response as described in C., above, is the only isolated finding, no, or minimal, additional mortality may be anticipated.

However, in the case of both B. and C. responses, a history of definite or suspected coronary disease, angina pectoris, irregular pulse, marked overweight, hypertension, diabetes, hypercholesterolemia, etc., combines badly with any T wave, ST segment, rhythm or conduction changes and final mortality evaluation must be made with caution so that an adequate rating is applied.

6.4. **False negative and false positive.** Incorrect interpretations of the electrocardiogram exercise test are possible and consideration of the factors which influence the electrocardiogram patterns as well as consultation with experienced electrocardiologists will considerably reduce the chance of such erroneous decisions.

It seems obvious, from the discussion of this test, that there will be technically perfect electrocardiograms properly interpreted according to accepted criteria which will, nevertheless, fail to present the true condition of the subject and therefore be false negative or false positive, as the case may be.

Determine the resting heart rate in the control electrocardiogram and then the rate immediately after exercise. Unless the heart rate at rest is quite slow, less than 60 per min, the amount of work done in the double standard two-step exercise test will almost always produce an increase in heart rate to over 90 per min. If this is lacking, the value of the test is lessened.

The ST segment may be seriously affected and rendered uninterpretable by a wandering (falling or rising) base line (isoelectric line). Good technique in preparing the subject and in recording the electrocardiogram can minimize this defect.

False negative tests may result because of insufficient stress, i. e., the exercise test is poorly done or carelessly controlled. They may also be due to poor standardization of the electrocardiograph string, i. e., it is too tight to record the deflections accurately. This is another reason why a technically good electrocardiogram always includes a record of string standardization. When it is omitted, through error or carelessness, these important judgments cannot be made accurately. Finally, a delay in recording the electrocardiogram after exercise may result in the omission of significant changes.

False positive tests may be the result of any circumstance associated with low potassium (K) ion content of the myocardium, e. g., rapid heart rate, hyperventilation, a recent meal, older ages, female sex, anxiety, hypertension (especially with low salt diet therapy), digitalis, myocardial disease, etc. Poor standardization, too loose a string, may cause the recording of suspiciously changed ST segments leading to errors in interpretation.

There is normally considerably decreased myocardial potassium (K) ion in women as compared with men, and also in older (over fifty) persons of both sexes. For this reason, slightly depressed ST segments in the resting electrocardiogram are not infrequently seen in these individuals and after exercise further lowering of the ST segments may occur and be interpreted as a positive test. Hence, the test is of limited value in women and in older men, unless marked ST segment changes occur.

The exercise electrocardiogram cannot be regarded as a valid diagnostic test in the presence of a baseline abnormal electrocardiogram. The presence of bundle branch block or the W-P-W pattern does not warrant meaningful interpretation of the exercise electrocardiogram should it be done when those conditions are known to be present at rest. The instability of ventricular conduction in the W-P-W pattern particularly, produces ST segment and T wave changes of positive degree after exercise, yet these may often be safely classed as false positive changes.

The exercise test may be done, however, in the presence of block patterns for whatever evidence it may present in efforts to reach a conclusion concerning the congenital or coronary sclerosis origin of the block. The development of multifocal arrhythmias or grossly abnormal ST segment and T wave alterations must be interpreted as increasing the serious evaluation placed on the basic clinical and electrocardiographic abnormality.

Coronary artery sclerosis has been proven to occur in many young men and fatal coronary occlusion, myocardial infarction, is not as infrequent among them as once thought. Myocardial infarction can occur with no, or very vague, signs and symptoms. Probably 25% to 30% of all myocardial infarctions are not recognized as such at the time of their occurrence. The electrocardiogram will not identify all of these "silent coronary" cases, but it will show residual changes or serial changes in many of them.

The electrocardiogram exercise test does not eliminate the possibility of a prior myocardial infarction, for its purpose is to show the adequacy of current coronary circulation. In a group with a known history of myocardial infarction, over 30% will have normal electrocardiogram exercise tests. The best method of establishing a diagnosis of past or current myocardial infarction is to study a series of electrocardiograms and demonstrate sequential changes in the QRS complexes, the ST segments and the T waves.

7. Conclusion

In evaluating some of the problems noted above, consultation will frequently be advisable. A discussion of a particular situation involving one or a series of electrocardiograms by several members of a medical department staff, or between the Medical Director of a direct writing company and the medical staff of a reassurance company, can be a most helpful procedure before final underwriting action is taken.

8. Electrocardiographic source references

BRADLOW, B. A.: How to produce a readable electrocardiogram. Textbook. C. C. Thomas 1964.
FRIEDBERG, CH. K.: Diseases of the heart. Textbook. W. B. Saunders 1966.
GUBNER, R. S.: An appraisal of the exercise electrocardiogram test. J. Occup. Med. 2 and 3 (1960); — Ann. Life Ins. Med. 1 (1962).
—, and H. E. UNGERLEIDER: Long-term prognosis and insurability in coronary heart disease. Amer. Heart J. 58, No. 3 (Sept. 1959).
LAMB, L. E.: Electrocardiography and Vectorcardiography. Textbook. W. B. Saunders 1965.
ROBB, G. P., and H. H. MARKS: Prognosis in coronary heart disease. Proceed. Med. Sect. A.L.C. 1964.
— — The postexercise electrocardiogram in arteriosclerotic heart disease. J. Amer. Med. Ass. 200, No. 11, June 12 (1967).
RODSTEIN, M., R. S. GUBNER, J. P. MILLS, J. F. LOVELL, and H. E. UNGERLEIDER: A mortality study in bundle branch block. Arch. Int. Med. 87, 663—668 (1951).
—, L. WOLLOCH, and R. S. GUBNER: The significance of minor electrocardiographic T wave changes. Amer. J. med. Sci. 252, No. 1 (July 1966).
SINGER, R. B.: Bundle branch block and related defects. Proceed. Med. Sect. A.L.C. 1962.
— Mortality in 966 Life Insurance Applicants with Bundle Branch Block or Wide QRS. Trans. Life Insur. Med. Dir. 1968.
UNGERLEIDER, H. E.: The prognostic implications of the electrocardiogram. Amer. J. Card. 6, No. 4 (July 1960); — Ann. Life Ins. Med. 1 (1962).
— The electrocardiogram in practical risk appraisal. Trans. Life Insur. Med. Dir. Amer. 1946.
—, and R. S. GUBNER: Life Insurance and Medicine. Textbook. C. C. Thomas 1958.
WILKINSON, R. S., JR., J. A. SCHAEFFER, and J. A. ABILDSKOV: Electrocardiographic and pathologic features of myocardial infarction in man. Ann. Life Ins. Med. 2 (1964).
ZION, M. D.: The role of the electrocardiogram in underwriting. Ann. Life Ins. Med. 2 (1964).

Right bundle branch block

Max Holzmann

The term right bundle branch block (RBBB) was originally anatomically and functionally strictly defined. The term is based on the experiments of Eppinger and Rothberger with animals (1909), in which the right branch of the atrioventricular bundle was cut. The functional consequences produced a typical change of the ECG which corresponds to a delayed activation of the right ventricle.

When the findings gathered from animal experiments were first used to study the ECG changes in the human being a mistake as to the localisation occurred. However later on this mistake was eliminated among other things by using the precordial leads of Wilson and a variety of functional tests.

By means of numerous pathological-anatomical examinations of the human heart the consequences of a pronounced functional impairment or an interruption of the right branch of the atrioventricular bundle were conclusively proved. Complete right bundle branch blocks are as a rule the result of a total or near-total interruption of the right branch whereas incomplete RBBB arise as a result of overdistention of the hypertrophied right ventricle without evidence of extensive histological damage of the right branch of the atrioventricular bundle (Lenègre). In these cases, we must assume that the delayed spread of impulse of the right ventricle is the result of functional damage to the whole ipsilateral specific conduction system as well as to the synapses of the working myocard. The left branch of the atrioventricular bundle shows similar features with regard to the left ventricle. I have therefore recommended the use of the term bundle branch block picture in typical ECG changes as it occurs in fact in a bundle branch block or as it also may result from peripheral damage to the specific conduction system. For the same reasons Katz suggested that the term "intraventricular block" be used instead of bundle branch block.

In order to justify the diagnosis of RBBB, it is imperative that the impulse of the entire right ventricle be delayed. As the activation of the ventricle originates normally on the left side of the ventricular septum no change takes place in the ECG within the first 20 milliseconds in the case of an RBBB. Only in the subsequent part of the initial ventricular deflection — as a result of the delay in depolarization of the right ventricle — do the vectors deviate to the right, forwards and upwards. As this spread of impulse does not take place through the fast conducting Purkinje fibres, the impulse travels more slowly and the resulting waves are wide in the scalar leads.

The delayed impulse of the right ventricle may be the result of a delay or a complete absence of the spread of impulse of the right branch of the atrioventricular bundle. Consequently different degrees of conduction disturbance can be distinguished. It has become practice to consider a QRS prolongation to 0.12 sec. or more as a complete RBBB and a prolongation to 0.105—0.115 as a partial or incomplete RBBB. However, in this way no account is taken of the fact that in the adult the spread of activation in the right ventricle, which has fewer muscles than the left, takes less time than in the left ventricle and that in the right ventricle it comes to an end before the QRS group is complete. A given prolongation of the QRS duration corresponds to a greater delay if it occurs in the right ventricle than if it occurs in the left. An incomplete bundle branch block can therefore already be present in an adult if the QRS duration is 0.09—0.105 sec. Such an assumption may be confirmed by comparison with the previous normal ECG pattern. In infancy and childhood this is anyway necessary. In adulthood one has to reckon with an average QRS duration of 0.09 sec. but it is also known that in tall men the duration may be up to 0.11 sec.

The delay of the final and highest peak (fhp) [= intrinsicoid deflection (Wilson) = onset of the highest negative deflection (Holzmann) upper reversal point (Gillmann)] in the precordial leads over the right ventricle ($V_{1, 2, E, r_3 - r_4}$) exceeding 0.04 sec. is therefore a better criterion for the activation delay of the right ventricle (0.05—0.09 sec. in an incomplete, $>$ 0.09 sec. in a complete RBBB).

This situation is however complicated by physiological variants and also pathological conditions with hypertrophy of the crista supraventricularis dextra. In this case the outflow tract of the right ventricle is activated last and there appear in the right precordial leads as well as in V_R small positive waves at the end of the QRS group. Analogous pictures may arise because of a focal block in this area or because of distortion of the electrical field in the case of a funnel chest (Portheine). If the QRS duration is 0.09—0.11 sec. pictures may occur which cannot be distinguished from those of an incomplete RBBB. This has been confirmed experimentally and also emerges from observations on supraventricular extrasystoles with different couplings and abnormal ventricular conduction of varying degrees as well as in residual findings after successful heart surgery in patients who previously had a complete RBBB. A safe genetic differentiation of such isolated ECG findings is not possible. Now and then the probable cause of such findings can only be assumed on the basis of the personal medical history and the accompanying clinical findings.

The most important variations in the ECG pattern are obtained from the leads which are taken over the right heart. In the majority of cases, the standard leads V_1 and V_2 are sufficient. Not infrequently the decisive finding only comes to light in the supplementary leads V_{r_3} or V_{r_4}. These leads must therefore be consulted in all cases where the leads V_1 and V_2 are not decisive.

Fig. 1 gives a survey of the most important classical patterns and the possibility of differentiating and classifying them.

Fig. 1

QRS patterns over the right heart in atypical and delayed right ventricular excitation

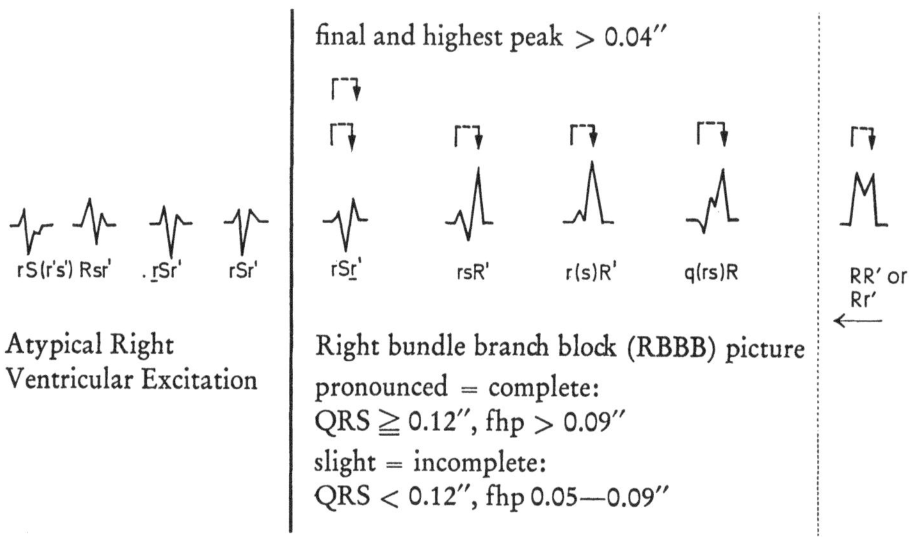

All patterns show two positive peaks which differ in proportion and in relation to a negative deflection. On this basis, two groups of patterns can be distinguished: Waves whose first peak is highest (R) or whose two peaks are of the same size (R = R′) and waves whose second peak is higher (R′). In the pronounced RBBB pictures the second positive peak is higher than the first and its delayed occurrence represents the characteristic finding of delayed right ventricular depolarisation. It corresponds as a rule to the onset of the intrinsic deflection. In the rSr′-type this latter feature does, however, not occur, whereas the pattern with the twofold quality of a "final and highest peak" is the essential characteristic and holds good for the whole group rSr′, rsR′, r(s)R′ and q(rs)R′. Its delay to 0.05 sec. or more and the width of the R wave can be related to a total delay of the spread of impulse of the right ventricle and these patterns may be classified as right bundle branch block pictures and depending on the duration of the delayed onset of the intrinsic deflection as complete or incomplete.

For the patterns rS(r′s′), Rsr′, rSr′ and rSr′, which also do not show in leads V_{r_3} and V_{r_4} a delayed final and highest peak, such an interruption cannot be safely assumed, but there are, as mentioned, various possibilities as to how it may arise. It is therefore recommended that a term be used which creates no prejudice, i. e. "atypical right ventricular depolarisation".

In a rightwards rotated heart, the typical pattern must always be looked for in leads V_{r_3} and V_{r_4}. Correspondingly an M-shape, an RR′ or Rr′ pattern respectively in lead V_1 permits the typical delay of the final and highest peak to be recognized only in these latter leads.

Various authors have classified the special patterns of the pronounced RBBB in groups. The following survery of LEPESCHKIN (with Fig. 2) gives a practical idea of the patterns that mainly occur, with indication of the occurrence in per cent.

Fig. 2

Grouping of patterns of RBBB pictures according to LEPESCHKIN

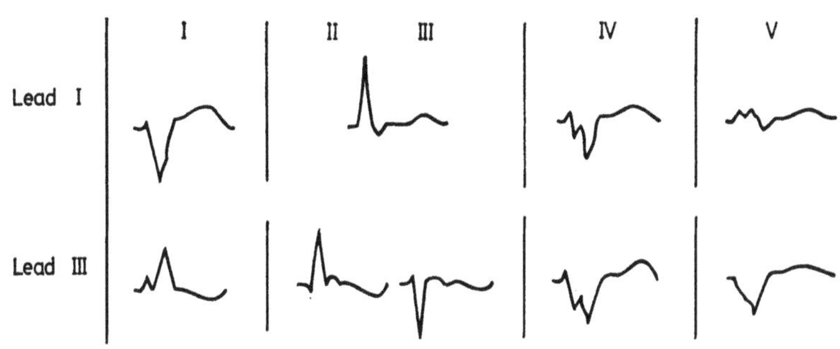

Type I	rare "classical" type with right axis deviation or predominant wide S_1 and dominant terminal wide R_{III}	18%
	"WILSON" block with predominant slender R_1 and wide S wave	
Type II	with tall slender qR_{III} and wide r'_{III} . . }	64%
Type III	with tall slender qR_{III} and wide r'_{III} . . }	
Type IV	rare concordant type with predominant wide S in leads I—III	7%
Type V	"Bayley type" with wide flat R_I and S_I and predominant wide S in leads II and III	11%

Among these patterns there are transitions and variants. Nevertheless they permit a limited clinical classification. The association with a very tall R wave in V_1 and a deep S wave in V_6 indicates an accompanying right ventricular hypertrophy, a very high R wave in V_6 indicates an accompanying left ventricular hypertrophy.

Occurrences

Among all bundle branch block pictures the WILSON type is with 55% the most frequent. The male sex predominates, the ratio being about 3 : 1. Approximately

80% come under observation after the age of 50. In about 7% the other heart findings appear to be normal. Slight RBBB pictures are with approx. 5% most frequent, pronounced WILSON block types and LBBB pictures follow, each with about 1%.

In a Parisian Cardiac Clinic it was found that out of 1,745 patients who had no other signs of cardiopathy 5.77% had a slight to pronounced RBBB (TAIMONT et al.).

A pronounced WILSON block not causing any symptons was found in about 2 permille of the flight service personnel under investigation (122,043) (FRIEDBERG):

The rSr′ pattern in lead V_1 occurs in about 5% of people with a healthy heart. It is even more frequent in children. It may also be the result of an artefact as it occurs in chest deformations, in particular in a funnel chest, by distortion of the electrical field and can be eliminated by correction (PORTHEINE).

In general the RBBB pictures show the following etiologic origins (FRIEDBERG):

Coronary heart disease and hypertrophy	75%
Rheumatic cardiopathy	15%
Acute chronic cor pulmonale	3%
Congenital angiocardiopathy	3%
Rare causes	4%

Today diphtheria is a rare cause; other causes are heart tumors, accidental heart traumas and heart surgery.

In casuistic investigations the different RBBB fall into the following classifications:

If the rare form of RBBB with right axis deviation (Type I) occurs permanently it is coupled with a cardiopathy, overload and hypertrophy of the right ventricle. Exceptions are rare.

The pronounced WILSON block (Type II/III) is to be found in cardiopathies which affect only or predominantly the right ventricle as well as in those which affect only the left ventricle. In right ventricular cardiopathies damage or interruption of the right bundle may thus occur or may be caused by an overdistension of the whole right ventricular conduction system; in left ventricular cardiopathies the cause is in most cases a disturbed blood circulation in the region of the right bundle which receives its supply from the descending branch of the left coronary artery.

Partial or incomplete RBBB pictures are particularly frequently found in cardiopathies with excentric right ventricular hypertrophy such as congenital heart defects, mitral defects and cor pulmonale. In particular in atrial septal defects there is often an incomplete, less often a complete RBBB present.

An accompanying right ventricular hypertrophy can be recognised by simultaneous writing of the leads V_1 and V_5. Thus simultaneously with the second passage of the initial ventricular deflection through the isoelectric line (from below to above) in V_1 the potential in V_5 is positive. From a vectorial point of view this means that the vector loop changes at that time from left to right ventrally of the zero point and not dorsally as in pure RBBB. If the electroventriculogram of a congenital defect with RBBB picture also shows left ventricular predominance with anticlockwise rotation of the axis in the frontal plane, either an ostium primum or canalis av communis, or more seldom an Ebstein's tricuspid anomaly is most probably involved.

Types IV and V occur rarely and are always linked with severe cardiopathies although in type IV vertical axis deviation and in type V horizontal axis deviation may also play a role. These types may occur in cor pulmonale, left ventricular hypertrophy as well as coronary heart disease. If the principal vectors are strongly distorted to the top left in the standard leads a divergent bundle branch block may arise which in the precordial leads corresponds to an RBBB and in the extremity leads to an LBBB. A strong distortion of the electrical field explains such a situation based on BURGER's triangle as derivation principle. By application of the corrected three-dimensional leads of FRANK it is possible to obtain a vectorial picture.

The combination of RBBB in the precordial leads and high grade left axis deviation in the extremity leads may be of congenital origin as well as acquired. In the first case there is most often a canalis av communis (primum type) with incomplete RBBB as a consequence of volume hypertrophy of the right ventricle and abnormal disposition of the division of the left bundle branch. More rarely an EBSTEIN's anomaly is involved with abnormal disposition of the right and left specific muscle system. In the acquired cases there is as a rule a disturbed septal blood circulation in the region of the descending branch of the left coronary artery often with an anteroseptal heart infarction, more rarely a myocardiopathy or a left ventricular hypertrophy with septal degenerative foci in aortic valvular disease. These pathological conditions lead to a functional disturbance in the right bundle branch and in the upper anterior ramus of the divided left branch which results in a delayed activation of the corresponding myocardial region.

As in all bundle branch block pictures right ventricular bundle branch blocks can occasionally be seen only intermittently in an ECG tracing or be seen only transitorily. They have the same significance as permanent findings. In rare cases RBBB pictures may disappear after they have been present for a number of years. As a rule there is an abrupt transition from the individual basic pattern of the electroventriculogram to the bundle branch block picture.

Sliding transition from an individual basic pattern to RBBB pictures which are dependent on the frequency arise under special circumstances.

Such abnormal right ventricular conductions, the degree of which is inversely proportional to the duration of the preceding ventricular interval can be observed on the one hand in premature supraventricular extrasystoles and on the other hand in atrial fibrillation. They should be considered as physiological aberrations in the sense that various degrees of the delay of activation of the right ventricle are dependent on the time factor in which the activation of the relative refractor phase of the right ventricle takes place.

Prognosis

In the first instance the following general rules apply for bundle branch block (BBB) pictures:

If a BBB picture occurs in acute heart disease (myocarditis, heart infarction) the involvement of the ventricular septum is proven and there is a great danger of arrhythmic complications with STOKES-ADAMS attacks. The prognosis becomes more serious in the presence of a BBB.

On the other hand, if a BBB is discovered during a medical check-up, the prognosis depends only on the accompanying findings, the age and the personal medical history. Below the age of 40 it is in the majority of cases a result of residuals of a myocarditis or a congenital anomaly, which has no serious significance if the other findings are favourable. If it is discovered after the age of 40, the probability increases that it is a sign of incipient coronary sclerosis. As a sole finding it does not worsen the prognosis but it has to be added to other risk factors.

Taking into account the frequent association with serious heart disease the RBBB pictures of type I, IV and V are as a rule a sign of grave significance.

RBBB pictures of the Wilson type have been observed for decades in individuals with a healthy heart and also in individuals with heart disease for more than 10 years.

To-day there is general agreement that prognostication of an RBBB picture should not be based too much on the particular ECG finding, but should be based much more on the overall picture.

References

EPPINGER, H., u. C. J. ROTHBERGER: Folgen der Durchschneidung der Tawara-Schenkel. Z. klin. Med. 70, I (1910).

FRIEDBERG, CH.: Diseases of the heart. 3 ed. Philadelphia 1966.

GILLMANN, H.: Das analysierte Potentialrelief der unipolaren Brustwand-Ableitungen. Z. Kreisl.-Forsch. 41, 325 (1952).

HOLZMANN, M.: Klinische Elektrokardiographie. 5. Aufl. Stuttgart 1965.

KATZ, L.: Electrocardiography. Philadelphia 1946.

LENÈGRE, J.: Contribution à l'étude des blocs de branche. Paris 1958.

LEPESCHKIN, E.: Modern Electrocardiography. Baltimore 1951.

PORTHEINE, H., u. K. AUSTERMANN: Zur Deutung der EKG-Veränderungen bei Trichterbrust. Verh. dtsch. Ges. 32, 192 (1966).

TAIMONT, F., G. CARUSO, A. NÈGE, J. LENÈGRE: Etude statistique des blocs de branche. Arch. mal. cœur 45, 927 (1952).

WILSON, F. N., A. G. MACLEOD, and P. S. BARKER: The order of ventricular excitation in human bundle branch block. Amer. Heart J. 7, 305 (1932).

Some reflections on the significance of vectorcardiography in diagnosing coronary and hypertrophic heart disease

P. LICHTLEN

Vectorcardiography, although for many years primarily of scientific value, has become today widely accepted as a clinical routine examination. The main reason for its propagation is due to considerable improvement of the technical aspects, including especially the development of efficient oscilloscopes, thus permitting a greatly advanced recording system. At the same time a world-wide search for better lead systems brought the necessary simplifications allowing an easy clinical approach. Several vectorcardiographic systems have been proposed during the past two decades (BURCH [1], DUCHOSAL [2], GRISHMAN [3], FRANK [4], MCFEE [5]), differing in their arrangement of the various leads or in the application of various numbers and location of electrodes as well as in the presence or absence of corrections for lead strength and orthogonalisation. It cannot be the purpose of this brief discussion to evaluate the advantages of the various systems, especially the difference between corrected orthogonal and uncorrected lead systems. However, it should be emphasized that the majority of investigators has adopted the corrected, orthogonal system, developed by FRANK or its modification by MCFEE. The requirement of only seven electrodes, five of them on the same thoracic level yields considerable clinical advantages. In addition, it was shown by FRANK's brillant theoretical studies [4, 6], confirmed by numerous experimental and clinical investigations, that this system is founded on sound physiological principles, providing a highly accurate representation of the activation of the heart.

As vectorcardiography is performed routinely, the question of its diagnostic significance in recognizing heart disease has become paramount. While its superiority to conventional electrocardiography is still debated, the facility in diagnosing abnormal heart conditions by the vectorcardiographic approach and its immense didactic value due to a more distinct and three-dimensional display of the activation pattern, are uniformly accepted.

Any comparative study between ECG and VCG has to take into account that — due to the diversity of techniques — the criteria for normality or abnormality are necessarily different for the two methods. Whereas conventional electrocardiography is recording variations of action potentials as projected on a circumscript area or line of the body surface, vectorcardiography is displaying the potential variations in its entire course of evolution, monitoring continuously the course of activation at any moment during depolarisation and repolarisation. This results in a continuous loop representing size and orientation of the action potentials throughout the entire heart cycle in the three planes of the space (horizontal, sagittal, frontal). Thus a three-dimensional representation of the manifest potential variations is being formed. As the vector loop is presenting a very high degree of resolution in time and quantity, a precise analysis of the action potentials generated at any moment, is possible. One has to remember, however, that the criteria for electrocardiography and vectorcardiography are mainly defined on a numerical background; it can therefore be expected that vectorcardiography will provide higher accuracy. This is, however, only true if the analysis is based on a thorough comparative study between statistical data and clinical or postmortal findings.

Electrocardiography and vectorcardiographic manifestations of cardiac abnormalities have thus to be verified by autopsy data as well as hemodynamic and angiographic studies. The following report, evaluating the significance of vectorcardiography as an additional tool in diagnosing electrophysiological abnormalities and comparing ECG and VCG is therefore based mainly on a comparative clinical study.

Methods:

1. Electrocardiography

Electrocardiograms were performed by the standard method, registering simultaneously the three extremity and unipolar leads and the six precordial leads using a 6 channel Elema recorder. No additional leads were taken into account in the comparative study as the investigation under discussion was based on the significance of VCG and ECG in daily routine examination. All standard ECG's were performed in close connection to the vectorcardiographic recording i. e. with no more delay than one day.

2. Vectorcardiography

For the above-mentioned reasons the Frank vectorcardiographic system was used. The recordings were in accordance with the standardisations of the Committee on Electrocardiography and Vectorcardiography of the American Heart Association [7]. The correct placement of the thoracic leads was given the greatest care. Buffer electrodes — according to the system of PIPBERGER [8] — were only applied in patients with high skin resistance, a modified buffer system being already built into the recording apparatus. Comparison of the vector loops recorded in 100 consecutive patients with and without use of buffer electrodes showed only minimal variations, the mean difference in potentialities being not more than 5—10%. Vectorcardiograms were always recorded in three planes (horizontal, left-sagittal and frontal) both as continuous and instantaneous loops. Furthermore an orthogonal electrocardiogram in the three axes of the space (x, y, z) was performed in each case.

3. Additional clinical investigations

a) *Coronary arteriography:* All patients with myocardial infarction and coronary disease resp. were submitted to selective coronary arteriography following the technique of SONES [9]. Only those angiograms were included into the study in which a satisfactory representation of the essential structures has been achieved (angiography in different positions, visualisation of vessels down to the size of the A-V node, atrial and septal arteries).

b) *Ventriculography:* In most of the patients with coronary artery disease and in all patients suspected of aneurysm, left ventricular angiocardiography was performed in addition to the coronary arteriography. Pictures were taken in the right (RAO) and often also in the left oblique (LAO) position, in order to visualize the anterior and posterior wall of the left ventricle as clearly as possible.

c) *Cardiac catheterisation:* All patients with valvular heart disease or cor pulmonale underwent cardiac catheterisation (right heart, transseptal left heart and retrograde left heart catheterisation). Regurgitant fractions in aortic or mitral incompetence were assessed by the dye dilution technique. In addition the great majority of these patients was submitted to selective angiocardiography of left ventricle, left atrium and aortic root.

Results

A. Coronary artery disease

Table I and II represent a comparison between the electrocardiographic and vectorcardiographic diagnosis of patients with angiographically proven coronary artery disease. There is a slightly better yield in positive diagnosis of myocardial infarction in vectorcardiography (70,7% in ECG versus 79,1% in VCG). This

Table I. *Diagnosis of myocardial infarction in patients with severe coronary artery disease, as shown at selective coronary arteriography.*
Only patients with total, subtotal or partial obstructions are included; only one infarction per patient is regarded

Number of patients	Diagnosis of infarction		Unspecific changes, LVH, LBBB, RBBB	Normal
	positive	questionable		
ECG 155	103 = 66.5%	17 =11.0%	23 =15.0%	12 = 7.5%
VCG 148	113 = 76.5%	12 = 7.9%	18 =12.2%	5 = 3.4%

ECG and VCG diagnosis in patients with normal coronary arteriography including patients with minimal lesions

ECG 95	11	5 PWI 6 AWI	13	35	36
VCG 92	8	5 PWI 3 AWI	14	59	11

difference is mainly due to a better vectorcardiographic recognition of combined posterior wall and anterior wall infarction in patients with obstructions of both the right coronary artery and left anterior descending branch (6 cases in ECG, 16 in VCG) (fig. 1, 2). Thus, in these cases electrocardiography revealed a clear tendency to misdiagnose either posterior wall (fig. 1) or anterior wall (fig. 2)

Table II. *Comparison between ECG and VCG, related to changes of major coronary branches. Only total or subtotal obstructions are considered. In contrast to Table I all myocardial infarctions are included*

Electrocardiogram							*Vectorcardiogram*							
Coronary artery lesions	Post. Wall Inf.		Ant. W.I.				Post. W.I.		Ant. W.I.				total	
	pos.	quest.	pos.	quest.	unspec.	normal	pos.	quest.	post.	quest.	unspec.	normal	ECG	VCG
RCA±LC	23	2	1	1	4	5	25	4	—	3	3	1	36	36
LC	4						4						4	4
LAD±LD	1	1	21		4	3	1		23	1	1	3	30	29
RCA+LAD	3	3	5 2 [a]	3 [a]	2	1	4	1	3 8 [a]		2		19	18
RCA/LAD/LC	17	2	16 6 [a]	3	7		11	1	11 16 [a]	1	7		51	47
	48= 34.3%	8= 5.7%	51= 36.4%	7= 5%	17= 12.1%	9= 6.5%	45= 33.6%	6= 4.5%	61= 45.5%	5= 3.8%	13= 9.7%	4= 2.9%	140	134

Positive diagnosis of infarction: ECG = 70,7%, VCG = 79,1%.
[a] Patients with both anterior and posterior wall infarction.
RCA = right coronary artery; LC = left circumflex branch; LAD = left anterior desc. branch.; LD = left diagonal branch.
Post. W.I.: posterior wall infarction; Ant. W.I.: anterior wall infarction.
pos.: positive diagnosis; quest.: questionable diagnosis; unspec.: unspecific changes.

infarctions. This was due partly to the application of rigid ECG criteria for the signs of posterior wall infarctions requiring a duration of the Q wave of 0,04 sec in lead III and aVF and a depth of the Q wave of at least 25% of the R wave [10]. Previous vectorcardiographic analyses of patients representing obstructions of the right coronary artery, of the left circumflex branch or both vessels together revealed however, that for a considerable number of these patients the abnormal initial superior loop deviation leading to a pathologic Q wave in the inferior electrocardiographic leads (lead II, III, aVF) may be significantly less than

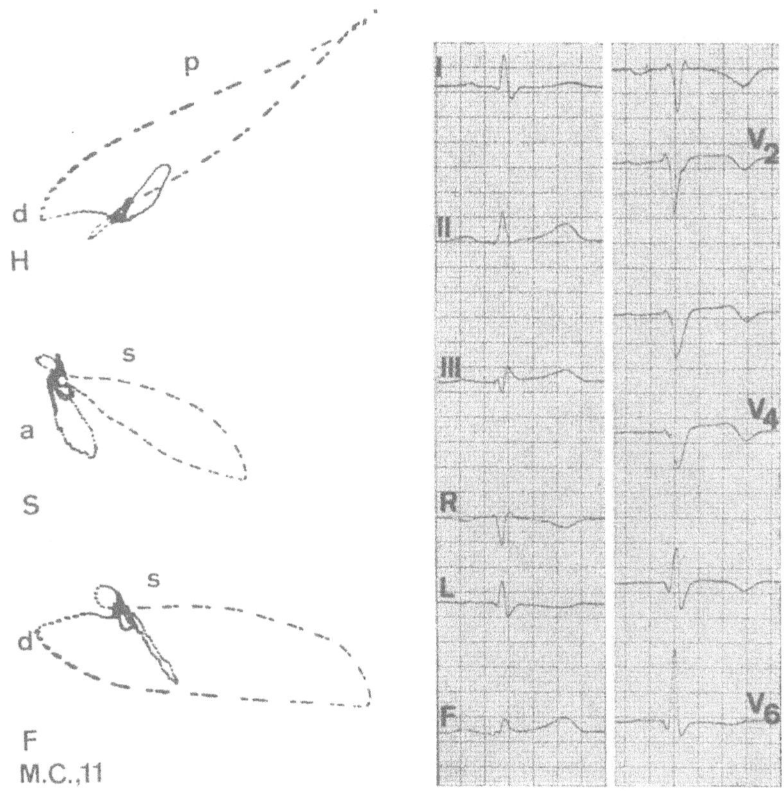

Fig. 1. M. C., 1911. In August 1968 hospitalized with acute anterior wall infarction. Coronary arteriography revealed a subtotal occlusion of the main RCA, a total obstruction of the LAD and diffuse alterations of the left circumflex branch. LV angiography showed imcomplete contractions of the anterior wall, but no aneurysm. On the left: Vectorcardiogram: H = horizontal plane, S = left sagittal plane, F = frontal plane, d = dexter, p = posterior, a = anterior, s = superior. Development of the QRS loop in dash-point-direction. Time interval 2 msec. (The VCG designations will be the same for all following figures.) In the VCG an anterior orientation of short duration is present, followed by a displacement of the early loop portion towards the right and the rear, expressing moderate anterior wall damage. Note the abnormal, clockwise rotation of the initial portion of the horizontal QRS loop. In addition there is an abnormal superior orientation of the initial loop, exceeding 20 msec. On the right: Electrocardiogram: extremity and precordial leads. Paper speed 50 mm/sec. Due to the initial anterior orientation lead V1 shows a rSr pattern, r waves being present also in lead V2 and V3. There are no diagnostic ECG changes of posterior wall infarction, a small r wave being present in lead III

40 msec [11, 12, 13, 14, 14, 16] (fig. 10). Based on this analysis the lower limit for the duration of the initial superior displacement, separating posteroseptal infarctions from normals ranged in the vicinity of 20 msec. Another very valuable parameter was found in the mean amplitude of the initial superior deviation, being about 0.04 mV [12, 14]. It seems therefore justified to lower the critical limit of positive vectorcardiographic criteria in posterior wall infarctions. This conclusion is mainly based on the evidence that — due to the orthogonalisation and spatial recording — initial superior deviations are registered more accurately in VCG than in conventional electrocardiography. Due to the fact that the conventional extremity leads are corresponding mainly to a strictly frontal plane and are lacking an additional neck lead detecting upward movements more readily, they remain often relatively insensible for superiorly orientated potential variations on the y axis, especially those not being located strictly in the frontal plane. Furthermore, posterior wall or diaphragmatic infarctions, especially when

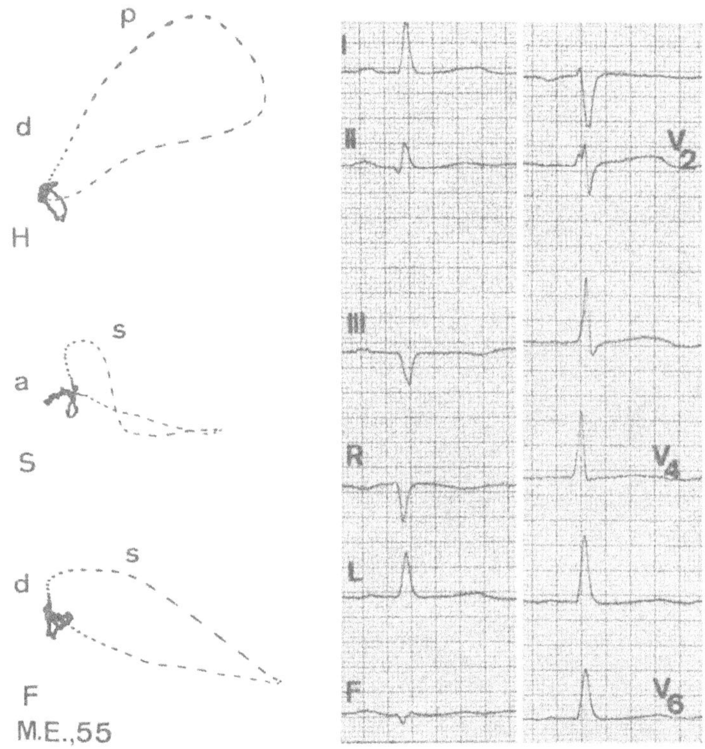

Fig. 2. M. E., 1955. Severe angina pectoris. Coronary arteriography revealing a subtotal occlusion of the main RCA and of the LAD as well as diffuse changes of the left circumflex and diagonal branches. The LV angiogram showed incomplete contractions of the apical area and the anterior and posterior wall, but no aneurysm was present. In the VCG a significant loss of anterior orientation is found, the initial forces of the horizontal QRS loop being shifted to the left, paralleling lead V1 and V2. In addition there is marked abnormal superior orientation of 36 msec duration. The ECG cannot be considered diagnostic for anterior wall infarction, normal progression of R waves being present in the precordial leads. However there are typical signs of posterior wall infarction

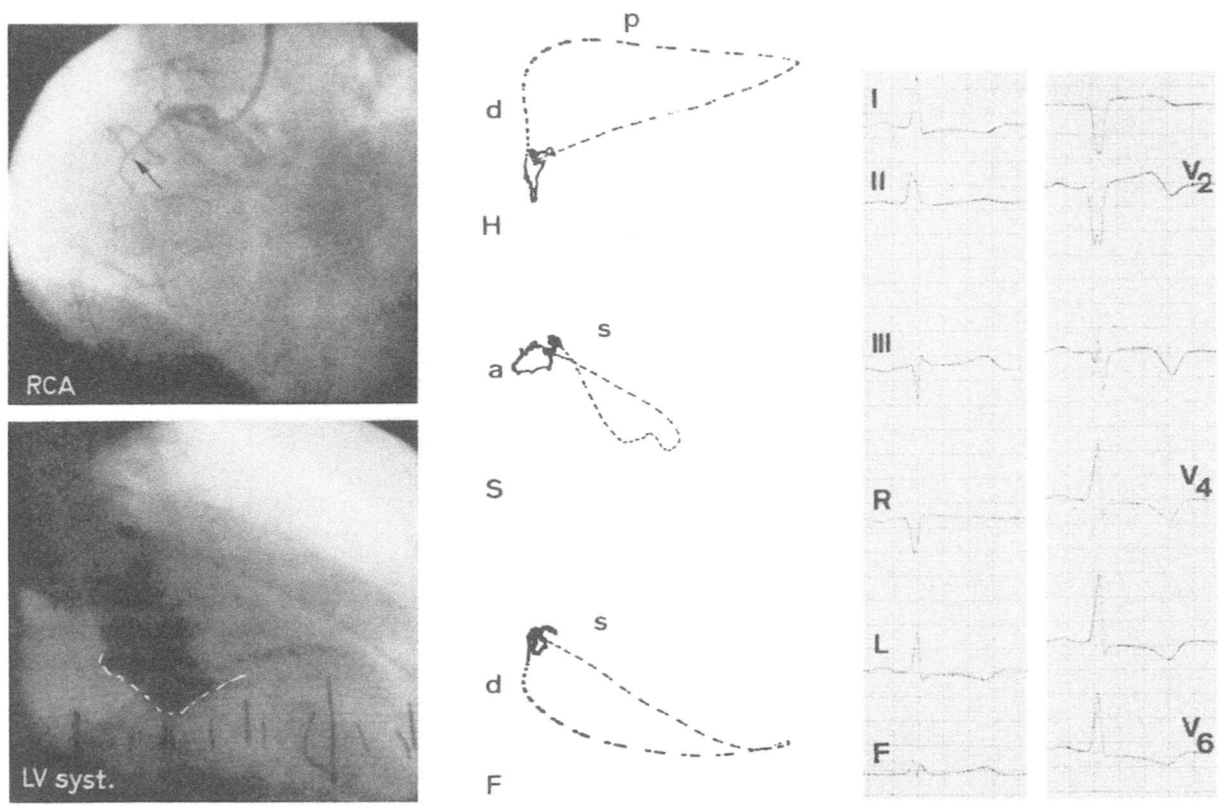

Fig. 3. Z. R., 1926. In October 1968 hospitalized with acute anterior wall myocardial infarction. ECG and VCG from February 1969, at the time of coronary arteriography. Injection into the right coronary artery (RCA) (left oblique projection [LAO]) reveals complete obstruction of the main branch shortly below its origin (arrow). In addition subtotal occlusion of the left anterior descending branch (LAD) and mild changes in left diagonal and circumflex branches were present. LV injection (lower left) shows posterior wall aneurysm and incomplete contraction of anterior wall. The VCG shows immediate orientation of the initial horizontal loop to the left, lacking any anterior development. No significant superior movement is seen, the initial superior deviation being less than 8 msec. Precordial leads are typical for anterior wall infarction. However, the rSr pattern in lead III and aVF is not diagnostic for loss of inferior potentials. T inversions from V2 to V6, expressing the abnormal orientation of the T loop. The posterior infarction is thus poorly reflected both in VCG and ECG

combined with anterior wall infarctions, may present a rS pattern in lead III due to a short initial downward movement of the spatial frontal loop, before turning definitely superior in a counterclockwise fashion (fig. 1). These ECG's usually show a marked left axis deviation. Thus, the presence of a small r wave in inferior leads does not absolutely exclude posterior wall infarctions. In these cases, the development of the midportion of the loop is of higher diagnostic value than the initial part and may be regarded as diagnostic for the loss of inferior potentials. Nevertheless, in combined anterior and posterior wall infarction, the latter may occasionally also be missed at vectorcardiography (fig. 3). — A further source of electrocardiographic misinterpretation is the insufficient display in posterobasal-lateral infarctions (strictly posterior infarctions), i. e. infarctions including mainly the area of the left ventricle situated

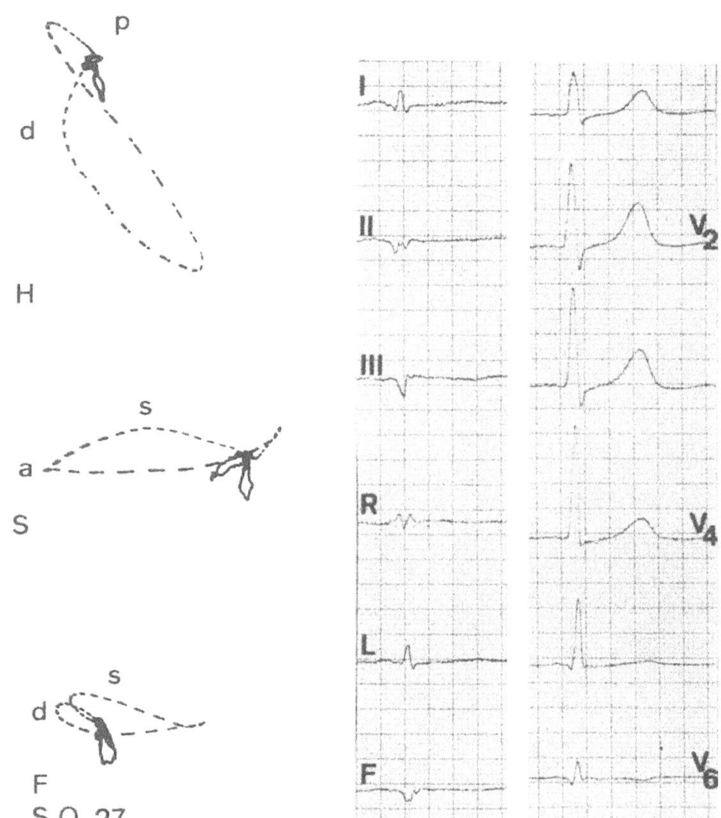

Fig. 4. S. O., 1927. Typical posterolateral infarction, demonstrated in an abnormal anterior development of the horizontal QRS loop, exceeding 40 msec, as well as in a mild rightward deviation of the terminal forces. The initial superior development is also greatly abnormal, the superior orientation being of 30 msec duration. Anterior and superior displacement are readily recognized in the ECG. — Coronary arteriography showed complete obstruction of the left circumflex branch and a small subtotal occlusion of the LAD as well as diffuse changes of the RCA. LV injection revealed incomplete contractions of the apical area and the lateral portions of LV

immediately adjacent to the mitral valve ring, often extending to the lateral wall of the left ventricle (fig. 4, 5). Such infarctions are usually associated with a significant anterior displacement of the early portion of the QRS loop especially including the segment from 20 to 40 msec [12, 14]. Unsatisfactory electrocardiographic recognition (fig. 5) may be due either to the absence of a back electrode recording opposite potential movements or to a strong upward direction of the entire QRS loop, out of the plane of the precordial leads. In addition to the duration of anterior displacement, exceeding 35 to 40 msec, again the quantitative aspects proved crucial in these cases. Anterior displacement of 0.4 mV or more — occurring 30 to 40 msec after the onset of the QRS loop — was found to be diagnostic for postero-lateral infarctions [12, 14]. Due to the considerable decrease in posterobasal forces, occurring late during the activation of the left ventricle, additional late manifestation of right ventricular potentials may be observed, expressed in a rightward movement of the terminal loops (fig. 4, 5).

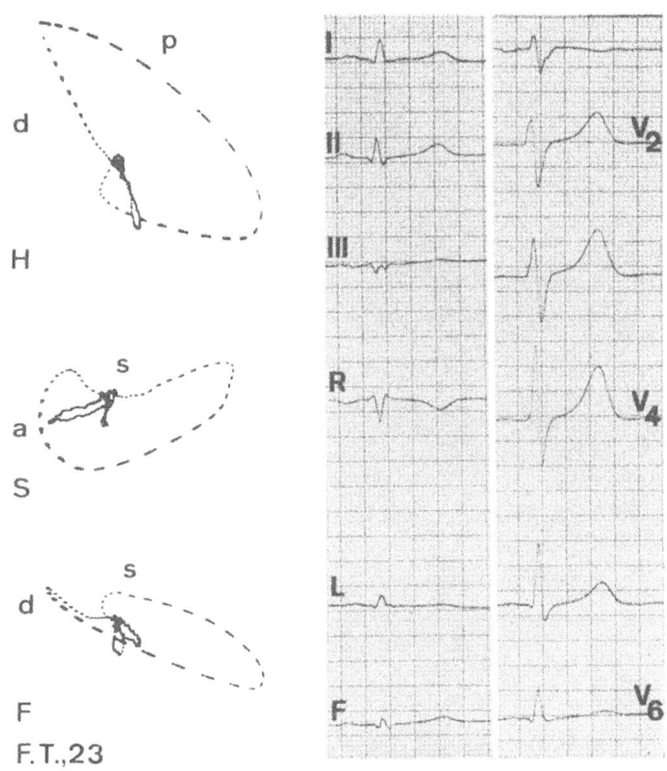

Fig. 5. F. T., 1923. Posterolateral infarction. In the VCG abnormal initial anterior and superior orientations of 40 resp. 22 msec duration are present. The ECG may be suggestive of postero-lateral infarction, regarding the mild increase of R potentials in V2 and V3, accompanied by some elevation of the T waves corresponding to the anterior displacement of the T loop. The superior orientation is poorly reflected in the extremity leads of the ECG, presenting a rSr pattern in lead III and a small, but insignificant Q wave in lead aVF. — Coronary arteriography revealed almost total obstruction of the left circumflex branch and a subtotal occlusion of the LAD. LV injection showed incomplete contractions of the lateral wall

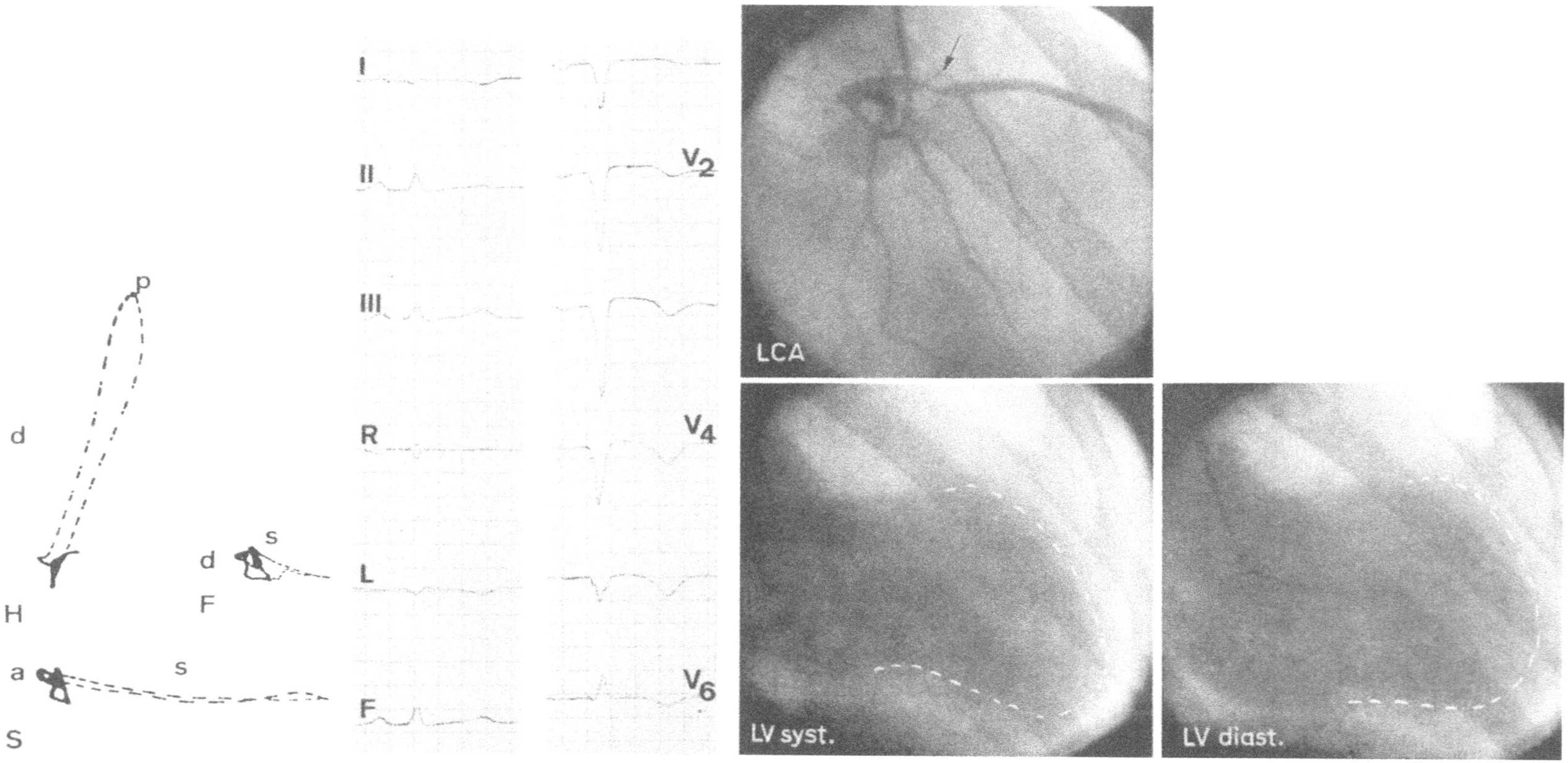

Fig. 6. E. K., 1911. There is almost complete obstruction of the LAD (upper left angiogram, LCA injection in RAO position), leading to an extensive aneurysm including the entire apical area and anterior wall of LV (LV angiogram in systole and diastole, RAO position, lower left and right). Poor contractions, being present only in the "constrictor plane". — VCG shows initial deviation of the horizontal QRS loop to the right and the rear, resulting in a clockwise rotation of the loop in the horizontal plane, typical for anterior wall aneurysm. The ST vector is only minimally displaced. ECG typical for extensive anterolateral infarction, but not diagnostic for LV aneursym, the ST segments being only slightly elevated. However the broad Q wave in lead I and aVL, a result of the initial rightward movement of the frontal loop, is considered as a reliable sign of LV aneurysm

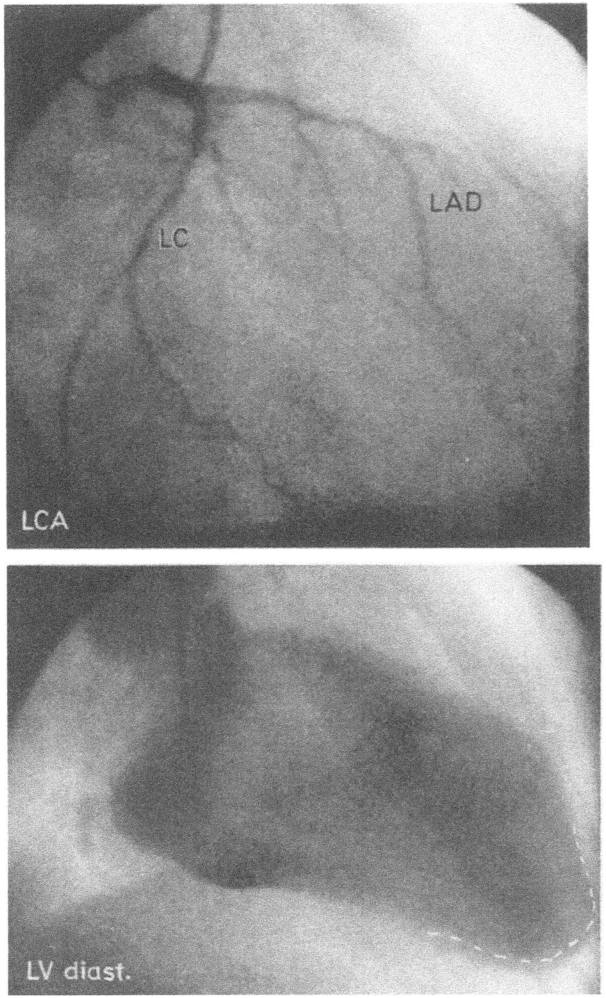

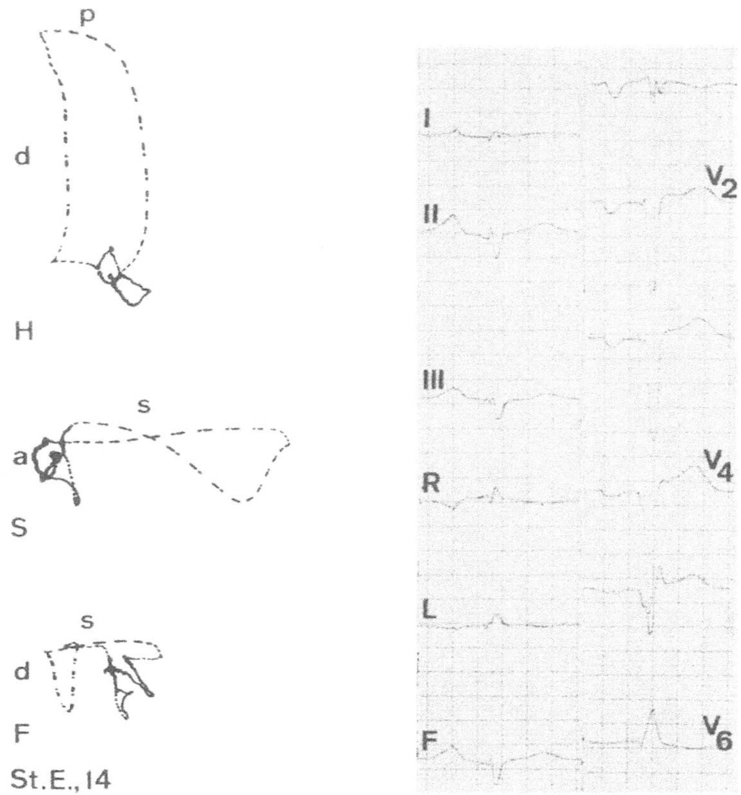

Fig. 7. ST. E., 1914. Severe diffuse narrowing of the LAD (upper left: LCA injection in RAO position). In addition a total obstruction of RCA and of the posterolateral branch of the left circumflex artery was present. LV angiogram (diastole) (RAO position) reveals an apical aneurysm. Typical VCG changes, the initial forces being displaced markedly to the right and the rear. There is also an abnormal initial superior orientation, confirming the posterior wall infarction, due to RCA obstruction. ECG shows small r waves in lead V1, expressing the initial rightward movement of the horizontal QRS loop. The QS pattern in V4 and V5, accompanied by ST elevations is diagnostic of anterior wall aneurysm. The posterior wall infarction however is not readily recognisable

The additional diagnostic gain through vectorcardiography was found to be less important in the presence of anterior wall infarctions. In general, the absence of an anterior development of the early forces and the immediate posterior orientation of the loop is clearly reflected in a loss of R waves in the precordial leads (fig. 6, 7). However, as shown by comparison with coronary arteriography, subtotal occlusions of the left anterior descending branch may still be accompanied by small r waves in leads V1 and V2, the initial loop being mainly deviated to the left, paralleling those leads, but not orientated significantly to

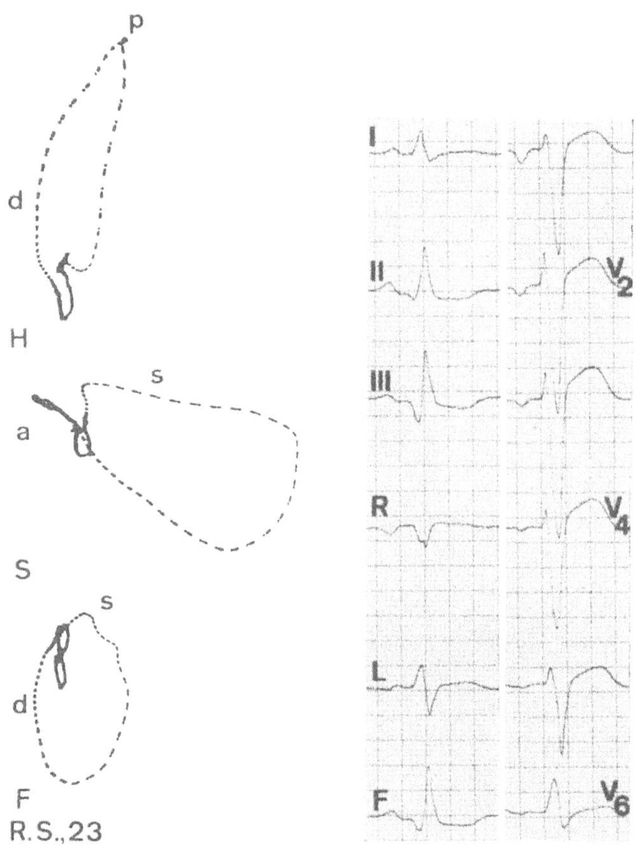

Fig. 8. R. S., 1923. Severe diffuse coronary artery disease was shown by selective angiography, including total obstruction of the RCA, subtotal occlusion of the LAD and total obstruction of the posterolateral branch of the left circumflex artery. An extensive aneurysm of the anterior wall and the LV apex, as well as an aneurysm of the posterior wall was present at LV injection. The angiographic findings were confirmed by autopsy, death occurring two weeks after angiography in progressive heart failure and terminal ventricular fibrillation. The VCG shows the initial forces still orientated anteriorly, however, subsequently the horizontal QRS loop is abnormally displaced towards the rear and the right, the rotation still being normal. There is greatly abnormal superior orientation of the initial forces, due to the loss of posterior wall potentials. Thus, the VCG is typical for anterior and posterior wall infarction, however, not diagnostic for anterior wall aneurysm. In the ECG normal R waves are present in precordial leads V1 to V4, followed by deep S waves up to V5, suggesting rather LVH or biventricular hypertrophy than anterior wall infarction. The pathological Q waves in leads III and aVF are concordant to the initial superior orientation of the loop

the rear (fig. 8, 9). Furthermore, some patients with extensive anterior wall infarctions and either total or subtotal obstructions of the left anterior descending branch may show anterior, but rightward orientation of the early forces, a constellation that is again accompanied by normal R waves in lead V1 and V2. In these cases recognition of infarction is based mainly on subsequent development of the QRS loop deviated to the right and the rear, indicating a massive loss of anterior forces usually being present in patients with anterior wall aneurysm (fig. 7). This early rightward and forward movement has to be explained by the overwhelming presence of early right ventricular forces, normally neutralized by those of the left ventricle. Although such a constellation is usually still recognized in electrocardiography as anterior wall infarction, its extent may be underestimated, pathological q waves being present only in V4 to V5 (V6) (fig. 7).

Based on the evidence of coronary arteriography and left ventricular angiography the significance and gain of vectorcardiography in coronary disease is therefore found to be a twofold one:

1. easier recognition and better confirmation of myocardial infarction due to a more accurate analysis of temporal and quantitative aspects of the abnormal loop.

2. better and safer judgment of the extent, localisation and size of the infarction, especially in patients with multiple infarctions. In addition the electrocardiographic changes are easier interpreted with the knowledge of underlying vectorial changes (fig. 10).

B. Ventricular hypertrophy

The vectorcardiographic diagnosis of ventricular hypertrophy is based mainly on two criteria: alteration of the morphological aspects of the QRS loop and increase in the amplitude of localized and maximal potentials. However, it is important to note that qualitative and quantitative changes do not necessarily occur simultaneously, typical morphological loop alterations being often present without any changes in vectorial forces. On the other hand, significant increase of potentials is practically always accompanied by characteristic deformations of the QRS loop. The continuous three dimensional display of the loop represents a major advantage offered by VCG in the recognition of an altered activation pattern and the safe detection of ventricular hypertrophy at an early stage of the disease. In addition, due to the better resolution of time and quantity, changes in the size of localized and maximal vector potentials are apprehended more accurately. The criteria for left and right ventricular hypertrophy, based on a close comparison with angiographic, hemodynamic and clinical data, are briefly outlined and the difficulties of electrocardiographic diagnosis are discussed.

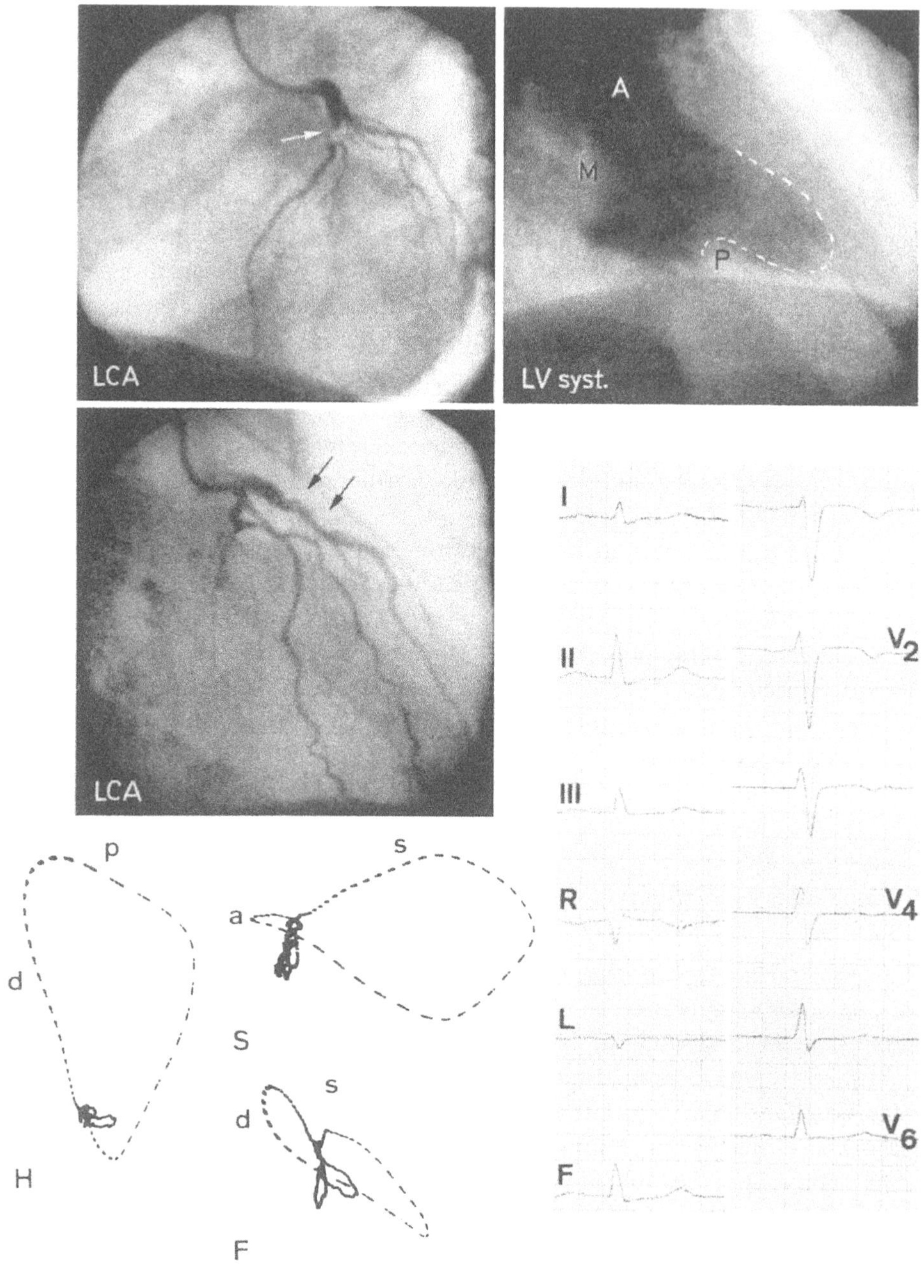

Fig. 9. W. F., 1909. Subtotal occlusion of the LAD (upper left: LCA injection in LAO position, lower left: LCA injection in RAO position), leading to anterior wall damage, as shown by incomplete contractions of the anterior wall (LV injection in RAO position). Contractions of the posterior wall are normal, the posterior papillary muscle (*P*) being clearly outlined (*M* = mitral valve, *A* = aortic valve). VCG shows shortening of the anterior orientation and deviation of the early portions of the horizontal QRS loop farther to the right, suggesting some loss of anterior wall potentials. T loop abnormally orientated to the left. The ECG is not diagnostic for anterior wall infarction

1. Right ventricular hypertrophy (RVH)

Whereas RVH is usually easy to recognize in the FRANK vectorcardiogram, its diagnosis by means of the conventional electrocardiogram may present considerable difficulties. This is especially true in mild RVH as well as at the onset of cor pulmonale. The better display of RVH in the FRANK vectorcardiogram may be due to the location of an electrode in the right axillary line registering the main feature of RVH, the increasing rightward movement of the terminal portion of the QRS loop, in a more accurate way (fig. 11, 12). For the same reason, the conventional electrocardiogram relying strongly on leftsided precordial electrodes, is prone to underestimate or miss a rightward orientation of the terminal forces. This may at least in part be due to proximity effects of precordial leads [17]. Thus, the ECG diagnosis of early RVH has to be based on a careful analysis of the S waves being present in all precordial leads including V5 and V6, accompanied by poor progression of R waves (fig. 11, 12). Furthermore, a leftward deflection of the ST and T vector, pointing away from the right ventricle, may provide additional evidence (fig. 11, 12, 13). Whether these changes of repolarisation are merely an expression of overwhelming right ventricular repolarisation, as is suggested from similar alterations in right bundle

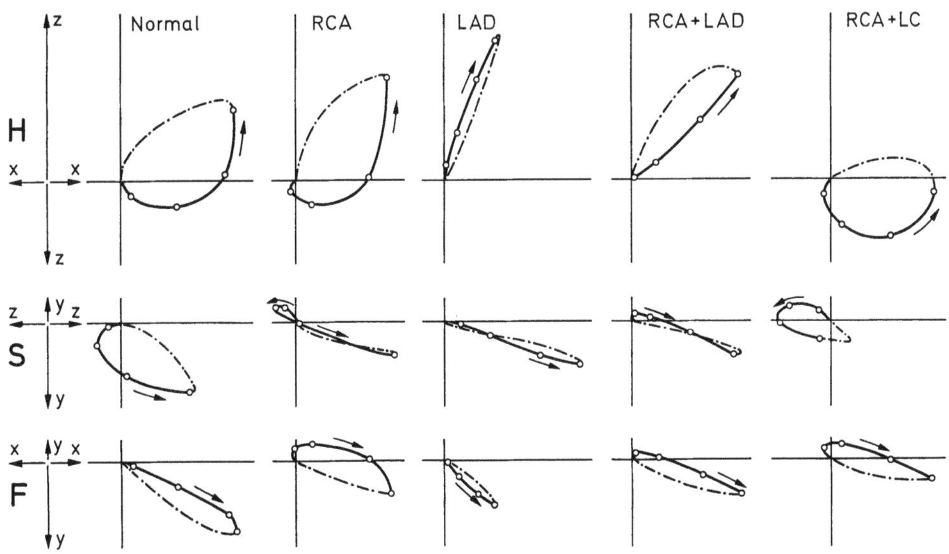

Fig. 10. Development of the horizontal (*H*), sagittal (*S*) and frontal (*F*) QRS loop during the first 40 msec (open circles at 10 msec intervals) or alternatively up to the maximal vector. The constructions of the average mean vector loop are based on the comparison with selective coronary arteriography; only patients with subtotal or total obstructions of at least one of the major branches are included. (Mean values derived from 70 patients.) RCA = right coronary artery occlusion; LAD = obstruction of left anterior descending branch; LC = obstruction of left circumflex branch. Note that the average superior orientation in RCA obstructions (posteroseptal infarctions) is 30 msec, the average anterior duration in obstructions of the left circumflex branch (with or without additional changes of RCA) (posterolateral infarction) is more than 40 msec. In combined obstructions of RCA and LAD the average of the initial superior orientation is still more than 20 msec

branch block (RBBB), or represent some ischemic alterations of the endocardial structure of the right ventricle, still remains open to discussion. Nevertheless, absence of normal R waves in lead V1 to V3, combined with considerable T inversions up to lead V4, may result in the incorrect diagnosis of anterior wall ischemia and thus, confounding cor pulmonale with anterior wall infarction, represent one of the major electrocardiographic pitfalls of mild RVH (fig. 13). Careful analysis of the extremity leads, expressing the rightward orientation of the terminal forces in the frontal plane by a SI-SII-(SIII) configuration, will, however, in the majority of cases be decisive. It should be mentioned that early recognition of RVH and cor pulmonale has become increasingly important, the number of such cases investigated in our VCG and catheterisation laboratories nearly quadrupling during the last year, a feature also seen in other laboratories in this country [18, 19]. This seems of special importance as the prognostic outlook of primary pulmonary hypertension proved to be uncertain, and the only treatment promising a certain success may consist in anticoagulation at the very early stage of the disease. Acute right ventricular overload, as found in large

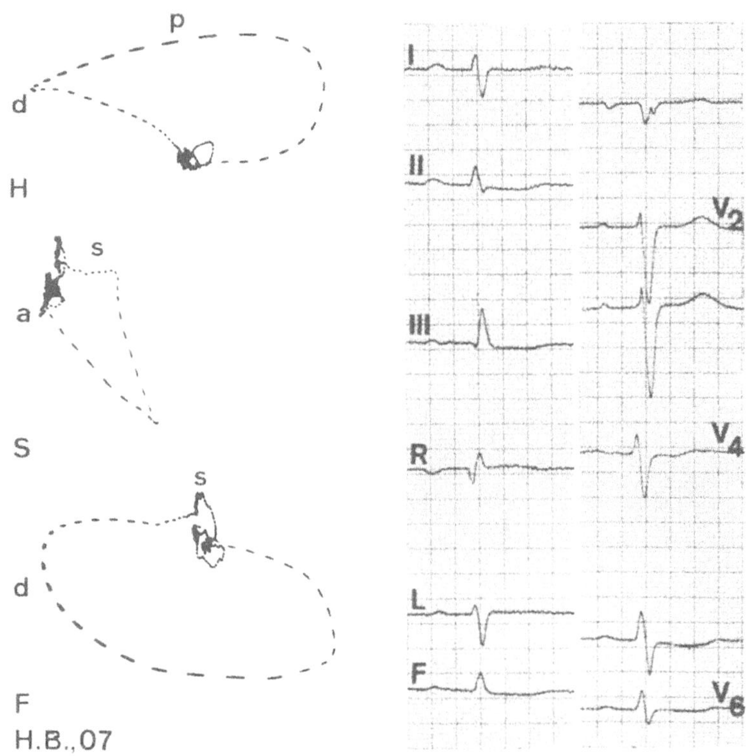

Fig. 11. H. B., 1907. Severe cor pulmonale due to pulmonary vascular obstructive disease. Pulmonary artery pressure 97/34; mean 54 mm Hg; CI 1.4 L/min/m²; pulmonary vascular resistance 1630 dyn sec cm⁻⁵. The VCG shows abnormal deviation of the terminal loop to the right and the rear, resulting in persistence of deep S waves of the precordial leads up to lead V6, as well as in a S wave in lead I. The T loop is oriented to the left, the rear and superiorly, pointing away from the right ventricle. VCG and ECG are typical for moderate cor pulmonale

pulmonary emboli is usually well recognized both in VCG as in the ECG, the classical signs described by McGinn and White [20] still being the leading criteria (fig. 12). Caution seems, however, advisable in judging the considerable T inversions usually present from lead V1 to V4 (V5) as they may not represent myocardial damage of such an extensive area as covered by the precordial leads. In view of the vectorcardiographic aspect of these T loop changes, it seems rather likely that the wide-spread electrocardiographic alterations of the repolarisation are merely an expression of the strong posterior orientation of the T vector being characteristic for transient systolic overload of the right ventricle. This is confirmed by the experience of a long persistence of these electrocardiographic changes despite of complete normalisation of the hemodynamic signs of pulmonary

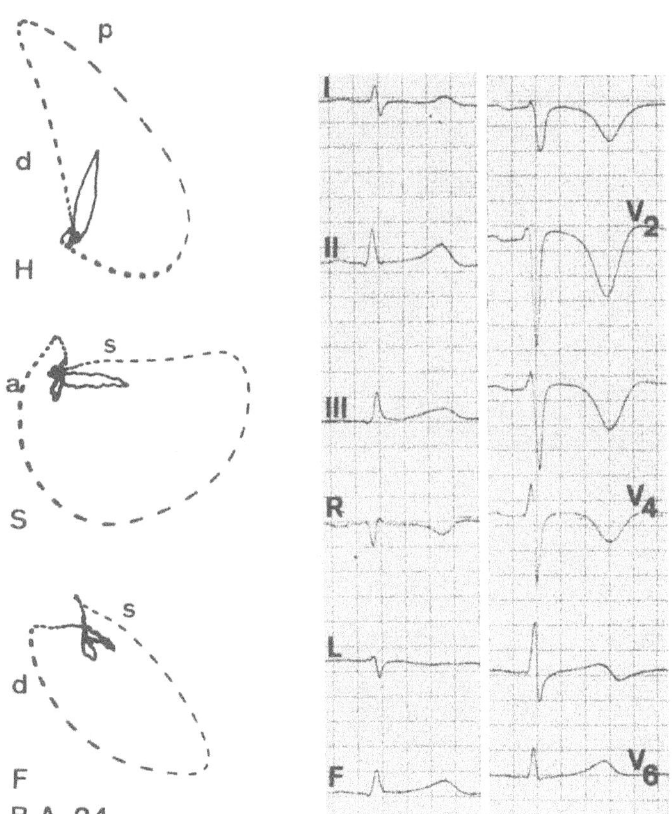

Fig. 12. B. A., 1924. Hospitalized due to recurrent pulmonary emboli to the right middle and lower lobe. VCG and ECG two weeks after the last attack, at the time of cardiac catheterisation. Pulmonary artery pressure 34/12, mean 19 mm Hg; CI 4.5 L/min/m²; pulm. vasc. resistance 119 dyn sec cm⁻⁵. The VCG shows mild deviation of the terminal QRS loop to the right as well as abnormal initial superior orientation (Signs of McGinn and White). The outstanding feature is a massive deviation of the T loop to the left and especially to the rear, the T vector being enlarged and widened. Consequently the ECG presents S waves up to lead V6 as well as a SI-QIII pattern. According to the T loop deviation to the rear, there are deep T inversions from leads V1 to V4. — Note that in spite of the typical changes of VCG and ECG, pulmonary artery pressure and resistance were almost normal

hypertension (fig. 12). In contrast, such a development was not observed in our patients with peripheral vascular obstructive disease, where the vectorcardiographic signs of RVH were usually rapidly progressing even in the presence of unaltered pulmonary vascular resistance [14].

In contrast to mild RVH, recognition of severe RVH usually presents no major problem in conventional electrocardiography. As the hypertrophy of the right ventricle is not only limited to the outflow tract but includes the entire right ventricle, the horizontal loop is deviated anteriorly, rotating in a clockwise fashion to the right (fig. 14). Due to this anterior displacement of the mid-portion of the loop, there is considerable increase of R waves in lead V1 to V3,

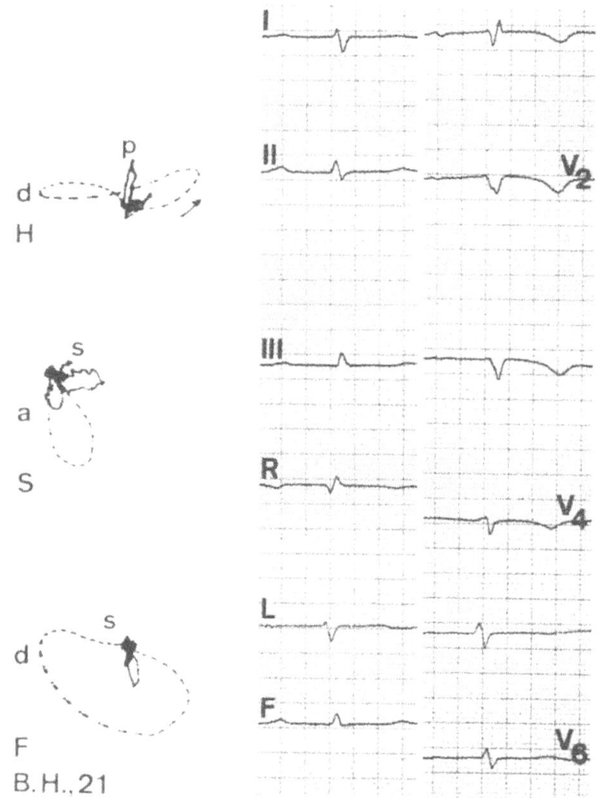

Fig. 13. B. H., 1921. In 1968 sudden onset of dyspnea associated with chest pains suggesting angina pectoris. In the presence of a loss of R waves in leads V2 to V4 accompanied by considerable T inversions, myocardial infarction was suggested. Cardiac catheterisation revealed primary pulmonary hypertension due to pulmonary vascular obstructive disease. Pulmonary artery pressure 70/34; mean 48 mm Hg; CI 1.95 L/min/m²; pulmonary vascular resistance 1150 dyn sec cm⁻⁵. — The VCG shows marked deviation of the terminal QRS loop to the right, the T vector deviating to the rear, pointing away from the right ventricle. The initial orientation of the horizontal QRS loop to the left is decreased, probably due to cancellation of LV potentials by increased early RV forces. — Thus, the ECG shows only small R waves in leads V2 to V4 and generalized low voltage. Deep S waves up to lead V6 as well as in leads I and II, are however present. The precordial T inversions, reflecting the posterior orientation of the T loop of RV repolarisation should not be confused with anterolateral ischemia

deep S waves up to lead V6 being still present as an expression of a further deviation of the terminal forces to the right. In addition the shift of the electrical axis to the right and the signs of "right ventricular strain" are unmistakable.

Further difficulties may be found in patients presenting a combination of RBBB and RVH. The criteria first mentioned by GRISHMAN and SHERLIS [3] consisting of anterior displacement of the midportion of the QRS loop, the horizontal loop rotating to the right in front of the 0 point, are still valid for the majority of cases. However, it has to be emphasized that in a considerable number of cases with RBBB and RVH, the midportion of the QRS loop may still rotate to the right behind the 0 point, as it does in uncomplicated RBBB. In contrast to the loop display in RBBB, the rightward development of such loops is however always very near to the 0 point! Their electrocardiographic analysis proves to be very difficult, and a differentiation between patients with RBBB with RVH and those without additional RVH is seldom possible.

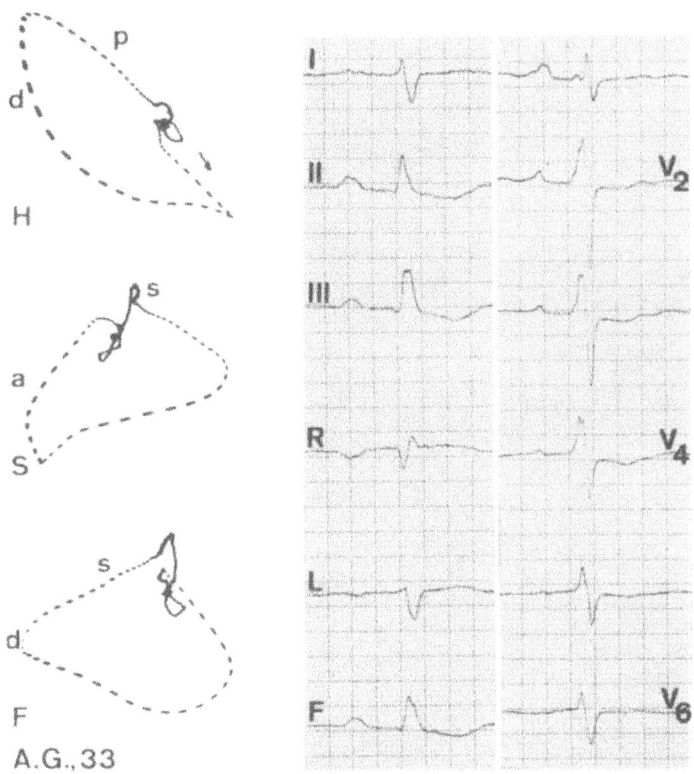

Fig. 14. A. G., 1933. Severe cor pulmonale due to pulmonary vascular obstructive disease. Pulmonary artery pressure 104/47 mm Hg; mean 66 mm Hg; CI 2.02 L/min/m²; pulmonary vascular resistance 1333 dyn sec cm^{-5}. Typical vectorcardiographic changes of severe RVH, the horizontal QRS loop rotating clockwise anteriorly and to the right, leading to increased R potentials in lead V1 to V3, as well as to deep S waves up to V6. The frontal loop is markedly shifted to the right, resulting in a deep S wave in lead I, but not in lead II. The T loop changes are typical of RVH

In summary, vectorcardiography is of special significance in detecting initial and mild forms of cor pulmonale. Furthermore, the advantages of readily assessing the course of the disease more accurately, in recognizing the increasing development of the terminal loop portion to the right or a reverse of the rotation of the horizontal loop, are evident.

2. *Left ventricular hypertrophy (LVH)*

In contrast to RVH, fewer discrepancies are found between ECG and VCG in recognizing LVH. The main reason may be found in the fact that the activation pattern of the hypertrophied left ventricle is oriented to the left, to the rear and upward, the development of the QRS loop following this direction very closely (fig. 15, 16, 17). The precordial leads, placed over the left chest and facing

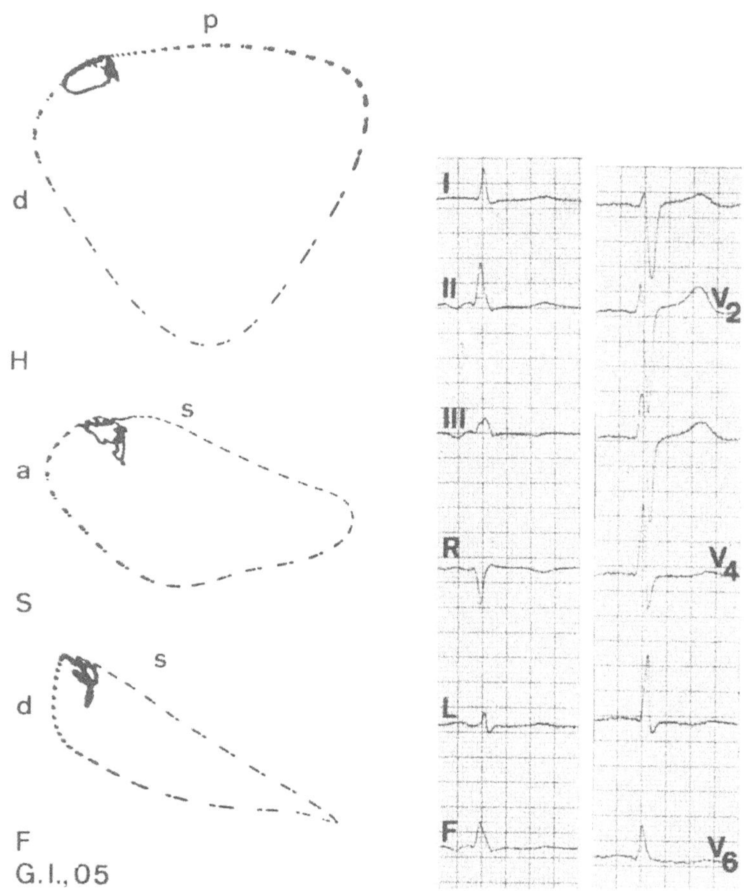

Fig. 15. G. I., 1905. Essential hypertension. Blood pressure 170/120 mm Hg. Normal renal function. Only minimal increase of potentials (maximal spatial vector 1.54 mV). The horizontal QRS loop is widened, "bulging" anteriorly and to the rear. Abnormal T loop due to shortening of repolarisation (no digitalis treatment). Typical VCG for mild LVH. ECG not typical of LVH. "Flattening" of T waves in leads V4 to V6, according to the abnormal repolarisation

mainly the left ventricle, are therefore ideally located to reflect such alterations in potential variations. However, mainly because of proximity effects [17], morphological loop alterations, like the increasing narrowing of the horizontal QRS loop or changes in its initial anterior orientation, are often wrongly interpreted or even missed from ECG. In contrast, alterations of the ST and T vector, deviating anteriorly and to the right, pointing away from the left ventricle, are readily recognized both in VCG and ECG. As in RVH, it is not decided as to what extent changes of repolarisation represent alterations of the endocardial structures (LV ischemia) or express simply overwhelming left ventricular repolarisation as in LBBB.

It is again the electrocardiographic diagnosis of *mild* LVH, which presents most of the difficulties. For reasons not yet clearly understood, early LVH is associated with a widening of the horizontal loop, the initial portion being ab-

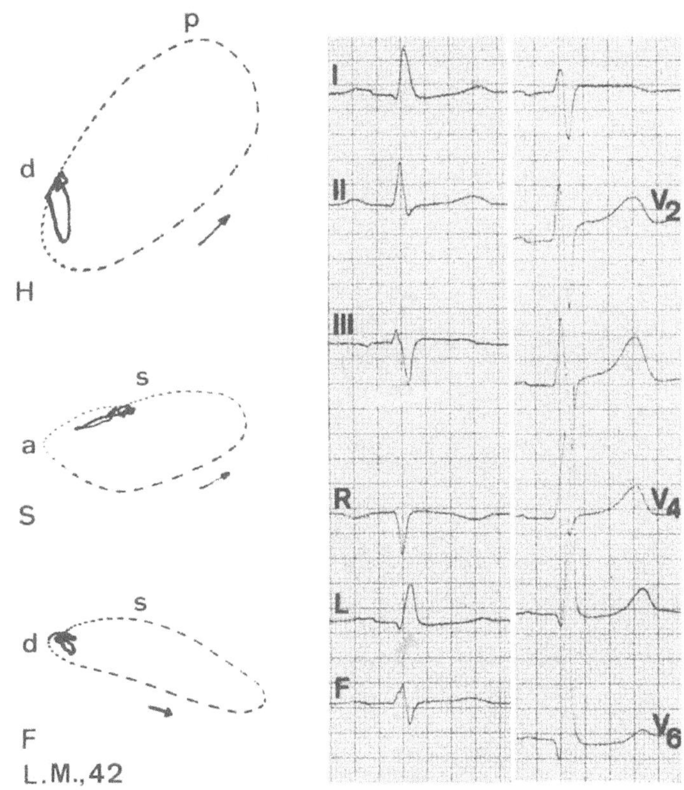

Fig. 16. L. M., 1942. Severe aortic regurgitation. LV pressure 120/0—10 mm Hg; aortic pressure 120/35; mean 78 mm Hg; CI 2.3 L/min/m². Cineangiography of the aortic root revealed massive reflux of contrast medium into the LV, filling the entire greatly entlarged LV cavity. Aortic regurgitation was confirmed at operation (Prof. A. SENNING). VCG shows increased potentials (spatial vector 2.26 mV), the QRS loop being shifted to the rear and the left as well as towards the horizontal axis. The normal anterior orientation of the QRS loop is still present, the frontal loop however is rotating counterclockwise. Normal orientation of the T vector. ECG is compatible with LVH; the small q waves in leads I and aVL suggest an initial rightward movement of the frontal loop, typical of volume overload of the LV in aortic insufficiency

normally displaced anteriorly, mid- and terminal-portions "bulging" towards the rear (fig. 15), the maximal potentials still being within the normal range. It is suggested that these changes, predominantly found in essential hypertension and in mild cases of aortic stenosis, mostly of congenital origin, represent focal left ventricular hypertrophy, especially of the left ventricular outflow tract. The difficulty of the electrocardiographic recognition of these cases may be due mainly to the absence of significant increase in potentials or specific ST-T wave changes (fig. 15). Important characteristics were found in the vectorcardiographic assessment of volume overload (diastolic overload) of the left ventricle, especially in mild forms of aortic regurgitation [21]. The relatively long per-

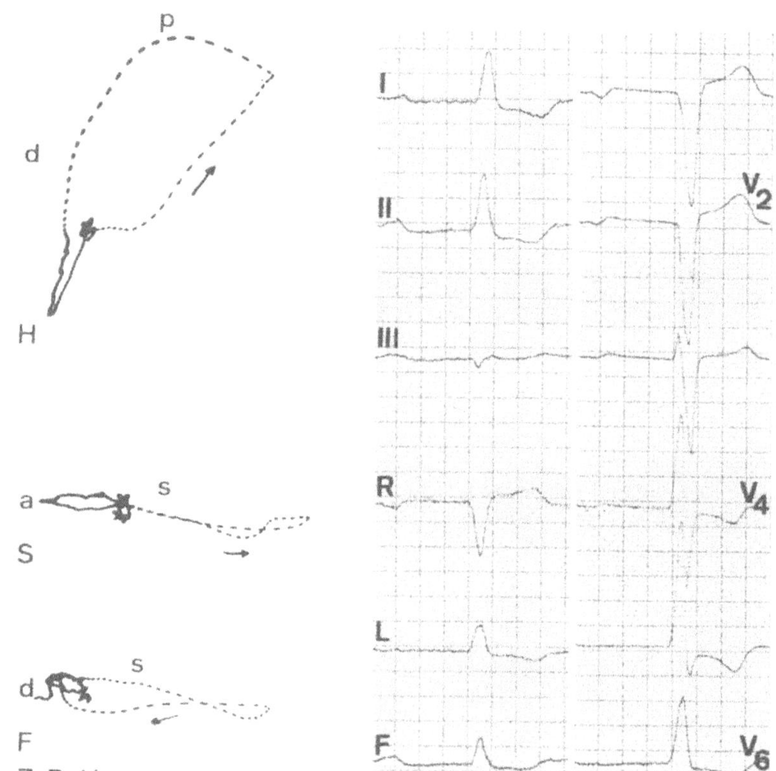

Fig. 17. Z. P., 1911. Severe aortic stenosis, minimal regurgitation. LV pressure 201/7—16 mm Hg; aortic pressure 106/53 mm Hg; mean systolic gradient 80 mm Hg; CI 2,45 L/min/m². Angiography revealed heavy calcification of the aortic area, the aortic valves being severely stenosed, the contrast medium leaving the hypertrophied LV through a small "jet". VCG shows posterior and leftward displacement of the QRS loop, as well as orientation towards the horizontal axis (maximal spatial vector 2.58 mV). The horizontal QRS loop is narrower than normal, the initial forces deviate to the left without significant anterior orientation. An anterior wall infarction is however unlikely in the presence of a strong leftward orientation of the early forces. ST and T vector are directed to the right and anteriorly, pointing away from the left ventricle. ECG shows severe LVH and "left ventricular strain". The absence of R waves in leads V1 and V2 is suggestive of an additional old anterior wall infarction. Coronary arteriography showed no signs of coronary artery disease, especially the LAD was absolutely normal

sistence of initial anterior forces in volume overload, even in the presence of considerable LVH, has been wellknown (fig. 16). However, a criterion of great significance and persistence was found in the abnormal, counterclockwise rotation of the frontal loop, being present in 80% of patients with pure or predominant aortic insufficiency [14, 21] (fig. 16). This additional criterion proved to be of special importance in diagnosing volume overload of the left ventricle as the wellknown sign of the persistence of normal repolarisation is often masked by unspecific alterations (Digitalis). It can still be seen even in the absence of normal anterior orientation of the horizontal QRS loop. A counter-clockwise rotation of the frontal loop may be recognized in the extremity leads of the ECG by the presence of small q waves in lead I and aVL as the initial vectors are orientated to the right, pointing away from these leads. However, when a small frontal loop is present or the initial vector is being directed not to the right but strictly downwards, such a change may be easily overlooked.

In contrast there are usually no major discrepancies between ECG and VCG in pressure overload (systolic overload) of the left ventricle. As most of these cases are accompanied by a considerable increase in potentials the known criteria for LVH are readily applicable. The major diagnostic difficulty is encountered in the judgment of a loss of R waves in leads V1 to V3, often present in the ECG of patients with severe LVH, suggestive of additional myocardial infarction (fig. 17). As can be seen from the horizontal QRS loop of these patients, a minimal duration of less than 5 msec. of anterior forces is quite often present. This small and short anterior orientation of the initial activation may however be absent in the ECG, either due to strong proximity effects or to a loop display paralleling lead V1 and V2 (fig. 17). Nevertheless, a number of patients remain presenting a lack of anterior forces also in the VCG. The reasons for this loss of anterior potentials are still subject to discussion; the existence of coronary artery disease is however rather unlikely as shown by coronary arteriography.

The significance of vectorcardiography in the diagnosis of LVH is therefore again mainly based on more precise recognition of the disease. In addition, at an early stage of development certain types of volume overload are more clearly outlined, specific loop alterations being present.

References

1. Burch, G., J. Abildskov, and J. Cronvich: Studies of the spatial vectorcardiogram in normal man. Circulation 7, 558 (1953).
2. Duchosal, P. W., et R. Sulzer: La vectorcardiographie. Basel: Karger 1949/1959.
3. Grishman, A., and L. Scherlis: Spatial vectorcardiography. Philadelphia: W. B. Saunders 1952.
4. Frank, E.: An accurate, clinically practical system for spatial vectorcardiography. Circulation 13, 737 (1956).
5. McFee, R., and A. Parungao: An orthogonal lead system for clinical electrocardiography. Amer. Heart J. 62, 93 (1961).

6. FRANK, E.: General theory of heart-vector projection. Circulat. Res. **9**, 258 (1954).
7. Report of the Committee on electrocardiography. American Heart Association. Recommandations for standardization of leads and of specification for instruments in electrocardiography and vectorcardiography. Circulation **35**, 583 (1967).
8. PIPBERGER, H. V.: Personal communication.
9. SONES, F. M., JR., and E. K. SHIREY: Cine coronary arteriography. Mod. Conc. cardiov. Dis. **31**, 735 (1962).
10. PARDEE, H. E. B.: The significance of an electrocardiogram with large Q in lead III. Arch. intern. Med. **46**, 470 (1930).
11. LICHTLEN, P., u. U. GUHL: Zur vektoriellen Analyse des Herzinfarktes. Cardiologia **49**, 177 (1966).
12. — Zur Analyse des räumlichen QRS-Vektors bei Koronarsklerose anhand der selektiven Koronarographie (Vektorkardiographie nach Frank). In: Aktuelle Probleme der Vektorkardiographie. VIII. Internat. Kolloquium für Vektorkardiographie, Wien, 1967. Stuttgart: Thieme 1968.
13. HOLZMANN, M., u. P. LICHTLEN: Vergleichende Untersuchungen über EKG, VKG und Koronarographie. In: Aktuelle Probleme der Vektorkardiographie, Wien, 1967. Stuttgart: Thieme 1968.
14. LICHTLEN, P.: Klinische Vektor-Elektrokardiographie. Berlin - Heidelberg - New York: Springer 1969.
15. YOUNG, W., and C. WILLIAMS: The frontal plane vectorcardiogram in old inferior myocardial infarction. Criteria for diagnosis and electrocardiographic correlation. Circulation **37**, 604 (1968).
16. HUGENHOLTZ, P. G., C. E. FORKNER, and D. LEVINE: A clinical appraisal of the vectorcardiogram in myocardial infarction. II. The Frank system. Circulation **24**, 825 (1961).
17. HARTMANN, I., R. VEYRAT, O. A. M. WYSS, and P. W. DUCHOSAL: Vectorcardiography as studied on the isolated mammalian heart suspended in a homogenous volume conductor. Cardiologia **27**, 129 (1955).
18. GATTIKER, H., F. NAGER, A. BÜHLMANN, and P. LICHTLEN: Pulmonary vascular obstructive disease. (In preparation.)
19. GURTNER, H. P., M. GERTSCH, C. SALZMANN, M. SCHERRER, P. STUCKI, und F. WYSS: Häufen sich die primär vasculären Formen des chronischen Cor pulmonale? Schweiz. med. Wschr. **98**, 1579, 1695 (1968).
20. MCGINN, S., and P. D. WHITE: Cor pulmonale resulting from pulmonary embolism. J. Amer. med. Ass. **104**, 1473 (1935).
21. LICHTLEN, P.: Die Volumenüberlastung des linken Ventrikels im Frank'schen Vektorkardiogramm. Schweiz. med. Wschr. **98**, 1267 (1968).

Electrocardiographic practice in the United States

RICHARD S. GUBNER, M.D.

The electrocardiograph has been in general employment for so many years, spanning the careers of almost all of us, that it may appear solely a descriptive exercise to analyze the actualities of electrocardiographic practice. Yet the state of things as they are is not necessarily the same as they might be, and it may be useful to survey electrocardiography as it is being practiced to derive some lessons. This, then, is quite apart from sophisticated techniques such as vectorcardiography, high speed wave study, computer analysis, telemetry, etc.; rather we are concerned with a consideration of material as it presents to us in our daily underwriting decisions.

Material for study

The material for this study comprises 500 consecutive electrocardiograms (representing as many physicians and all sections of the nation), made on insurance applicants who had had medical attention, in which connection an attending physician's statement had been obtained; and electrocardiograms made on the applicant, prior to his insurance examination, were submitted together with the medical report. Electrocardiograms made in our home or regional offices or requested by us in connection with the insurance application were not included. Thus, the sampling is a cross section of electrocardiographic practice by physicians in practice, and to lesser degree derives from clinics and hospital sources. This study supplements a similar one [1], also comprising 500 tracings, conducted a decade earlier in our home office and so offers some insight into changes which have occurred in electrocardiographic practice in this interval. Factors analyzed include reasons for taking the electrocardiogram, details of technique, type of apparatus, leads recorded, exercise tests and other special features, an evaluation of the interpretation made by the physician, and errors of commission and omission.

I know of no other source than this type of insurance material which so uniquely lends itself to obtaining a cross sectional insight into an aspect of medical practice; and this is one further illustration of the opportunities for investigation uniquely provided by insurance material. In some respects the data for a study of electrocardiography is more objective and accurate than material, for example, on blood pressure and heart murmurs which have been subjected to so many actuarial studies. Any analysis can be no better than the data from which it derives. We all recognize limitations of our blood pressure records on insurance applicants, with bunching and rounding out around the zero digit such as 90 for example. With heart murmurs we may have some degree of confidence in the systolic murmurs reported to us, but certainly diastolic murmurs are neither heard nor interpreted reliably, so that we have no adequate information for mortality analysis of either mitral stenosis or aortic insufficiency. The electrocardiogram, however, is an objective record, and we can see plainly the adequacy of both technique and interpretation.

Coefficient of utility

The electrocardiogram has taken its place directly alongside the stethoscope and sphygmomanometer, and together with fluoroscopy or a chest x-ray just about comprises the usual cardiac examination. I think it may be purposeful to consider briefly the concept of clinical utility, on all of which these procedures obviously score highly, in contrast for example to the ballistocardiogram, and roentgen, electro or kinetocardiogram, which, for clinical purposes remain esoteric.

We may define the coefficient of clinical utility of a particular procedure as the ratio of its usefulness (as numerator) to its limitations as denominator. Limitations include such considerations as availability, cost, sensitivity and specificity, and complexity of use, and of course hazards. Stated differently, it is an empirical ratio of what we get out to what we put in. Thus, if we grade numerator and denominator 1 to 10, to give us a possible range of 10/1 to 1/10, we would grade the usefulness of the stethoscope or sphygmomanometer as 10 and its limitations in proper hands as 1, and the electrocardiograph — again in proper hands, much in the same category.

The appropriate way to look at the numerator of usefulness, at least clinically, is not what one can do with it or use it for, but rather what can one not do *without* it, in other words for what is it indispensable. The blood pressure apparatus is indispensable to recognize hypertension, the stethoscope to diagnose mitral stenosis, and the electrocardiograph to detect myocardial ischemia. Consider, by contrast, the history of ballistocardiography. Initially, when introduced by ISAAC STARR its usefulness was an enigma, and the complexities of the Starr platform structurally and in application so involved that it was employed only in a few physiological laboratories. At this point the coefficient of utility was a ratio of 1/10 or not much better. In 1949 Dr. WILLIAM DOCK simplified the apparatus almost to a reductio ad absurdum in the form of a very inexpensive electro-magnetic shin bar producing a record which could be easily recorded on a standard electrocardiograph. Immediately the denominator which we had weighted at a maximum 10 because of complexity, cost and unavailability fell to a low order, and the numerator of clinical use climbed, as hundreds of eager investigators swarmed in to see what uses the now generally available ballistocardiography could be put to. The chief uses, it must be said from the vantage point of time, were to provide papers for jounals and further the careers of budding cardiologists. From the more sober judgment not of what can one use the ballistocardiograph for, but for what clinical purpose it is indispensable the numerator, I am afraid still falls relatively low and its coefficient of utility is still not a high one. This is not to deprecate the interesting applications of the ballistocardiogram as an exquisitely sensitive method for studying the force of the heart and the influence of drugs; and a useful area of clinical application may yet emerge, since long term follow-up studies by STARR [2] at the University of Pennsylvania, and BAKER [3] and co-workers at JOHNS HOPKINS, have shown significant correlation with future coronary heart disease and mortality.

In this fashion one can, and should, evaluate the various procedures we employ in medicine; and while the electrocardiograph in its proper perspective rates very high, we must subject this to scrutiny, and our other procedures also to determine when such techniques as coronary arteriography and other angiographic procedures, and catheterization, are indispensable, and what they are apt to tell us for what is put in, in complexity, cost and hazard to the patient.

Realistically the chief utility of the stethoscope often is to identify the physician in a hospital, acting as a wand and pass to allow him access to elevators and other areas where he would otherwise need a visitor's permit. The blood pressure machine is, often as not, the official seal of the medical examination. How much does it contribute in persons who are not hypertensive, to have blood pressure taken whenever patient meets the doctor? We must look at our other diagnostic aids, such as the electrocardiograph in the same candid manner.

For example, in the 500 electrocardiograms comprising the present analysis standard 12 lead tracings were taken in 83%. Does this mean that the unipolar limb leads, aAR, aVL, and aVF, taken in all these have a high coefficient of clinical utility? Not at all! They come as a standard attachment on all the machines presently used, and, requiring no more than a flick of the dial to record, are routinely included. Conversely in the entire sample of material there were two vectorcardiograms and one esophageal lead recording. Does this comparison reflect the lack of utility of the latter versus the unipolar limb leads? Again, not at all, but merely that there is still a difficult denominator of limitation of applicability for these.

We will come back to the technique for electrocardiography presently. I wish to address this question of the coefficient of clinical utility to a more basic question. How useful is electrocardiography in specific clinical situations, for this is the way we must evaluate it.

Indications for electrocardiography and findings

Let us first consider then what the indications were for taking electrocardiograms and what information they provided in each category. In 167 of the 500 cases or 33%, the tracings were taken as part of a routine examination without any symptomatic complaints. In 69, or 14%, the electrocardiogram was made as part of an examination for symptoms other than those suggesting a cardiovascular association. Together then, 33 plus 14 or 47% of the records were made for other than cardiovascular reasons. In 53% of the 500 cases, presently to be considered, the electrocardiograms were made for chest pain, history of coronary attack, hypertension, heart murmurs, cardiac enlargement, arrhythmias, or history of some cardiac disorder.

Let us return to our primary question. What is the coefficient of utility of the electrocardiogram when it is taken for other than a specific cardiac diagnostic purpose, in other words of how much value is it as part of a check-up examination, or a screening test when examining for miscellaneous unrelated symptoms? The answer is, that in this perspective, the electrocardiogram has a relatively low order of utility as it is being used. In only 6 of 167 cases where tracings were made for so-called check-ups was there a distinct abnormality. In our earlier study also of 500 similarly selected cases significant abnormalities were present in 10 of 200 persons, or 5%, in whom electrocardiograms were taken during routine or periodic examinations. Four showed major T abnormalities indicating myocardial disease, and two showed a right bundle branch block. However, there is an important group of 15 borderline tracings in this group almost all of which had been called negative, which showed QRS voltage changes or minor T changes suggesting left ventricular hypertrophy. I will return to this in our discussion of hypertension for in some respects I think the usefulness of the electrocardiogram to document the significance of a hypertensive background, and as an indicator of a presumptive hypertensive background and left ventricular hypertrophy is the most important lesson to be drawn from this study and one of the most important applications of electrocardiography.

There was a similar low yield of abnormal electrocardiograms among the 69 cases in which tracings were made for symptoms other than cardiovascular reasons. There were 6 definitely abnormal tracings, 3 of which occurred in applicants with pulmonary disease.

The relatively low diagnostic sensitivity of the electrocardiogram as a screening procedure when applied in the manner employed, and I will underscore the term *manner employed*, since there is a crucial failure in our standard technique, and we will return to this; may be contrasted with the much higher incidence of electrocardiographic abnormalities among the 53% of the 500 cases in which electrocardiograms had been made for the reason of some suspected or known cardiovascular abnormality. Whereas significant electrocardiographic abnormalities were present in 6 of 167 cases or 4% among electrocardiograms made as part of a check-up examination, distinctly abnormal electrocardiograms were present in 64 of 177, or 38% of persons with history of chest pain or coronary attack, 24 of 45 or 53% of hypertensive applicants, and 20 of 42 persons or 38% with miscellaneous other cardiovascular abnormalities such as murmurs arrhythmia history etc. These statistics are not surprising but there are some lessons to learn from reviewing them.

Coronary disease

We must put our observations into the context of what we are looking for in the electrocardiogram. The cardinal diagnostic application of electrocardiography, at least in the United States, is in coronary heart disease. In other parts of the world Chagas Disease or other cardiomyopathies might be a more significant area of application, but as our analysis indicates ischemic heart disease is the most frequent indication in our employment of the electrocardiograph and the type of heart disorder where it is most important and offers the greatest yield of diagnostic and prognostic information.

Statistics will vary according to their source, but a particularly good series is that of Dr. Richard Gorlin [4] who has correlated clinical picture, coronary arteriography, and double-two-step exercise tests in a large series of patients. His observations may be quoted: "Out of any given hundred patients we know to have coronary atherosclerosis, approximately 70 to 75% of this pre-selected group will have an abnormality in a resting tracing, irrespective of the type, leaving you a full 25 to 30% of all the people with documented atherosclerosis, who have an absolutely clean tracing. In our hands, of that number, 60%, of the total group, 15% of what you started with, will have an abnormal exercise two-step test of carried out to the double Master's criteria; this leaves a residual of ten."

In other words, the resting electrocardiogram plus the double-two-step exercise test may be expected to detect significant coronary disease producing myocardial ischemia in fully 90%, an impressive documentation of the value of electrocardiography.

There are ways to improve still further on the yield of positive exercise tests, such as progressive exercise to attain near maximal heart rates as developed by Sheffield and Reeves [5], which is not practicable in insurance medicine, or a simple procedure I reported at the American Therapeutic Society [6]. This involves giving a 15 mg tablet of Isuprel sublingually 10 to 15 minutes before performing the double-two-step test, which considerably augments post exercise tachycardia and heart work and induced abnormal post exercise ST segment depression, where the standard double-two-step test fails to evoke an abnormal response.

In any event the utility of the Master double-two-step exercise test is considerable, and it is discouraging to note that exercise tests were carried out in only 24 of 177 persons complaining of chest pain, a small number of these 177 total having had a background of myocardial infarction. The figure of exercise tests in 13% of persons with chest pain is precisely the same as it was in the study we carried out a decade earlier. Despite the large literature attesting the value of the exercise test in eliciting myocardial ischemia, and the safety of the test, practitioners are evidently still loathe to employ this diagnostic procedure. It must be reported further that such exercise tests as are being carried out are poorly performed. Of the 24 persons in whom exercise was performed a positive response was elicited in only 4, and this low yield is a commentary on the failings of technique rather than the procedure itself. Among 166 persons in whom electrocardiograms were made on asymptomatic applicants as part of a check-up, exercise tests were done in only 16, or 9.4%, and in none was the test positive.

It is interesting to note that the same low yield of abnormal exercise tests was found by Dr. MAURICE ROUGRAFF [8], of the American United Life Insurance Company. He analyzed 500 consecutive exercise electrocardiogram tests received in his home office, and among these 80 showed positive, ischemic changes after exercise. It was ROUGRAFF's observation, as it was ours, that, all too often, in our experience a majority of instances, a true Master double-two-step test was not carried out. Rarely was the amount of exercise specified, and the most varied amounts and types of exercise including knee-bends, running or hopping in place or mounting a stool were used. Any of these might be satisfactory if they resulted in a significant acceleration of heart rate, which is a sine qua non of a properly performed exercise test. It is absolutely essential to raise the heart rate (which reflects heart work) significantly, if one is to elicit ischemia; and if one does not push the heart rate to 150 as in the submaximal test as done by SHEFFIELD and REEVES, at least one should see the heart rate accelerate to over 100. In our group only a relatively small number showed appreciable acceleration of the heart rate. The chief virtue of the immediate post-exercise tracing lies not so much in exhibiting ischemic abnormalities (for these are often most conspicious in the 2 or 3-minute post-exercise records) but in providing proof that sufficient exercise to accelerate the heart was indeed performed. ROUGRAFF noted that when a Master style exercise test was carried out the average post-exercise acceleration was 27 beats per minute, in those with positive exercise tests it was 32, and in persons who had other than Master type tests the average acceleration of the heart rate was only 15 to 20 beats per minute.

Many tests are reported to us as "Master" tests when they are not. It seems clear that the term Master test has become identified with exercise electrocardiograms, but that exercise tests are in fact not being widely or satisfactorily carried out, and the name but not the procedure has been adopted. There are many aspects of the exercise test both in technique and interpretation, upon which I could expand, and new facets such as telemetered exercise electrocardiography, but I will defer this to our meeting in St. Louis this October where I will be discussing this subject at the Association of Life Insurance Medical Directors, as part of a symposium on electrocardiography (1968 annual meeting).

The electrocardiogram in hypertension

Other than in coronary disease, and of course in arrhythmias, one of the most useful areas of application of the electrocardiogram, and too often unappreciated, is in hypertension. Among 45 insurance applicants in our study who had hypertension the electrocardiogram was abnormal in 22, or just about half, and in an additional 11 instances there were borderline patterns in voltage or in T waves. This is a very high yield indeed and attests to the value of the electrocardiogram in hypertension.

Among the many QRS voltage criteria proposed for detecting left ventricular hypertrophy, an R wave amplitude in lead I exceeding 15 mm (1.5 mv) is the most specific; and the precordial lead criterion R in V5(6)+S in V1 exceeding 35 mm (3.5 mv) is the most sensitive [9]. Other commonly observed changes include total QRS voltage in single precordial lead V3 or V4 exceeding 35 mm, abnormally low R waves in precordial leads V1, V2 and V3; T wave in lead 1 lower than T in lead 3, and T in precordial leads V5 and V6 lower than T in precordial lead V1.

Evaluation of the hypertensive applicant is one of the most frequent and most important problems in our daily underwriting decisions, and the electrocardiogram is helpful in many ways. Hypertensive applicants with the voltage pattern of left ventricular hypertrophy have a mortality rate fully double that of persons with the same blood pressure whose electrocardiograms are normal, as we showed in a study many years ago [10]. The electrocardiogram not only tells us something about the past background of the hypertensive applicant and his prospects for the future, it also indicates in an increasingly important manner his present situation, about which he does not always provide entirely candid information. By this I mean that the electrocardiogram gives us clues to whether an applicant is taking antihypertensive drugs. The two most widely employed agents, reserpine and the thiazide diuretics, produce characteristic changes in the electrocardiogram which often lead us to suspect that these agents are being taken. Reserpine causes significant bradycardia, and thiazides, by causing potassium depletion produce a typical hypokalemic pattern, with low broad T waves and prominent U waves. Such suspicion, aroused by the electrocardiogram, may be confirmed by chromatographic analysis of the urine, a procedure we have been employing on a large scale in our home office laboratory.

Another aspect of the electrocardiogram in hypertension is worthy of brief comment. In many persons with hypertension whose resting electrocardiograms are normal, a double-two-step exercise test will evoke the pattern of "left ventricular strain". Accordingly an abnormal exercise test in a hypertensive person is less specific of coronary disease and myocardial ischemia, but it does serve to elicit a latent pattern of hypertrophy and is thereby useful.

For the above reasons I would urge that electrocardiograms be obtained in all insurance applicants with elevated blood pressure. The result will be not only to assure proper substandard ratings where these are indicated, but to offer the prospect of more favorable contracts in doubtful situations when the electrocardiogram proves normal.

The female electrocardiogram

I think it is appropriate, because it simply has not been recognized, to speak of a circumstance in which ST segment changes, of a type often seen in hypertension, may occur normally. This is the electrocardiogram of the normal older female, characterized by a prolonged, flat instead of rising or even slightly depressed ST segment in limb and particularly lateral precordial leads. In collaboration with my associate, Dr. MANUEL RODSTEIN [11], we have made a quantitative analysis of normal males and females in the second through seventh decades and the changes in the ST segment noted above are very characteristic. The point is an important one for the changes may lead to an erroneous diagnosis of myocardial ischemia or left ventricular strain, and predispose to abnormalities after exercise, accounting for a high incidence of false positive exercise tests in females. The cause of the ST change appears to lie in a decreased myocardial calcium, as well as potassium, content, which may have a bearing also on the decreased contractile force of the female heart as well as other muscles. At any rate as Mozart titled his opera, Cosi fan tutte, — women are like that! This study was presented at the American Heart Association in 1968, but not with the title which would have been most properly descriptive, i. e., Sex and the Electrocardiogram, The Older Female ST Sag.

Errors in interpreting electrocardiograms

Table I represents a summary of the physician's interpretation of the electrocardiogram divided into negative, abnormal and borderline classifications in each of the six major categories for which the electrocardiogram was taken. Among the 500 cases there were 24 major errors of commission, in which negative electrocardiograms were falsely reported as abnormal; and 15 errors of omission, in which abnormal electrocardiograms were erroneously interpreted as negative.

The greatest number of significant errors occurred among the group of persons with a history of chest pain or coronary attack. In 12 persons with normal electrocardiograms an erroneous diagnosis of posterior wall infarct was made in

7, and an unjustified diagnosis of myocardial disease was made in 5 on the basis of supposed ST and T changes which actually did not exist or were spurious due to technical errors. Contrariwise, there were 5 instances with patterns of acute infarction (3 posterior, 2 anterior) which were overlooked and misinterpreted as normal. 2 electrocardiograms which showed significant abnormalities were misread as negative. In two young men, both 31, an erroneous diagnosis of acute infarction was made where electrocardiograms (and clinical history) quite clearly indicated the correct diagnosis to be acute pericarditis. Three errors occurred in interpreting arrhythmias among the group of 177 persons with chest pain or coronary attack history. A case with nodal rhythm was erroneously interpreted called a Wolff-Parkinson-White syndrome. In another instance a W-P-W pattern was not recognized and the diagnosis of myocardial disease was made. In the third supraventricular tachycardia was called atrial fibrillation.

The above recitation of diagnostic errors relates only to the 177 of the 500 cases with chest pain, where errors of commission and omission are probably most serious. Among the 500 cases of the entire study a very substantial glossary of errors was assembled. It would serve little purpose to relate these individually; collectively they provide good documentation of the inexorable operation of Murphy's Law, i. e., if something can go wrong it will.

This comment concerning significant errors in interpretation of electrocardiograms does not relate to the considerable gray zone area of the borderline, of which there were 47 in the author's judgement. These had been variously interpreted as negative, abnormal or borderline, using the considerable number of qualifying equivocal expressions which have become part of the lexicon of electrocardiography, such as "non-specific ST and T changes". The complexities of evaluating the prognostic significance of minor electrocardiographic changes

Table I. *Reasons for taking electrocardiogram and interpretation in 500 insurance applicants*

Findings	Interpretation reported	History of Chest pain No. 177 (35.4%)	Hypertension No. 45 (9.0%)	Heart murmur, enlargement, and misc. cardiovasc. findings No. 23 (4.6%)	Arrhythmias No. 19 (3.8%)	Other symptoms No. 69 (13.8%)	Check-up No. 167 (33.4%)
Negative	Negative	90	9	12	5	48	139
Negative	Abnormal	12	2	0	1	3	1
Negative	Borderline	0	1	0	0	2	6
Abnormal	Negative	7	2	1	1	2	2
Abnormal	Abnormal	56	20	5	12	4	6
Abnormal	Borderline	1	2	1	0	0	0
Borderline	Negative	4	4	1	0	2	8
Borderline	Abnormal	1	2	0	0	2	2
Borderline	Borderline	6	3	3	0	6	3

has been considered by us elsewhere [12]. In addition observer variation among trained readers is considerable, so that, particularly in minor changes in the electrocardiograms there is understandable latitude in interpretation [13].

Electrocardiographic technique

Conventional 12 lead electrocardiograms (1, 2, 3, aVR, aVL, aVF and V1—6) with proper standardization were made in 313 of the 500 cases, and in another 98 adequate technique employing 12 leads was used, although no standardization was recorded. Thus, in 411 of the total 500, or 82%, standard electrocardiographic procedure was followed. This compared to 70% in which 12 lead tracings were made in the analysis of 500 tracings a decade earlier.

The most common deviation from standard 12 lead technique was the employment of less than 6 precordial leads. In 62 instances 3 or 4 V leads were recorded. This is not a serious omission as a rule; although leads V1, 2, and 3 are often needed to evaluate anteroseptal infarction, V4 and V5 are important for voltage changes in hypertrophy, and V5 and V6 for ST and T changes in ischemia, so that all the chest leads are useful. On occasion only a single chest lead, such as V4 or V5 was recorded, and this is inadequate. On the other hand extra leads were made in some, occasionally totalling 20 leads.

Among the special procedures and leads employed the following may be tabulated:

exercise tests	53
telemetered exercise tests	3
double speed tracings	6
photomotogram	1
ballistocardiogram	2
deep inspiration Lead 3	9
lead V3R	4
vectorcardiogram	2
esophageal leads	1
high V leads (3rd interspace)	1
ensiform lead	1

Each of the above has special areas of application. Double or higher speed tracings permit careful study of the QRS excitation wave; and we have found, for example, that a slurred initial downstroke helps characterize an anteroseptal Q in V1—V3 as distinguished from normal variants or similar findings in left ventricular hypertrophy. The photomotogram is a record of the Achilles tendon jerk recorded on the electrocardiograph, the rate of muscle relaxation correlating with thyroid function. The ballistocardiogram also may be recorded on the electrocardiograph, using the simple Dock electromagnetic shinbar for example; and gives sensitive information about the force of the heart. High V leads, lateral V leads, and esophageal leads may be used to detect elusive high anterior, lateral, and posterior infarcts respectively. Vectorcardiography is a major topic in itself, but its usage remains limited, and specific applications most clear in certain instances of posterior infarct and in distinguishing right ventricular hypertrophy from right bundle branch block. The esoterica of electrocardiography could be multiplied many fold beyond the permutations and variations cited. The next chapter, and it may rewrite the book, will be contributed by computer read-outs which offer a versatility of analysis of the electrocardiogram the naked eye cannot readily match.

A final observation may be made concerning errors in technique, which were significant in 12 instances. In 1 there was the classic reversal of polarity due to switching of right and left arm electrodes. I have known this common error to cause a tragically erroneous diagnosis of anterior infarction. In 5 there was inadequate low frequency response and high resistance due to poor electrode application causing a lag in stylus movement and spurious ST changes. In 2 major A-C interference was present, and in 3 instances there was a double stylus recording, leading in one to erroneous interpretation of right bundle branch block. These gross technical errors in 12 of the 500 cases are similar in number to 13 in 500 in the earlier series analyzed a decade before the present study.

For a more complete analysis of technical errors in the electrocardiogram, and where these may lead, the reader is referred to the book, "How to Produce a Readable Electrocardiogram", by Dr. Bertram Bradlow, of Johannesburg, to which the author had the privilege of contributing a foreword [14]. Also relevant is an article, Disorders of Electrocardiographers, which unfortunately is more factual than facetious [15].

Summary

Evidently electrocardiographic practice has not changed greatly in recent years. Analysis of 500 consecutive electrocardiograms submitted to the Home Office of the Equitable Life Assurance Society, made on insurance applicants by their physicians, revealed findings similar to a series of the same number studied a decade earlier.

Direct writing instruments were employed in 99 per cent of the present series, whereas in the earlier study 80 per cent of tracings were direct writing and 20 per cent photographic. Standard 12 lead tracings are increasingly used (82 per cent, vs. 70 per cent in the earlier study). Errors of technique are still not uncommon and of the same frequency and type as previously reported. In an occasional instance this may lead to a serious diagnostic error, where technical artifacts are mistaken for organic abnormalities.

Errors of commission and omission persist, but in some respects are less than in the previous analysis. In the initial study an erroneous interpretation that the electrocardiogram was abnormal and false diagnosis of heart disease was made in 24 of the 500 cases, in the present group the number was identical. However, whereas in the earlier study abnormalities present were not recognized in 40 tracings, this was true in the present series in only 15 cases.

Exercise electrocardiogram tests remain infrequently done; with generally inadequate exercise stress, and frequent improper technique and interpretation of post-exercise tracings.

Chest pain was the most frequent indication for taking electrocardiograms, i. e., 177 (35.4%) of the present study of 500 cases, with electrocardiograms as part of a check-up 167 (33.4%) a close second. Exercise tests were done in only 40 of these two groups of 344 persons. Since resting electrocardiograms are so often normal in persons with coronary disease, an adequate electrocardiogram stress test is essential for the detection of myocardial ischemia.

Another area of great value of the electrocardiogram is in evaluating persons with hypertension. The electrocardiogram provides useful clues to the presence of left ventricular hypertrophy, of considerable prognostic value; and also exhibits characteristic changes in persons taking antihypertensive drugs such as reserpine and thiazide diuretics. It is recommended that electrocardiograms be requested more often in applicants with elevated blood pressure to assist in proper underwriting decisions.

References

1. GUBNER, R. S., and H. E. UNGERLEIDER: Survey of electrocardiographic practice in the United States. Circulation **14**, 947 (1956).
2. STARR, I.: Prognostic value of ballistocardiograms. J. Amer. med. Ass. **187**, 511 (1964).
3. BAKER, B. M.: Ballistocardiography: predictor of coronary heart disease. Circulation **37**, 1 (1968).
4. GORLIN, R.: Conference on coronary artery disease. Trans. Ass. Life Insur. med. Dir. Amer. **51**, 221 (1967).
5. SHEFFIELD, L. T., and T. J. REEVES: Graded exercises in the diagnosis of angina pectoris. Mod. Conc. cardiov. Dis. **34**, 1 (1965).
6. LI, Y., et al.: Electrocardiographic response to maximal exercise. Amer. J. Cardiol. **20**, 541 (1967).
7. GUBNER, R. S.: Diagnostic and therapeutic applications of beta adrenergic stimulation and blockade in chest pain. Presented at Amer. Therapeutic Society, San Francisco, June 14, 1968. Reported in Medical Tribune, June 24, 1968; — Internist Observer **6**, 1 (August 1968).
8. ROUGRAFF, M. E.: How significant are "exercise" electrocardiograms? J. Indiana med. Ass. **59**, 1440 (1966).
9. RODSTEIN, M., and R. S. GUBNER: Specificity and sensitivity of QRS voltage criteria of left ventricular hypertrophy. Amer. J. Cardiol. **13**, 619 (1964).
10. DALEY, R. M., H. E. UNGERLEIDER, and R. S. GUBNER: Prognosis and insurability of hypertension with particular reference to the electrocardiogram. Trans. Ass. Life Insur. med. Dir. Amer. **28**, 18 (1941); — J. Amer. med. Ass. **121**, 383 (1943).
11. GUBNER, R. S., and M. RODSTEIN: Age and sex changes in the ST segment in a normal population; some physiological and clinical implications. Presented at Annual Meeting of American Heart Ass., Miami, November 24, 1968.
12. RODSTEIN, M., L. WOLLOCH, and R. S. GUBNER: The significance of minor electrocardiographic T wave changes: a mortality study of 518 applicants for insurance. Amer. J. med. Sci. **252**, 55 (1966).
13. CALATAYRUD, J. B., et al.: Observer variation in electrocardiographic interpretation. Amer. J. Cardiol. **13**, 99 (1964).
14. BRADLOW, B. A.: How to produce a readable electrocardiogram. C. C. Thomas 1964.
15. GUBNER, R. S.: Disorders of electrocardiographers. Resident Physician **11**, 170 (1965).

The next decade in cardiovascular surgery

LAURENCE MISCALL, M. D.

Less than a generation ago only a few hardy souls had the courage to deny that the summit in Cardiovascular Surgery had been attained. As late as 1947 Castiglione listed repair of heart wounds, myocardial revascularization, blood vessel anastomosis, repair of aneurysms, closure of the patent ductus and resection of the constrictive pericardium as significant advances. He cited the latter two as the best surgical accomplishments in heart disease. The record was not unimpressive but the story was bleak since it exhibited not even an inkling of the intellectual dissatisfaction and investigative effort which produced the advances which daily contribute so much to human welfare. Anyone who has been active in this field through this period of explosive progress has a perspective radically different from previous generations. It is clear that the surface hardly has been scratched and that the summit is not discernible in the forseeable future. From the defects which become apparent with each day's experience with these brilliant achievements one can identify these areas in which improvement can be expected rather promptly.

Present equipment is excellent and a far cry from that available in the early days of open heart surgery. The safety in its use is such that now no patient need be denied surgery because of inadequate machinery. However, since all this is run by people, the performance can be no better than the operator. When one considers the number of variables in this work it is amazing that more difficulties do not arise. A start has already been made in maximal eradication of chance for error by automation. Continued progress in this area offers almost endless improvement.

Artificial hearts designed primarily to support a failing circulation have received much attention. They have been used with some success in a few cases and are bound to find increasing application particularly in a society that beats coronary vessel so unmercifully.

An artificial heart to replace a hopelessly damaged organ has been an attractive idea. However success must await development of suitable material for its construction and a reliable source of energy to regulate and drive it. There is little doubt that such a unit can and will be built but imposing problems for which no solutions are in sight indicates its perfection to be in the distant future. Such a mechanism has one great virtue. If practicality and reliability can be insured, such units could be stored and readily available at any time and place. This is not the situation with cardiac transplantation.

In the short space of time that pacemakers have been available the improvement has been phenomenal. They now meet more nearly the functional requirements. With the use of new power sources and methods of instrumentation one can expect compact units which will abolish failure which still is too frequent.

Every type of valve surgery has its limitations. This makes it imperative not to abandon any but rather to use them either singly or in concert for specific indications. Closed technique is very satisfactory in some cases but its deficiencies are well recognized. For others with more advanced changes only open operation is acceptable. Even here certain defects are constant.

Artificial prostheses have been a poor substitute. They are not everlasting and mechanical failure has been too common. Turbulence, valvular gradients, interference with blood flow, infection, thrombosis and an adverse affect upon blood elements vitiate the results. Two changes are necessary. The valves need redesigning to more closely approximate the hemodynamics of the valve being replaced. They must be constructed of material which is durable and can be incorporated in the body tissue or which exerts only minimal or no adverse effect on it. Each new model has made its contribution. Pending final perfection there should be no hesitation in using the present valves since they have produced handsomely for many patients. If meticulous attention is given to every detail of treatment the risk of failure can be reduced to a minimum. The record is far superior to surgery for many forms of cancer which no one even thinks of abandoning at this time.

Some may wish to persevere in the plastic reconstruction of damaged valves. To date the results from operative reconstruction have been disappointing. Perhaps in the future, biochemical methods of inducing resolution of changes may be effective but as of now little promise is in view.

Homografts and heterografts have been difficult to insert and follow-up has indicated that they are subject to changes which if progressive could well indicate the desirability of abandoning them.

At the present time the prospect for developing a satisfactory artificial prosthesis seems to have the greatest promise of all methods.

As the age of the population increases and living becomes more complex an increase rather than a decrease in the incidence of coronary artery disease can be expected. The success of the internist and the cardiologist in their intensive care units justifies rapid multiplication of them. For the patient who does not respond satisfactorily to conservative measures surgery will play an increasing role. Temporary support of a failing circulation may carry many into a phase of illness permitting ultimate recovery. In chronic coronary insufficiency revascularization can not only relieve symptoms but does rehabilitate many. It has been superior to direct operation on the coronary vessels.

If further progress in the treatment of hypertensive disease and atherosclerosis can be gained particularly by conservative measures a decrease in this problem may be a dividend.

The years 1968 and 1969 had at least two almost miraculous events. Transplantation of the human heart became a reality and Apollo XI returned safely to the earth after two men had set foot on the moon for the first time in history. Although the problem of transplantation has only been scratched it has been demonstrated that it can be done. Improvement will follow intensive investigation of every detail. As success mounts the black areas of ignorance take on a grey tint of beginning light. Soon it, like open heart surgery, may not appear so astounding.

It seems destined at this time to have ever widening possibilities. The number of totally correctable congenital lesions of the heart has grown markedly since the start of open technique. However many of them receive only variable benefit from a variety of procedures. If heart transplant lives up to its promise the young patients may become the most desirable group for application of this method. A venture in this area should be one of the most satisfying explorations facing the profession. For intractable heart failure it has no substitute. It should supplant lesser procedures for aneurysms involving a major portion of the ventricle.

If technical considerations were the only difficulties in the path of ultimate success the course would be shorter than expected. However, other factors will have a tremendous impact on the solution of this problem and it will tax the ingenuity of the profession which must take the helm in order to emerge from the wilderness. Murmurings already define some of the obstructions. A good segment of the population recoils in horror from the idea of donating a heart or other organs to a bank. Some of this has a basis in religious belief but a good portion arises from simple ignorance. Voices begin to raise legal questions. Rampant moralistic discussion too often is on a superficial plane and not without bias. A segment of the profession expresses either overt objection or registers indecision. The simple problem of delivery of the organs to the proper site at the proper time will tax the imagination of the most expert planner. It is rather elementary to observe that this will require substantial financial support much of which must come from the government. Under such circumstances the simple job of keeping the effort in high gear will command the time and thought of many.

It is difficult to envision greater benefits than those which accrue from surgery for P.D.A., coarctation, great vessel anomalies, aortic aneurysm, septal defects and others. It must be remembered that only vision, faith, hope and long hard work wrought this change. A lackadaisical attitude did not and cannot now contribute any progress. A great mass of new information concerning basic abnormal and normal cardiac physiology must be assembled. The progress of pathological change must be more carefully documented. The pharmacology of agents with significant cardiac action must be elucidated. These are but a few of the projects waiting solution. In an economy capable of visioning, planning and completing a project such as Apollo XI, it is juvenile to even suspect that the problems of cardiac surgery cannot be resolved. More than half a century has elapsed since Carrol wrote and talked about many of these problems. Much has been done but much more remains to be done. It is high time we got on with the job.

Relationships between lipid and carbohydrate metabolism; their influence on the arterial wall

G. HARTMANN

With 7 Figures

In other terms the relationships between hyperlipidemia and diabetes as well as their respective influence on atherogenesis, i. e. on the development of occlusive vascular disease are discussed in the following paper. — It is easier to comprehend the problem once the main characteristics of the physiology and pathophysiology of lipid and carbohydrate metabolism are known, as they form the basis for understanding the statistically ascertained links with atherogenesis.

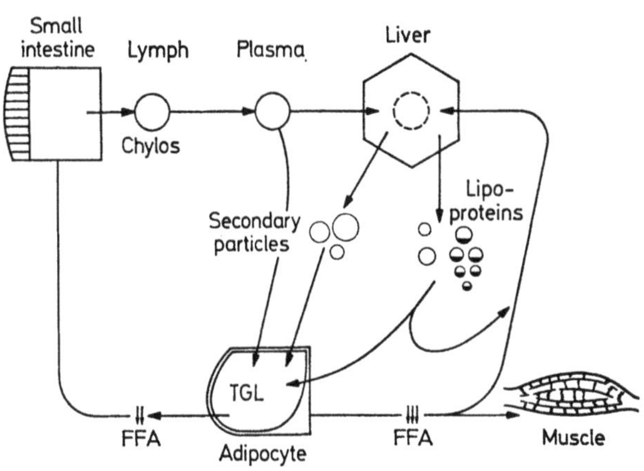

Fig. 1. Main routes of fat transport

Small intestine = epithelial cell of the small intestine
Chylos = chylomicrons
FFA = free fatty acids
TGL = triglycerides

As regards *lipid metabolism* in connection with atherosclerosis, we are first of all interested in the problem of intravascular lipid accumulation, i. e. the hyperlipidemia. Hyperlipidemias represent for the most part disorders of lipid transport. Figure 1 shows in a schematic diagram the principal routes of lipid transport in the organism. Five classes of lipid vehicles may be distinguished

(Table I). For a good comprehension of disorders in the transport of lipids, the following facts are important:

1. Chylomicrons are synthesized by the cells of the small intestine depending exclusively on the amount of exogenous fat. Accumulation thereof in the intravascular space results from an impaired elimination mechanism, i. e. to a large extent from a deficiency in lipoprotein lipase.

2. The free fatty acids are released mainly by the adipose tissue.

3. All the other lipoproteins derive almost exclusively from the liver; they are carried partly to the adipose tissue and partly back to the liver.

Table I. *The lipid vehicles*

Class	Origin	t/2	Diagnostic significance for hyperlipidemias
Free fatty acids	endogenous	2—3 min.	– –
α-lipoproteins	endogenous	~ 4 days	– –
β-lipoproteins	endogenous	~ 4 days	++
Pre-β-lipoproteins	endogenous	? hours	++
Chylomicrons	exogenous	5—10 min.	++

t/2 = half-life period.

The flow of lipids from the fatty tissues to the liver and to other organs occurs only in the form of free fatty acids, which are loosely bound to albumin. Their concentration of 10 to 15 mg% in the normal individual is very small compared to the total amount of serum lipids (from 500—800 mg% on an average). Their turnover rate may reach, however, extremely high levels and rise up to 500 g a day, i. e. far more than any other fraction.

There are two important links with carbohydrate metabolism which we may anticipate:

Insulin and glucose inhibit the release of free fatty acids (the lipolysis) from the adipose tissue, whereas epinephrine, fasting, growth hormone etc. promote it.

A very imbalanced intake of carbohydrates stimulates the formation of triglyceride-rich pre-β-lipoproteins in the liver, especially in the case of a hereditary disposition thereto, as in carbohydrate-induced hyperlipidemias. A relative lack of lipoprotein-lipase combined with such an imbalanced diet is an additional factor for a delayed elimination of the triglyceride-rich particles, as recent investigations have shown (BIERMAN).

A disproportion between formation of the various lipoproteins and their elimination from the vascular system leads to hyperlipidemia resp. to *hyperlipoproteinemia.* The various types can be classified from the pathogenesis on one hand and observing the lipoprotein pattern of the serum on the other hand. The different participating components are shown in Table I. For clinical purposes the various fractions are best separated by electrophoresis on paper or agarose; however, these two methods give only qualitative results. Clinical methods exist for the quantitative determination of the chemical fractions (cholesterol, phospholipids, triglycerides) which are commonly known today and most frequently used. However the determination of cholesterol alone is still too often used for the screening of hyperlipidemias. Due to a relatively constant composition of the individual lipoprotein classes — as shown by figure 2 — it is possible, in a large number of cases, to evaluate the prevailing lipoprotein pattern from the mere chemical fractions.

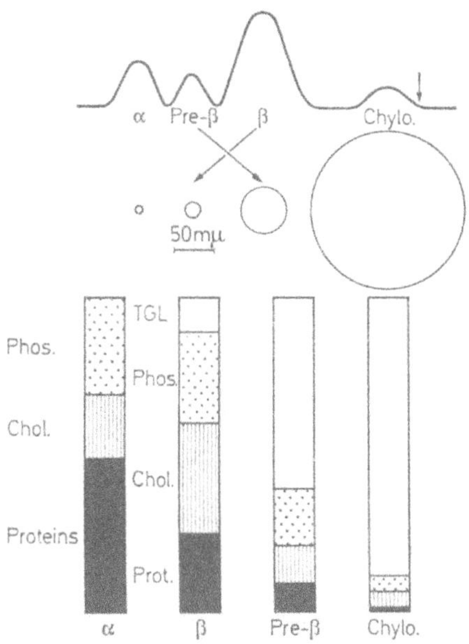

Fig. 2. The individual lipoprotein fractions in the electrophoresis (above), the approximate size (middle) and the chemical composition (below) of the different molecules

The most useful classification for the primary hyperlipidemias has been worked out by FREDRICKSON and LEES (Table II). The various types differ in their lipoprotein pattern as well as in a number of other characteristics as for instance the kind of xanthomas, the susceptibility to exogenous fat or carbohydrates, differences in heredity and so on. It is interesting to note in connection with this problem the frequently impaired glucose tolerance among the types III and IV and more rarely in type V. In many cases, it is impossible at first to distinguish between a hyperlipidemia with impaired glucose tolerance and a diabetes mellitus with hyperlipidemia. Apart from diabetes mellitus, clinically important secondary or symptomatic hyperlipidemias are observed with hypothyroidism, ethylic and other forms of hepatopathy, the nephrotic syndrome as well as pancreatitis (which may in turn be a consequence of a more severe case

Table II. *Primary hyperlipidemias*

Type	I	II	III	IV	V
Chylomicrons	+++	normal	normal	normal	++
β-lipoproteins	normal	+++	+++ [b]	normal	normal
Pre-β-lipoproteins	normal	normal	+++ [b]	+++	++
Glucose tolerance	normal	normal	(reduced)	reduced	(reduced)
Lipoproteinlipase	reduced	normal	normal	normal	(reduced)
Susceptible to carbohydrates	–	–	(+)	+++	(++)
Susceptible to fat	+++	–	–	–	++
Xanthomas [a]	eruptive	tendinous tuberous	all	eruptive	eruptive
Hepatosplenomegaly	++	–	(+)	+	+
Atherosclerosis	?	+++	++	++	+?

[a] Xanthomas and Hepatosplenomegaly appear only in severe hyerlipidemias.

[b] A subclass of pre-β-lipoproteins and to a smaller part of β-lipoproteins is increased (so-called "broad-beta").

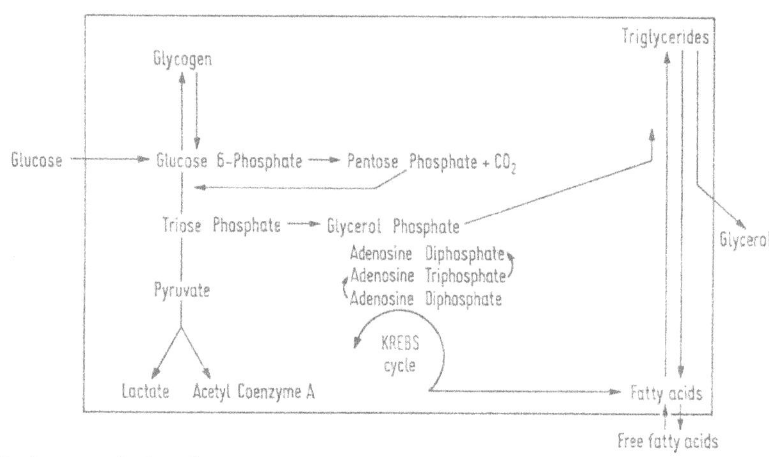

Fig. 3. Pathways of the glucose metabolism and its relationships to fat metabolism in an adipocyte. Basal conditions (according to B. JEANRENAUD)

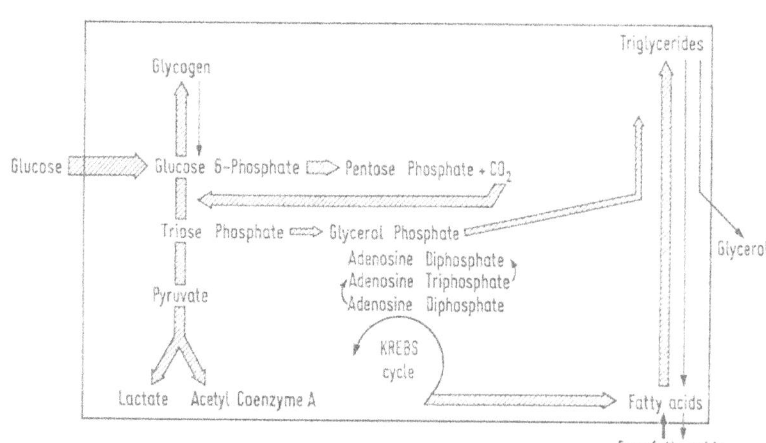

Fig. 4. Same as Figure 3. Effect of insulin (according to B. JEANRENAUD)

of hypertriglyceridemia). The increase of serum lipids during pregnancy is a physiological feature whereas hyperlipidemias in Cushing syndrome, plasmocytoma, glycogen storage disease are more rare conditions.

Figure 3 shows the main routes of glucose as they can be traced in a fat cell. The close relation with the intermediate lipid metabolism is obvious. The effect of the administration of insulin on the various mechanisms is demonstrated in Figure 4. The net result is an increased storage of fat. A marked insulin deficiency has the opposite effect and results in a considerable release of triglycerides in the form of free fatty acids due to the reduced uptake of glucose. The final result in this case is a heavy increase of the plasma free fatty acids as is commonly observed with decompensated diabetes.

Diabetes mellitus is by far the most important disturbance of carbohydrate metabolism. The current concepts of its pathogenesis are schematically represented in the diagram of Table III. Noteworthy is the partial or total ineffi-

Table III. *Pathogenesis of diabetes mellitus (according to* S. FRANKHAUSER)

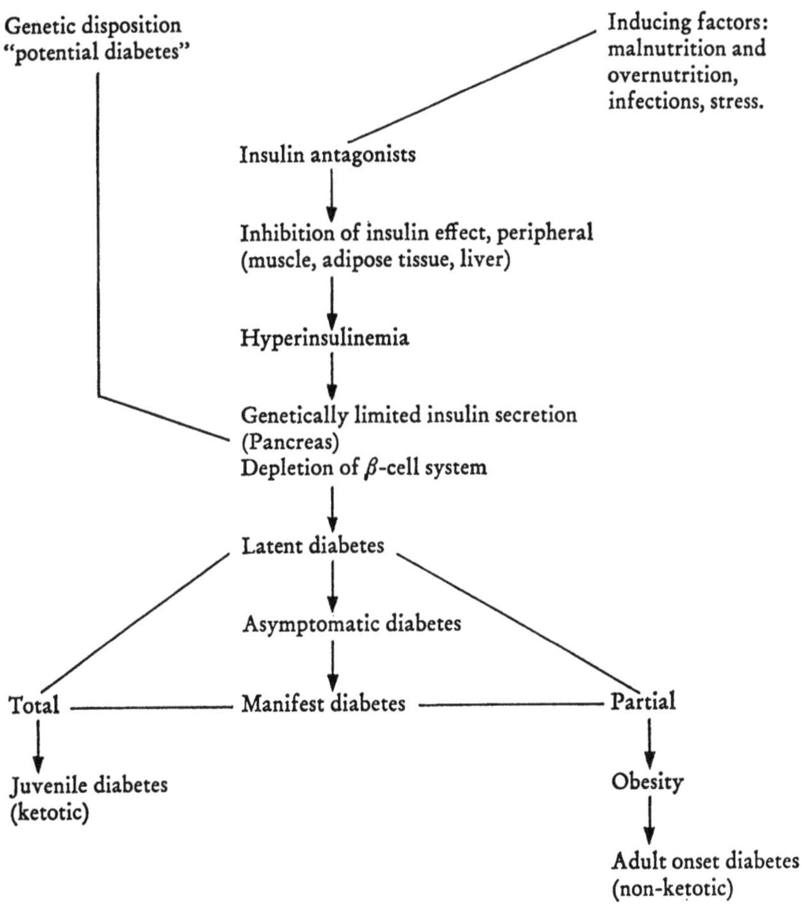

ciency of the hormone on the cellular level at an early stage and the ensuing hyperinsulinemia, whereas the number of cases with primary insulin deficiency is relatively small. In most instances the islets of Langerhans are exhausted only secondarily. Therefore substitution of insulin is in many cases not the optimal therapeutic measure as it was for many years thought to be. Methods which are aimed at improving the response of the muscles, the liver or the adipose tissue to endogenous insulin are very often much more effective, achieving an inhibition among others of increased lipolysis and decreasing consequently the accumulation of serum triglyceride. In order to achieve this we must first reduce the amount of adipose tissue as shown quite clearly by the results of weight reduction and most dramatically by complete fasting.

According to RENOLD, body fat is the only tissue which cannot fulfil its function in the absence of insulin, in contrast e. g. to the muscle or the liver cell. (Active) insulin accelerates the transport of glucose and of free fatty acids

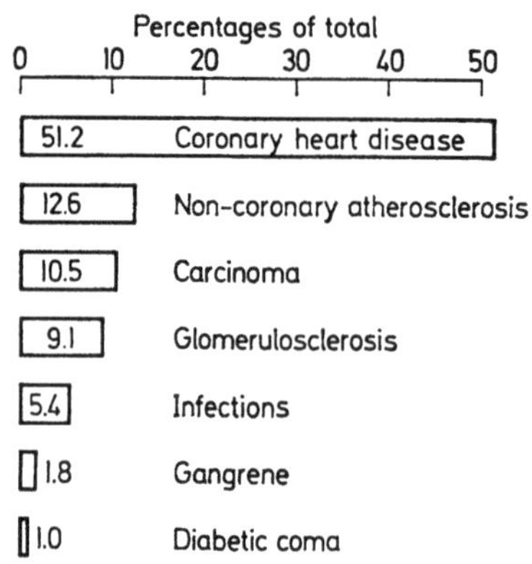

Fig. 5. Principal causes of death of diabetics (Joslin Clinic, 1956—1962)

through the cell membrane of the adipocyte and as a result of the high activity of hexokinase, glucose-6-phosphate is immediately formed. All further processes are secondary to this one, e. g. the reduced lipolysis, the increased triglyceride synthesis in the cell, etc.

What are then the *effects on the arterial wall* of diabetes on the one hand and of hyperlipidemia on the other? How can we visualize the relation between the two diseases and atherosclerosis?

Our knowledge in this field is full of gaps. Starting from the final results of obliterating atherosclerosis, of myocardial infarction or of peripheral arterial occlusion, the statistics reveal the following:

a) At the Joslin Clinic in Boston, 2/3 of all diabetics die from atherosclerotic diseases of the vessels, more than half from myocardial infarction (Figure 5); the latter figure is about three times higher than the number of deaths from myocardial infarction in the average population of Switzerland (irrespective of their higher mean age). If the frequency of diabetes among patients with coronary disease is investigated, percentages ranging from 6.7 (Hochrein) to 11.2 (Master), and among Jewish groups of up to 25% are found. The frequency varies of course with the respective criteria. Our own investigations carried out together with Widmer at the University Medical Clinic in Basle among patients suffering from arterial occlusion of the limbs (in the male age group 55—64 years), revealed a frequency of impaired glucose tolerance of up to 30%.

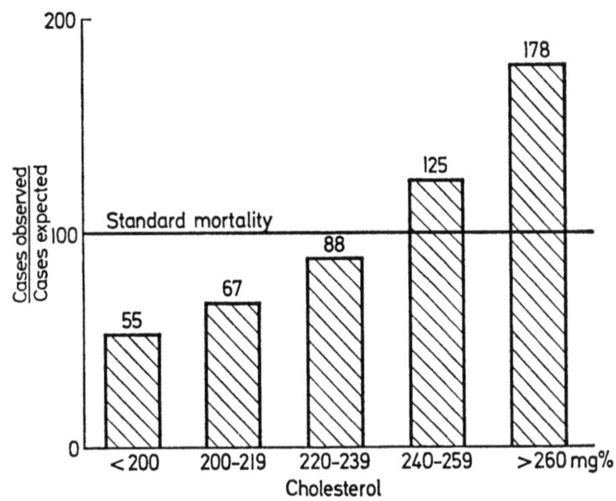

Coronary heart disease	<200	200-219	220-239	240-259	>260 mg%
observed	27	24	36	35	73
expected	49	36	41	28	41
Examined	591	389	432	297	414

Fig. 6. Morbidity of coronary heart disease in the course of 10 years in relation to serum cholesterol (Framingham). The incidence in males with an initial serum cholesterol level exceeding 260 mg% is three times greater than in individuals with a serum cholesterol below 200 mg%

b) The prognostic significance of hyperlipidemia has been established particularly by the Framingham study in the United States. Figure 6 shows the increasing risk for coronary heart disease with a rising level of serum cholesterol. Highly interesting is the fact that there is no critical concentration limit, i. e. people with abnormally low values are less prone than the average. — Our own studies showed more often an increase of the total β-lipoprotein content than of cholesterol in patients with peripheral arterial occlusion in comparison with an age-matched sample of working people. Albrink, Cramèr and Carlson found independently that abnormally high triglyceride levels occur more often than hypercholesteremia among patients with myocardial infarction. Our own observations in Basle confirm this finding. There is no doubt today that — bearing in mind the lipoprotein pattern of hyperlipidemias — both cholesterol *and* triglyceride must be taken into consideration as factors of risk although reliable prospective data for the latter are still outstanding.

These statistical relationships (a few mentioned among a huge body of data) are of course only of relative significance as arguments for the causal role of hyperlipidemia in atherosclerosis. As a matter of fact, however, a number of further observations give support to the so-called lipid theory:

— It is only possible to induce experimental atherosclerosis in animals, similar to that of human beings, with a diet rich in lipids. The same does, however, not occur with a diet rich in carbohydrates or proteins or after malnutrition. VASTESAEGER recently observed a first case of myocardial infarction in a chimpanzee after feeding a diet with a high content of saturated fat and cholesterol.

— Populations or population groups with low average serum lipid concentrations have a lower incidence of myocardial infarctions.

— Lowering of the serum lipid concentrations induced in certain cases an improvement of the symptoms in coronary heart disease, and in several studies a lower incidence of myocardial infarction was observed (LERÉN et al., TURPEINEN et al.).

— The vascular atheromas consist of lipids which are at present interpreted to have been deposited mainly from serum lipoproteins.

On a pathophysiological level, fat and carbohydrate metabolism seem to be linked in their common adverse effects on the vascular wall by increased serum lipid concentrations which are found in a large percentage of diabetics. Atherosclerosis of the greater arteries has to be clearly distinguished from the diabetic microangiopathy which seems to evolve independently from hyperlipidemia and fat metabolism.

To what extent does the *formal genesis* of atherosclerosis, as it is conceived today, fit in with the so-called lipid theory? Results of the static and dynamic angiochemistry as well as morphological studies support the concept that the major part of the lipid material in atheromatous arteries derive from the intravascular space. It is, however, important to stress that this is not the result of a purely passive filtration mechanism, but that indeed variable propensity of myogenic elements to be transformed into foam cells represents one of the essential factors of the primary fatty degeneration. This so-called "wall factor" which includes the terms of heredity, disposition, constitution etc. might be the decisive factor in many cases as to whether obliterating atherosclerosis develops or not. It may at the same time explain the absence of serious atherosclerosis in the presence of massive hyperlipidemia as well as formation of atheromas with normal quantities of serum lipids, i. e. the existence of a purely relative hyperlipidemia.

After this very simplified sketch of complex mechanisms, it must be remembered that the arterial wall is exposed to numerous influences and that stenosing atherosclerosis is the result of a process involving several factors, one of which is thrombogenesis which plays at least a secondary role.

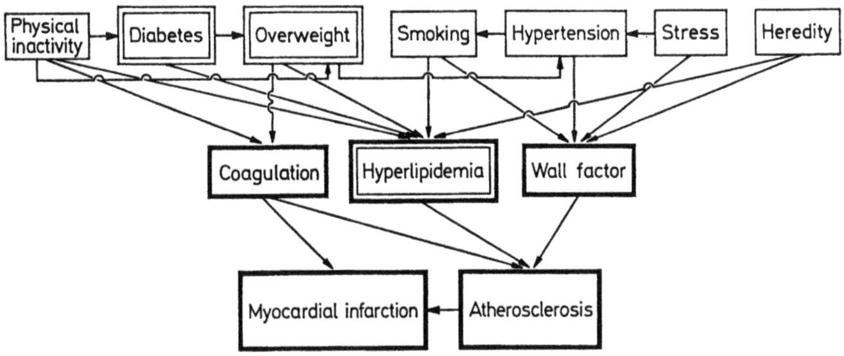

Fig. 7. Pathophysiological interrelations between risk factors found epidemiologically and atherosclerosis or myocardial infarction respectively

In considering the problem to what extent the observed statistical relationships in terms of risk factors can be explained from a pathophysiological point of view, we would refer to the synopsis in Figure 7. It shows in a schematic form that all effects centre on two principal key points: the hyperlipidemia on the one hand and the wall factor on the other hand. It may be that with diabetes, changes of the arterial wall even of greater vessels occur independently of hyperlipidemia, but we do not have yet any concrete information in this respect.

A long term study of insured and declined diabetics

George Goodkin, M.D. · Leon B. Wolloch, M.A.

Mortality studies by Life Insurance Companies in the past have been deficient in the respect that only the mortality of insurance applicants who were offered a policy and who had accepted the contract was investigated. The mortality of the applicants who were declined, who had not accepted the life insurance offer, or who had accepted but lapsed the policy within the period of the study was unknown.

While this deficiency is a minor one in impairments where there is a large body of statistical data and where the natural history of the disease is known, it assumes larger proportions in those diseases or disorders which are still classified as experimental underwriting impairments.

In experimental underwriting certain criteria are set up which are largely determined by clinical experience and which are through to be conservative enough to protect the insurance company from unacceptable losses. Dependence is then placed upon future mortality studies to confirm or disprove the reliability of the assessed ratings and to draw up a balance sheet comparing the predicted experience with the actual and determining whether the premiums charged were correct, excessive or inadequate.

Satisfactory though this may be in determining which underwriting criteria are too liberal, it does not answer the question on the opposite side of the coin. Are the underwriting criteria eliminating from consideration many diabetics who may very well be insurable within our mortality limits?

From our point of view, therefore, two overriding questions have remained unanswered:

1. What is the mortality of those diabetics who fail to pass the underwriting criteria?

2. What ist the mortality of all diabetics who apply for insurance?

In order to obtain valid answers to these pertinent questions, The Equitable Life Assurance Society embarked upon a mortality study of all diabetics who applied for life insurance with the Society, regardless of whether the insurance was in force, lapsed, not taken out or declined.

Applicants for life insurance were considered diabetics for the purpose of this study if: (1) They were diagnosed as diabetics by their attending physician, (2) They were taking insulin or oral hypoglycemic agents in addition to a diet at the time of application, (3) The insurance record showed a history of diabetes confirmed by a physician's statement. Individuals with a history of glycosuria without dietary treatment or medication or both or who had an abnormal glucose tolerance test at the time of examination, were excluded from the study as well as diabetics who applied for Major Medical or Disability Income Insurance but had not applied for life insurance.

The underwriting criteria for the insurability of diabetics consisted of the following:

1. *Age limits at time of application* — 15 to 60 years.
2. *Age at onset of diabetes* — Not less than 10 years of age or more than 60 years of age.
3. *Build* — Must qualify for standard insurance on the basis of build alone.
4. *Weight* — Must be stable unless diagnosis of diabetes has been made within the past year.
5. *Observation* — Should have been under adequate and competent observation since date of diagnosis.
6. *History of blood pressure* — Not more than a debit of +15 mortality points.
7. *Blood sugar* — The fasting blood sugar within 6 months of application should not have exceeded 200 mgs-%.
8. *Diabetic coma* — No history of coma after initial period of observation unless adequately explained.
9. *Insulin dosage* — Daily dosage not to exceed 100 units (all types).
10. *Pregnancy* — Not pregnant at time of application.
11. *Urine* — Should not contain albumin in amounts of 20 mgms or more.
12. *Family history* — Should not have more than two cases of cardiovascular-renal disease under age 60 in the immediate family (parents, brothers or sisters).
13. *Physical condition or history* — History of any impairment or any impairment on examination with the exception of diabetes which would make the applicant a substandard risk.

Any of the following factors was cause for declination:

1. History or present condition of any cardiovascular or renal disease or any other impairment with the exception of diabetes that would require a substandard rate.
2. A two-hour postprandial blood sugar on examination exceeding 250 mgs-%.
3. Glycosuria exceeding 4%.
4. History of severe insulin shock.
5. Poor control or supervision of diabetes.

Medical requirements

All diabetics who applied for insurance and who qualified on the basis of the preceding were given a medical examination and filled out an applicant's diabetes questionnaire. The examiner also secured two-hour postprandial blood and urine specimens which were sent to the Home Office for analysis. The venous blood was analyzed by the Auto-Analyzer using the Hagedorn-Jensen method for true blood glucose. A special Attending Physician's Statement was sent to the applicant's attending physician for completion.

In addition, in applications of over $ 10,000 in which the applicant was age 40 or over an electrocardiogram completed either at the Home Office or by a specified Board Certified Cardiologist was required.

Methodology

All diabetics who applied for insurance with the Equitable Life Insurance Society of the United States from the years 1951 through 1961 were observed to the anniversaries of their applications in 1966. Inasmuch as these cases were not homogeneous from an underwriting point of view, they were divided into three groups:

Group "A" consisted of those diabetic individuals who successfully passed the underwriting criteria and were issued policies regardless of whether they paid for them, did not accept the offer or subsequently lapsed their policies.

Group "B" consisted of diabetic individuals who were declined for non-medical reasons or who were declined because they failed to complete the underwriting requirements.

Group "C" consisted of diabetic individuals who were declined for insurance because they failed to pass the medical underwriting criteria.

In the investigation of factors thought to be important in determining the mortality of the diabetic it was found necessary to combine groups "A", "B" and "C" when group "A" had an insufficient number of deaths to be statistically significant. Similarly groups "B" and "C" were combined when group "B" had an insufficient number of deaths or when the variation between the mortality ratios was not significant.

The investigation of applicants who were declined, applicants who were offered policies but did not pay for them, and the insureds who subsequently lapsed their policies presented us with problems in tracing the large numbers of individuals involved because of their migratory habits and the passage of as much as fifteen years since the time of application.

Although this was a laborious and tedious procedure in tracing the status of these applicants, we were fortunate in being able to trace all but 215 individuals, making a total of 95.7% successfully traced in the declined, not taken out, and lapsed cases.

The procedure in tracing all individuals in the study that were not insured with the Society consisted of nine sequential steps:

Step No. 1 — *The M.I.B. record.* All individuals who had a record of applying for insurance subsequent to the cutoff date of December 1966 were considered to be living for the purpose of the study.

Step No. 2 — *Insurance in other companies.* Individuals who at the time of application indicated that they had insurance in force in other companies were tabulated and the individual companies were contacted as to their status — whether living or dead, and if the latter, the date and cause of death.

Step No. 3 — *National Service Life Insurance.* The same procedure was followed in those applicants who at time of application indicated that they had National Service Life Insurance in force. The Veterans Administration was contacted for the status of these applicants.

Step No. 4 — *The agency that submitted the application.* Each agency was contacted to determine whether the agent of record could advise us of the status of his applicant. This procedure was unproductive, as in most cases, the agent of record had lost contact with the applicant or was no longer employed by the Society.

Step No. 5 — *The applicant.* In rare cases the applicant was contacted directly by mail at the last known mailing address.

Step No. 6 — *The employer.* The last known employer was contacted by mail. If the status of his employee could not be determined, the employer was asked to provide us with the employee's Social Security Number.

Step No. 7 — *Social Security Administration.* The Social Security Administration was contacted for the status of the applicant. To date this line of investigation has been unproductive as the Social Security Administration has not as yet decided whether their policy would permit release of this information.

Step No. 8 — *Inspection of applicant.* Unlike other companies, we have our own Inspection Bureau so that the remainder of the unknown cases, including the list sent to the Social Security Administration, were sent to our Inspection Bureau for investigation.

Step No. 9 — *Final M.I.B. checking.* This consisted of a repetition of Step No. 1. Some cases could be traced for a limited number of years before the cutoff date and were included in the study for the observed period.

The remainder of the unknown cases (94) consisted of those who could not be traced within the period of one year after application and were dropped from the study. All deaths were verified by obtaining a copy of the death certificate and both primary and secondary causes of death were recorded.

Results

General characteristics of the study

Four thousand nine hundred and seventy-four applicants for life insurance who applied between the years of 1951 and 1961 were observed to the anniversaries of their applications in 1966. The expected deaths were computed using the Equitable's Select Mortality Table covering the period 1953—1958.

Table I. *Diabetes mortality study, 1951—1961*

General characteristics of the study

	Number	Percent
Applications traced to the 1966 anniversary of application	4,759	95.7
Contact lost one year before the 1966 anniversary	55	1.1
Contact lost two years before the 1966 anniversary	36	.7
Contact lost three or more years before the 1966 anniversary	124	2.5
All cases	4,974	100.0

	Issued	Declined	All
Entrants	1,342	3,632	4,974
Lives	1,151	3,330	4,481
Total exposure years	11,267	28,876	40,143
Average exposure years	8.4	7.9	8.1
Actual deaths	77	645	722
Tabular deaths [a]	41.43	126.48	167.91
Relative mortality	186%	510%	430%
Proportion of males	96%	90%	92%
Average age at application	39.4	40.0	39.8
Median age at application	36.5	37.7	37.3

[a] Tabular deaths were computed using the Equitable standard select mortality table 1953—1958.

The total exposure years was 40,143 with an average exposure of 8.1 years. The average age was 39.8 years and the median age 37.3 years. 92% of the entrants were males. There were 722 actual deaths compared to 167.91 expected giving a mortality ratio of 430% for the entire study.

Out of 1,342 entrants who were issued policies, (group A), 96% of whom were males, there were 77 actual deaths giving a mortality ratio of 186%.

Out of 3,632 declined cases, both medical and non-medical, (groups "B" and "C"), 90% of whom were males, there were 645 deaths with a mortality ratio of 510%.

Issued versus declined

Table II shows a further breakdown between those declined medically and those declined on a non-medical basis. The mortality ratio for applicants declined medically, (group C) was 429% compared to a mortality ratio of 540% for those declined for non-medical reasons (group B) and 186% for the issued cases (group A).

Table II. *Diabetic mortality study, 1951—1961*
Observed through 1966 anniversary of application
Expected deaths based on the Equitable's select mortality table 1953—1958

Issued versus declined

A) Relative mortality

	Entrants	Actual deaths	Expected deaths	A/E ratio %
Declined for medical reasons	1,118	146	34.04	429
Declined for non-medical reasons	2,514	499	92.44	540
Issued	1,342	77	41.43	186
All	4,974	722	167.91	430

B) Percentage of issued within specified age group at application

Age	Issued	Declined	All entrants	Issued as percent of all entrants in the same age group
10—29	236	907	1,143	21
30—39	457	846	1,303	35
40—49	407	915	1,322	31
50—59	221	720	941	23
60 and over	21	244	265	8
All	1,342	3,632	4,974	27

The distribution of entrants within specified age groups at application were as follows:

To age 29	1,143 or 23.0%
30—39	1,303 or 26.2%
40—49	1,322 or 26.6%
50—59	941 or 18.9%
60 and over . . .	265 or 5.3%

There was in this study a heavier concentration, (49%), in the age group under 40 than in the age group over 40 in diabetic applicants as contrasted to the age distribution in the general diabetic population where only 20% of diabetics are under the age of 40. Whether this is due to the nature of the insurance business because of the need for greater insurance protection in the younger families with dependents or whether this is merely a reflection of antiselection in the younger, more severe diabetics is difficult to determine. Nevertheless, this age distribution must be taken into account in considering the relative weight of factors which are believed to have a significant effect in determining the mortality of diabetics.

Mortality of issued cases by rating classification

Table III shows the mortality of insured cases by substandard classifications. It would appear that our best diabetics (135—195% predicted mortality) were within standard mortality limits. However, the number of deaths is too small to be statistically significant.

In the predicted 200—245% mortality class the actual experience was 156% with only fifteen deaths. The 250—295% predicted mortality class showed a mortality ratio of 231% and the 300—395% class, a mortality ratio of 386%.

The most important single factor in the prognosis of diabetes is considered to be the severity of the disease as reflected by the age of onset with duration of the disease the next in importance. Although it appears that we are making a profit on our insured diabetics at the present time and that our criteria for insurability are too conservative, the number of deaths in the series is still too small to be confident of our mortality ratios. In addition, one must wait for a longer average duration for the experience before coming to definite conclusions. In our next mortality study we may be able to answer this debatable point with more confidence in the reliability of our data.

Mortality by age at application

Table IV shows the results of mortality by Age at time of Application. In the Issued Cases (group "A") there were no deaths in the age group 10—19. The mortality ratio was highest for the age group 20—29 (333%) and lowest for the age group 40—49 years (118%) with the mortality ratio for all ages being 186% based upon 77 deaths.

In the declined cases (groups "B" and "C"), the mortality ratios declined with increasing age at time of application except for the age group 10—19 where there were only 8 actual deaths. The highest mortality ratio was 1741% for the age group 20—29 and progressively decreased to a low of 298% for ages 60 and over. This same pattern of declining mortality ratios with advancing age at time of application is seen when the total experience, both issued and declined is considered.

Mortality by duration of diabetes at time of application

Table V shows mortality by duration at time of application. In both the issued and declined cases the effect of duration was significant. There was a progressive increase in mortality ratios with increasing durations of the disease. The mortality data indicates that the mortality in diabetes of 5 years duration or less is most favorable in the issued cases and that there was a marked increase in mortality in the entire experience with a duration of 11—19 years and even more with a duration of 20 years or more. It is generally recognized that the duration of diabetes is a significant factor in underwriting this impairment and the mortality data bears this out.

Table III. *Diabetic mortality study, 1951—1961.* Observed through 1966 anniversary of application. Expected deaths based on the Equitable's select mortality table 1953—1958

All issued cases by rating

		Entrants	Actual deaths	Expected deaths	Ratio actual to expected		Ratio actual to expected premium basis	
Standard	Up to 130%	25	1	0.93	[a]	122%	[a]	73%
B	(135—145%)	59	5	2.70	185%		132%	
C	(150—195%)	398	17	15.23	112		64	
D	(200—245%)	381	15	9.62	156		69	
E	(250—295%)	225	14	6.07	231		84	
F	(300—395%)	183	21	5.44	386	368%	110	100%
G	(400—500%)	69	4	1.35	[a]		66	
Combinations		2	—	0.09	—		—	
All		1,342	77	41.43	186%		81%	

[a] A/E ratios not shown for less than 5 deaths.

Table IV. *Diabetic mortality study, 1951—1961.* Observed through 1966 anniversary of application. Expected deaths based on the Equitable's select mortality table 1953—1958

Mortality by age at application

Age at application	Issued				Declined				All			
	Entrants	Actual deaths	Expected deaths	A/E ratio	Entrants	Actual deaths	Expected deaths	A/E ratio	Entrants	Actual deaths	Expected deaths	A/E ratio
10—19	23	—	0.14	—	172	8	1.04	769%	195	8	1.18	678%
20—29	213	6	1.80	333%	735	101	5.80	1,741	948	107	7.60	1,408
30—39	457	18	6.43	280	846	112	11.82	948	1,303	130	18.25	712
40—49	407	18	15.31	118	915	160	32.58	491	1,322	178	47.89	372
50—59	221	32	15.30	209	720	187	49.38	379	941	219	64.68	339
60 and over	21	3	2.45	[a]	244	77	25.86	298	265	80	28.31	283
All ages	1,342	77	41.43	186%	3,632	645	126.48	510%	4,974	722	167.91	430%

[a] A/E ratios not shown for less than 5 deaths.

Table V. *Diabetic mortality study, 1951—1961.* Observed through 1966 anniversary of application. Expected deaths based on the Equitable's select mortality table 1953—1958

By duration of diabetes at time of application all ages combined

Duration in years	Issued				Declined				All			
	Entrants	Actual deaths	Expected deaths	A/E ratio	Entrants	Actual deaths	Expected deaths	A/E ratio	Entrants	Actual deaths	Expected deaths	A/E ratio
0— 5	752	32	23.78	135%	1,669	241	67.80	355%	2,421	273	91.58	298%
6—10	272	20	9.46	211	819	139	27.91	498	1,091	159	37.37	425
11—14	140	9	3.28	274	443	92	11.59	794	583	101	14.87	679
15—19	107	9	3.09	291	355	87	10.27	847	462	96	13.36	719
20 and over	71	7	1.82	385	346	86	8.91	965	417	93	10.73	867
All	1,342	77	41.43	186%	3,632	645	126.48	510%	4,974	722	167.91	430%

Mortality by age and duration of diabetes at time of application

Table VI which is a combined table of Age at Time of Application and Duration at Time of Application shows a trend of increasing mortality ratios with increasing durations of the disease at all ages, but particularly in the age groups below age 40. It should be noted that in the Age Group 20—29 which largely represents Juvenile Growth Onset Diabetes the mortality ratios are markedly higher for the same durations of the disease than in the Adult Maturity Onset Type of Diabetes.

Table VI. *Diabetic mortality study, 1951—1961*
Observed through 1966 anniversary of application
Expected deaths based on the Equitable's select mortality table 1953—1958

By age and duration of diabetes at time of application

	Issued and declined					
Duration of diabetes at time of application in years	Entrants	Actual deaths	A/E ratio	Entrants	Actual deaths	A/E ratio
		Ages 10—19			Ages 40—49	
0— 5	110	7	[a]	687	85	336%
6—10	48	—	—	291	40	375
11—14	29	1	[a]	122	12	282
15—19	5	—	—	110	19	488
20 and over	3	—	—	112	22	587
All	195	8	678%	1,322	178	372%
		Ages 20—29			Ages 50—59	
0— 5	345	19	686%	567	95	240%
6—10	246	22	1,146	182	57	427
11—14	177	31	2,153	79	29	642
15—19	109	19	2,159	62	21	504
20 and over	71	16	2,712	51	17	572
All	948	107	1,408%	941	219	339%
		Ages 30—39			Ages 60 and over	
0— 5	567	32	411%	145	35	227%
6—10	258	18	465	66	22	302
11—14	160	22	944	16	6	288
15—19	155	28	1,315	21	9	396
20 and over	163	30	1,408	17	8	620
All	1,303	130	712%	265	80	283%

[a] A/E ratios not shown for less than 5 deaths.

Mortality by age at diagnosis of diabetes

The pattern of mortality ratios as seen in Table VII reflects the severity of diabetes at the earlier ages of onset. It indicates that the Juvenile Diabetic is a severe diabetic and a poor mortality risk while the Adult or Maturity Onset Diabetic is a relatively mild diabetic with a better survival pattern. With the high mortality ratios shown in the diabetics who developed the disease before the age of twenty, it is doubtful if the Juvenile Diabetic is insurable at all and that perhaps only those diabetics who have had the onset of their disease at age 20 or over can be safely considered within our usual mortality limits.

Table VII. *Diabetic mortality study, 1951—1961*
Observed through 1966 anniversary of application
Expected deaths based on the Equitable's select mortality table 1953—1958

Mortality by age at diagnosis of diabetes

	Issued				Declined				All			
Age	Entrants	Actual deaths	Expected deaths	A/E ratio	Entrants	Actual deaths	Expected deaths	A/E ratio	Entrants	Actual deaths	Expected deaths	A/E ratio
Under 15	111	8	1.40	571%	598	97	5.38	1803%	709	105	6.78	1,549%
15—19	121	8	1.37	584	359	60	3.92	1531	480	68	5.29	1,285
20—29	324	7	5.10	137	678	80	11.68	685	1,002	87	16.78	518
30—39	357	12	8.50	141	721	104	20.94	497	1,078	116	29.44	394
40—49	300	28	14.72	190	723	180	37.75	477	1,023	208	52.47	396
50—59	124	14	9.89	142	452	96	35.92	267	576	110	45.81	240
60 and over	5	—	0.45	[a]	101	28	10.89	257	106	28	11.34	247
All ages	1,342	77	41.43	186%	3,632	645	126.48	510%	4,974	722	167.91	430%

[a] A/E ratios not shown for less than 5 deaths.

Mortality by control of diabetes

The quality of control is difficult to evaluate on a consistent basis as it is composed of many variable factors — postprandial blood sugar determinations, urinary sugar determinations, degree and frequency of supervision, history of insulin shock or coma and the type of management given by diverse schools of treatment. The general practitioner in remote areas does not have the facilities to do postprandial blood sugars and depends mainly upon urinary sugar determinations for control. The sophisticated diabetic specialist in the large cities exercises a greater degree of supervision, both qualitatively and quantitatively than his colleague in the rural areas. In addition, different philosophies of management prevail in different parts of the country — rigid control of diet and insulin in some clinics as opposed to free diet management in others. The diabetic himself is apt to mislead his attending physician. In order to avoid a lecture he is inclined to behave and watch his diet and insulin just before a scheduled visit to his physician and relapse into his customary habits after the visit is over. Some of the prize patients of well known clinics were found to have a high two-hour postprandial blood sugar when they were examined for insurance without advance knowledge of the blood sugar requirement.

Each applicant was judged individually by the underwriter for evidence of the quality of control taking into account the attending physician's report, the applicant's questionnaire, the medical examiner's report, and the two-hour postprandial blood sugar completed at the time of examination.

For the purpose of the study, only a certain percentage of the declined cases were considered as showing poor control. Any applicant who was issued a policy was deemed by the underwriter to be fairly well controlled. Of the declined cases, only the ones declined for the following reasons were considered to have poor control: 1. excessive glycosuria (over 4%) or two-hour postprandial blood sugar of over 250 mgs-%; 2. history of recent high blood sugar; 3. history of severe insulin shock or onset of coma after the initial period of observation.

The mortality ratios of the poorly controlled cases was approximately two and a half times that of the well controlled cases — 468% contrasted with 191% as shown in Table VIII.

Mortality by type of medication

The results as shown in Table IX confirm the clinical experience that diabetics who are controlled by diet alone (mortality ratio 241%) or diet and oral medication alone (mortality ratio 328%) are milder diabetics than those controlled by insulin and diet (mortality ratio 530%).

Mortality by units of insulin

The group treated by insulin and diet was further subdivided by the number of units of insulin of all types taken daily. The mortality ratios are shown in Table X.

In the issued cases the mortality ratios increased with increasing number of units of insulin taken daily. The same trend held true for both the declined and combined experience. The increase in mortality ratios with increasing number of units of insulin taken daily appears to be due to the increasing proportion of juvenile diabetics at the higher insulin dosages and is more a reflection of the age at diagnosis than the amount of insulin taken. In diabetics who developed the disease between 10 and 20 years of age there is no appreciable difference in the very high mortality ratios with increasing number of units of insulin taken daily. The same holds true of the older age groups where the mortality ratios are markedly lower.

Table VIII. *Diabetic mortality study, 1951—1961*
Observed through 1966 anniversary of application
Expected deaths based on the Equitable's select mortality table 1953—1958

Mortality by control of diabetes

Type of control	Controlled[a]				Poor control[b]			
	Entrants	Actual deaths	Expected deaths	A/E ratio	Entrants	Actual deaths	Expected deaths	A/E ratio
Insulin, less than 50 units	560	35	17.84	196%	292	34	7.87	432%
50 to 74 units	192	13	3.64	357	155	20	2.41	830
75 or more units	44	1	1.12	c	55	6	1.14	526
Amount unknown	8	1	0.35	c	14	—	0.17	—
All with insulin	804	50	22.95	218	516	60	11.59	518
No insulin, oral medication or diet only	460	24	15.83	152	140	22	5.93	371
All cases	1,264	74	38.78	191%	656	82	17.52	468%

[a] Issued cases
[b] Cases declined for the following reasons:
1. Excessive glycosuria or poor blood sugar tests on examination only
2. History of recent high blood sugar
3. History of coma or insulin shock only

[c] A/E ratios not shown for less than 5 deaths.

Table IX. *Diabetic mortality study, 1951—1691*
Observed through 1966 anniversary of application
Expected deaths based on the Equitable's select mortality table 1953—1958

Mortality by medication

Type of medication	Issued				Declined				All			
	Entrants	Actual deaths	Expected deaths	A/E ratio	Entrants	Actual deaths	Expected deaths	A/E ratio	Entrants	Actual deaths	Expected deaths	A/E ratio
Diet only No medication	277	10	11.08	90%	480	79	25.82	306%	757	89	36.90	241%
Insulin	804	50	22.95	218	2,324	438	69.07	634	3,128	488	92.02	530
Oral medication	183	14	4.75	295	330	40	11.73	341	513	54	16.48	328
Unknown	78	3	2.65	a	498	88	19.86	443	576	91	22.51	404
All	1,342	77	41.43	186%	3,632	645	126.48	510%	4,974	722	167.91	430%

[a] A/E ratios not shown for less than 5 deaths.

Table X. *Diabetic mortality study, 1951—1961*
Observed through 1966 anniversary of application
Expected deaths based on the Equitable's select mortality table 1953—1958

a) Mortality by units of insulin

	Issued				Declined				All			
Units of insulin	Entrants	Actual deaths	Expected deaths	A/E ratio	Entrants	Actual deaths	Expected deaths	A/E ratio	Entrants	Actual deaths	Expected deaths	A/E ratio
Less than 10	6	1	0.13	[a]	28	7	1.72	407%	34	8	1.85	432%
10—24	181	13	8.02	162%	398	76	19.56	389	579	89	27.58	323
25—49	373	21	9.69	217	949	188	27.15	692	1,322	209	36.84	567
50—74	192	13	3.64	357	591	102	11.03	925	783	115	14.67	784
75—100	40	1	1.04	[a]	204	33	3.53	935	244	34	4.57	744
Over 100	4	—	0.08	[a]	41	6	0.80	750	45	6	.88	682
Unknown	8	1	0.35	[a]	113	26	5.28	492	121	27	5.63	480
All	804	50	22.95	218%	2,324	438	69.07	634%	3,128	488	92.02	530%

b) Mortality by units of insulin and age at diagnosis

	Units of insulin											
	10—24			25—49			50—74			75—100		
Age at diagnosis	Entrants	Actual deaths	A/E ratio	Entrants	Actual deaths	A/E ratio	Entrants	Actual deaths	A/E ratio	Entrants	Actual deaths	A/E ratio
10—19	60	6	811%	403	63	1,514%	387	62	1,610%	146	19	1,450%
20—29	97	5	338	391	40	591	238	19	470	62	6	455
30—39	170	19	373	289	37	416	111	21	519	19	1	[a]
40—49	164	38	384	172	45	403	39	9	398	14	6	526
50—59	79	19	207	62	20	396	10	4	656	3	2	[a]
60—over	9	2	[a]	9	4	[a]	2	—	—	—	—	—
All ages	579	89	323%	1,326	209	567%	787	115	784%	244	34	744%
Ages 20 and over	519	83	309%	923	146	447%	400	53	490%	98	15	460%

[a] A/E ratios not shown for less than 5 deaths.

Mortality by reason for declination

The results are tabulated in Table XI.

Hypertension alone showed a mortality ratio of 541% but when combined with a non-circulatory impairment showed a slightly higher mortality ratio of 682%.

Unfavorable EKG only showed a mortality ratio of 436% but the number of deaths was too low to be significant.

Other circulatory impairments alone or in combination showed a mortality ratio of 734%.

Albumin, casts or other urinary findings other than glycosuria showed a very high mortality ratio of 1,197%.

Table XI. *Diabetic mortality study, 1951—1961*
Observed through 1966 anniversary of application

Mortality by reason for declination

Reason	Number of Entrants	Actual deaths	Expected deaths	A/E ratio
Hypertension only	268	68	12.56	541%
Hypertension combined with non-circulatory impairments	181	57	8.36	682
Unfavorable EKG only	52	12	2.75	436
Other circulatory impairments alone or in combination	195	55	7.49	734
Albumin, casts or other urinary findings other than glycosuria only	115	34	2.84	1,197
Albuminuria, in combination with impairments other than hypertension	56	17	1.67	1,018
Excessive glycosuria or poor blood sugar tests on examination only	513	59	13.88	425
Not under good supervision	377	64	14.50	441
History of recent high blood sugar	64	13	2.00	650
History of coma or insulin shock only	87	12	1.77	678
Not standard build only	66	6	2.40	250
Combination of impairments excluding hypertension or albuminuria only	167	38	7.81	487
Miscellaneous single impairments not listed above	191	34	6.05	562
Age of applicant only	89	18	8.74	206
Age at onset of diabetes only	158	23	1.33	1729
Other non-medical reasons	218	35	7.57	462
Incomplete data	835	100	24.76	404
All declined	3,632	645	126.48	510%

High postprandial blood sugar or excessive glycosuria (over 4%) on examination showed a mortality ratio of 425%.

Applicants who were declined for a history of a recent high blood sugar showed a mortality ratio of 650%.

The group with a history of coma or insulin shock only had a mortality ratio of 678%.

Age of onset of diabetes below the age of 10 showed one of the highest mortality ratios of the entire study — 1,729%.

Miscellaneous impairments of sufficient severity to classify the applicant as a substandard risk showed a mortality ratio of 562%.

It seems from an analysis of these mortality ratios that Hypertension Alone showed a lower mortality ratio than we expected although it was still almost three times that of the insured controlled diabetic. Albuminuria alone resulted in a very high mortality ratio and is an adverse prognostic factor in Diabetes. The Juvenile Diabetic who develops his disease at an early age is also a poor risk and cannot be considered to be insurable within our present mortality limits. Poor control showed moderately high but not uninsurable ratios. Poor supervision does not appear to render the applicant uninsurable but it is doubtful whether it is wise to insure a diabetic individual who has had insufficient exposure to a trained medical observer.

Causes of death

Clinically, Diabetes is known to accelerate the development of atherosclerotic lesions with advancing age. In addition, coronary heart disease of significant degree is common in juvenile diabetics in the third or fourth decade when microangiopathy, especially nephropathy, is advanced and when terminal myocardial infarction occurs in approximately 25% of these cases. Thus, the increased incidence of ischemic heart disease involves older diabetics in whom arteriosclerosis has been accelerated and younger diabetics who have severe diabetes of long duration in which age per se or hypertension has little effect.

In our mortality study (Tables XII and XIII) 41.3% of all deaths by number of individuals were due to Arteriosclerotic Heart Disease. At ages 20—39 there were 21% of deaths compared to 10% in the United States for the year 1962 as listed in the Vital Statistics for that year — a percentage increase of 110%. At ages 40—69 the percentage increase varied from 20% to 24%. These percentages demonstrate an increased incidence of Arteriosclerotic Heart Disease in the diabetic individual at all ages being most marked however in the younger age groups.

Out of 633 deaths by number of individuals in the study, 392 or 59.1% were due to Cardiovascular Disease and 9.2% to Renal Disease. 6.3% of deaths were due to malignant neoplasms, 4.4% to Diabetes (Coma and unspecified cause other than Diabetes) 1.7% to Diseases of the Digestive System, 4.1% to Accidents and 15.2% to other diseases.

Conclusions

We have accumulated a body of data which is unique in insurance and clinical medicine in that it pertains to a population which may be considered to be a cross section of the diabetic population of the United States. It reflects varying philosophies of diabetic management, transcending the experience of a single clinician or groups of clinicians working together in specific geographic sections of the country. It embraces mechanics, farmers, physicians, clerks, executives and laborers of all types from all economic and social classes. It, however, does not include the very old, the very poor and the very sick — the groups who are not insurance applicants. It is the first mortality study of diabetic applicants in the Life Insurance Industry in which both the issued and declined cases were traced to determine the mortality ratios for both groups.

Table XII. *Diabetic mortality study, 1951—1961*
Observed through 1966 anniversary of application

Classification of causes of death

Causes of death	Number of deaths	Percent distribution	Number of individuals	Percent distribution
Malignant neoplasms	48	6.6	42	6.3
Diseases of the cardio-vascular system	424	58.7	392	59.1
Renal diseases	65	9.0	61	9.2
Diabetes (coma and unspecified)	31	4.3	29	4.4
Diseases of digestive system	13	1.8	11	1.7
Other diseases including unknown	113	15.7	101	15.2
Accidents and suicides	28	3.9	27	4.1
All causes	722	100.0%	663	100.0%

Cardio-vascular-renal diseases

Diseases of cardio-vascular system	Number of deaths	Percent distribution	Number of individuals	Percent distribution
Arterio-sclerotic heart disease with or without angina	33	6.7	30	6.6
Acute coronary occlusion	264	54.0	244	53.8
Other diseases of the heart	80	16.4	75	16.6
Vascular lesions affecting the central nervous system	44	9.0	40	8.8
Other vascular diseases	3	0.6	3	0.7
Total cardio-vascular disease	424	86.7%	392	86.5%
Renal diseases				
Kimmelstiel-Wilson's disease	57	11.7	53	11.7
Nephritis	8	1.6	8	1.8
Total renal disease	65	13.3%	61	13.5%
Total cardio-vascular-renal disease	489	100.0%	453	100.0%

Table XIII. *Diabetic mortality study, 1951—1961*
Observed through 1966 anniversary of application
Expected deaths based on the Equitable's select mortality table 1953—1958

Deaths due to arteriosclerotic heart disease including coronary heart disease as a proportion of all deaths in the same age group

Age at death	Number of deaths by individuals	Proportion in study	Proportion white male in U.S. population 1962	Percentage increase of study over general population
20—29	4	12% } 21%	2% } 10%	500%
30—39	26	23	16	44
40—49	51	42	34	24
50—59	97	49	40	23
60—69	80	49	41	20
70—79	16	44	39	13

In summary, we believe that this mortality study has shown that certain conclusions may be drawn from diabetics who apply for life insurance:

1. The mortality declines progressively with increasing age at time of application.

2. The mortality increases with increasing duration of the disease particularly in the age groups below 40. The mortality ratios are markedly higher for the same durations of the disease in the Juvenile Growth Onset Diabetic than in the Adult Maturity Onset Diabetic.

3. The age at Onset of Diabetes is the most significant factor in mortality and showed the highest mortality ratio of the study at ages 14 and under. The Juvenile, insulin dependent diabetic, is a poor insurance risk and it is doubtful whether he can be safely insured within our current mortality limits.

4. Poor control shows about two and a half times the mortality of the well controlled group.

5. Diabetics on diet alone or diet and oral medication show lower mortality ratios than the insulin dependent diabetics.

6. The presence of albuminuria on examination was an extremely unfavorable prognostic factor with a mortality ratio of 1,197%.

7. 68.3% of the deaths were due to Cardiovascular-Renal Disease with almost 60% due to Cardiovascular Disease Alone.

In closing I would like to express my thanks and appreciation to all the companies that furnished us with data on the status of the individuals in our declined cases. Without your cooperation this mortality study would not have been possible.

The prognosis of lung sarcoidosis on the basis of catamnestic investigations

K. Wurm · E. G. Ewert · M. Romacker

It is estimated that in the Federal Republic of Germany there are about 10,000 to 20,000 people suffering from lung sarcoidosis. On the basis of this figure it is however not possible to judge the significance of this disease, either in relation to those concerned or in relation to public health. We require details as regards the average duration of the disease, its consequences on the ability to work and its final outcome, be it disablement or death.

There are no usable statistics available although the world literature on sarcoidosis has extended beyond range of sight. First of all there is a lack of morbidity statistics. There is no legal duty to report sarcoidosis and there are still many cases which are not recognised as such and even a higher percentage is not discovered because of the latent course of the disease.

Mass X-ray and enlistment examinations have improved the detection of sarcoidosis in recent times. These results relate however only to a limited part of the population and the observation period is too short in comparison to the duration of the disease which is often of long-standing, so that up to now no reliable morbidity statistics are available. It comes therefore as no surprise that the mortality figures given in the literature vary from 5.5 to 28.1% (Sones). There is a total lack of representative information covering the duration of the disease and its consequences from the socio-medical point of view.

Our case records at the Höchenschwand Clinic of 5400 patients suffering from sarcoidosis, covering the period 1950 to 1968 appeared to us to be suitable to make a useful report on the subject of the prognosis of this disease. In connection with an extensive documentation on sarcoidosis that is being made possible by the financial support of the Institute for documentation at Frankfurt, 1000 patients who stayed at the Höchenschwand Clinic between the years 1953 and 1963 were this year subjected to a catamnestic investigation on the basis of suitable questionnaires. The doctors who treated the patients after discharge from the clinic were requested to put all X-ray plates taken by them after discharge at the disposal of the clinic. Our catamnestic investigations are therefore based on our own case records, our interpretation of the X-ray plates, including those received from other sources, and the information given by the patients or their survivors.

Results of questionnaires of 1000 patients suffering from sarcoidosis covering the years 1953—1963

No reply		No X-ray films		Reply and X-ray films	
no reply received	could not be delivered	not sent	not examined	still alive	dead
305	134	108	31	390	32
439=43.9%		139=13.9%		422=42.2%	

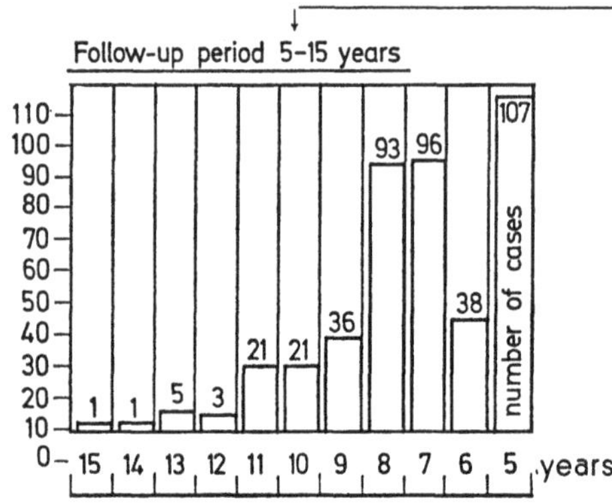

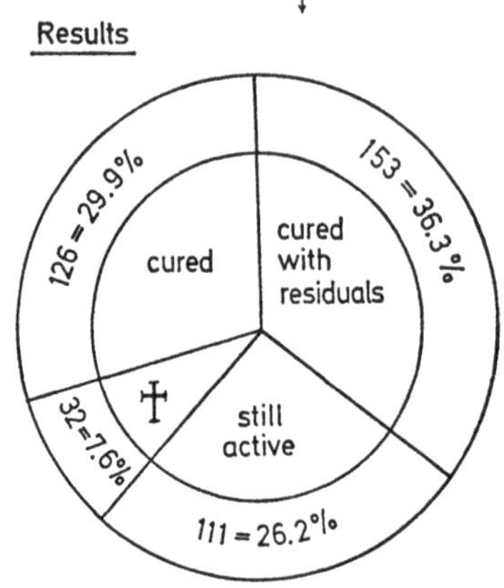

On the basis of the result of our inquiries we divided the 1000 patients into three groups as follows:

We received no reply from 439 patients of whom there were 134 cases in which the questionnaire could not be delivered.

Another 139 patients filled in our questionnaire but did not enclose the requested X-ray films.

The remaining 422 patients returned the completed questionnaire together with the desired X-ray films. The histories of these 422 patients suffering from sarcoidosis were fully investigated. The duration of the follow-up periods were from 5 to 15 years, on average 8 years.

Of these 422 patients 29.9% were cured in 1968. We considered a patient as cured when he was free from subjective symptoms, when he was fully capable of work, when roentgenologically there was restitutio ad integrum at the utmost slight anatomical residuals without any indication of diminished respiratory function and no relapse for 3 years after termination of corticoid therapy.

In 36.3% of cases a cure was effected, with residuals, that means that there were no signs of active disease judged by the absence of any relapse for at least three years, but there were permanent anatomical changes of a greater degree combined with functional impairment. Still active lung sarcoidosis was present in 111 patients, i. e. in 26.2% of the cases which still required treatment in 1968.

32 of the patients were no longer alive in 1968. In 12 cases only sarcoidosis was the cause of death; in 10 other cases it was certain that death was not in

Initial findings of the 422 patients under investigation

Stages			Course of disease		Age of patient			Known duration of disease		Lung findings			Trend of disease		
I	II	III	acute	chronic	<30	30—50	>50	→ 2 y.	>2 years	slight	moderate	serious	regressive	static	progressive
129	241	52	39	383	189	156	77	308	114	82	285	55	180	107	135

any causal relationship with sarcoidosis and in the remaining 10 cases the cause of death was not known. The survival time of those patients who died of sarcoidosis was on average 12 years reckoned from the date of discharge from the Höchenschwand clinic.

The survival time is however not identical with the duration of the disease because in many instances the disease had already been present for a number of years on admission to the clinic.

In 111 patients out of 422 under observation, i. e. 26.2% of the cases, sarcoidosis was still active and rerequiring treatment so that the final outcome of the disease is not yet known. A change for the worse has to be expected because in this group there are above all patients showing poor response to treatment or extensive findings. It is to be expected that a considerable number of them will have a cure with after-effects and also an increased mortality is likely. Nevertheless we feel that the figures ascertained so far are probably representative for the entire case records. If we compare the group that is being investigated with the group of patients from whom no reply was received, it is striking to see that according to our records the average age in the latter group is lower and that on an average the initial findings are less extensive, factors which speak for a favourable prognosis.

In the following survey we gain an insight into the state of the disease with the 422 patients under investigation at the time of the first course of medical treatment.

In the majority of cases, i. e. in 241 patients stage II had already been reached and in two thirds, i. e. in 285 cases the roentgenological findings were of a moderate and in another 55 cases of a serious nature. The acute course of the disease with its great tendency to spontaneous healing was present in 9.2%, i. e. in only 39 cases, whereas the primary chronic course of the disease with 383 cases represented more than 90% of those under observation.

The following figures provide us with some information about the further development of sarcoidosis after the first course of medical treatment.

Method of therapy during first course of medical treatment		Number of courses of medical treatment					Early results upon termination of the first course of medical treatment	
No medication	Corticoid therapy	1	2	3	4	5—8	0 → +	++ → +++
128	294	264	93	47	13	5	213	209

late results after 5—15 years							
roentgenological				†	socio-medical		
regr.	progr. → regr.	static	progr.		capable of work	disabled as a result of sarcoidosis	disabled as a result of other disease
45	75	205	75	32	335	41	14

Course of disease

During the first course of medical treatment 294 patients were subjected to corticoid therapy while the remaining 128 patients had only a climatic cure without any specified medicinal treatment.

On termination of the first course of medical treatment about half of the patients, namely 209, showed a good to very good remission while the other half had roentgenological findings which did not improve at all, or only slightly. In respect of late results it is surprising that during the observation period 5 to 15 years after termination of treatment only 45 patients had a continued progressive regression, 205 patients had stationary findings and the remaining 150 patients experienced recurrences which necessitated fresh medical treatment. The number of recurrences of 35.6% is surprisingly high. It follows that the first course of treatment has to be considered unsatisfactory.

If we look for the causes of the recurrences we see that there are a number of conspicuous distinctions as compared to the group of 238 patients without recurrences.

The character of the group under observation is for the following reasons a priori less favourable than for the group with which comparison is made: The advanced stages II and III occur much more frequently, the initial roentgenological findings are distinctly more serious, higher ages are much more frequent, the duration of the previous illness was on average considerably longer but above all the tendency to a progressive course of the disease was much more distinct in the group with recurrences and in 45% of the cases was more than twice as high as the corresponding share in the group without recurrences. Furthermore the group without recurrences had a much higher percentage of spontaneous healings of the acute form of the disease, i. e. 13.8% in contrast to 3.9% in the group with recurrences.

The coincidence of all these factors produces a negative aspect in respect to the course the disease is expected to take. The high frequency of recurrences is a result of inadequate treatment. In the group of recurrences the cases with

Comparison of the cases with and without recurrences following the first course of medical treatment

	No recurrences in 238 cases	1 or more recurrences occurred in 152 cases	Number of deaths 32
Classification of stage of disease			
Acute attack	33=13.8%	6= 3.9%	—
Stage I	68=28.6%	21=13.8%	1
Stage II	126=52.9%	97=63.9%	18
Stage III	11= 4.7%	28=18.4%	13
Age of patient			
up to 30 years	133=55.8%	54=35.5%	2= 6.2%
31 to 50 years	75=31.6%	71=46.8%	10=31.3%
over 50 years	30=12.6%	27=17.7%	20=62.5%
Known duration of disease			
up to 2 years	217=91.2%	79=52.1%	12=37.5%
more than 2 years	21= 8.8%	73=47.9%	20=62.5%
Roentgenological findings			
slight	68=28.6%	14= 9.2%	
moderate	157=65.0%	106=69.8%	22=68.7%
very marked	13= 5.5%	32=21.0%	10=31.3%
Previous course of disease			
spontaneous regression	67=28.1%	16=10.5%	1= 3.6%
regression following corticoid therapy	72=30.3%	20=13.1%	4=12.5%
stationary without treatment	39=16.4%	38=24.9%	6=18.8%
stationary despite corticoid therapy	14= 5.9%	9= 5.9%	1= 3.6%
progressive without treatment	25=10.5%	30=19.7%	11=34.4%
progressive despite corticoid therapy	21= 8.8%	38=25.9%	9=27.1%
Therapy during the first course of medical treatment			
no medications	101=42.5%	26=17.1%	1= 3.6%
corticoid therapy	137=57.5%	126=82.9%	31=96.4%

Of the 32 deaths 12 died of sarcoidosis.
In 10 cases the cause of death was not sarcoidosis, and
in 10 cases the cause of death was unknown.

treatment of short duration on low dosage corticoid medications prior to admission to the clinic occurred conspicuously often. Of a more serious nature is the fact that after discharge of the first course of treatment the necessary long-term treatment was discontinued prematurely, either on the instigation of the medical attendant, sometimes in order to avoid claims for regress on the part of the sickness fund or because of want of understanding. Very frequently the attending physician who continued treatment feared the side-effects of corticoid medications and administered insufficient and therefore ineffective dosages. In three-fourths of these 150 patients the cause of recurrence was the insufficient corticoid long-term therapy. It is however gratifying to note that according to our observations the number of recurrences has decreased over the past few years, most likely as a result of greater experience of the doctors with corticoid therapy. Today the early results are likewise more favourable than those obtained in respect of the first 1000 sarcoidosis patients. In any case we would recommend that the initial treatment with corticoids be carried out under stationary conditions. Depending upon therapeutic indication, responsiveness, compatibility and side-effects the subsequent treatment of the individual case as out-patient is determined. Treatment under optimal conditions and a sound attitude of the patient are decisive factors for the further course and therefore the final outcome of the disease. Special therapeutic complications may arise in those relatively rare cases in which a long-term corticoid treatment is not possible because of incompatibility (excessive corticoid side-effects), because of existing contra-indications or corticoid-resistance.

From a socio-medical point of view there were 41 patients who were classified as disabled as a result of sarcoidosis. We feel, however, that such a classification was not in all cases justified. In contrast to tuberculosis where it is assumed that an active process which requires treatment disables a person to such an extent that he is not able to work, this does generally not apply to an active sarcoidosis under treatment because the general health and general performance are often only insignificantly impaired. The decisive factor for disablement in lung sarcoidosis is the functional picture and not the X-ray finding.

As regards the often discussed question whether there is any causal relationship between sarcoidosis and tuberculosis it seems to me worthy of mention that in none of the 422 catamnestically investigated sarcoidosis cases, was sarcoidosis followed by tuberculosis. We do not wish to discuss what final conclusions can be drawn from such an apparent existing antagonism between the two diseases.

It should be noted that calcifications may occur in sarcoidosis. In our total cases under investigation we have seen so far 150 cases in which calcifications which are characteristic of sarcoidosis have taken place. These appeared for the most part in great number and extensively in the region of the mediastinal lymph nodes. In earlier times if calcifications were present one was inclined to diagnose tuberculosis rather than sarcoidosis.

The realization that calcifications may occur with sarcoidosis is not only of diagnostic interest. Calcifications appear mostly in the early stages of healing so that evidence thereof is of importance for therapeutic indications and prognostic interpretation.

The results of the foregoing investigations enable us to discern the fundamental principles which characterize the course of sarcoidosis and offer us a preliminary basis for the prognostic interpretation of sarcoidosis from a clinical and sociomedical point of view.

The case records of the patients of the Höchenschwand clinic are in more than one respect not free from selection and therefore the figures mentioned are not yet definitely binding. Definite conclusions may only be expected when the results of the extensive sarcoidosis documentation started recently, in which also other institutions in the Federal Republic of Germany are taking part, are known.

What can be done to retard ageing and to increase expectation of life? *

Alexander R. P. Walker, D. Sc.

Introduction

In the young, to what extent can sequelae of ageing be delayed? In the adult, among whom degenerative conditions or diseases are already clearly apparent, can these changes be slowed down, or even arrested? Still further, if heroic endeavours be made, is it all feasible to put the clock back a little and cause stigmata to regress? These questions have occupied man's contemplation, imagination, and ingenuity since early times, when the desire for long life was very much heightened because of its brevity from famine, pestilence and war. Down through the ages, the search for an "elixer of life" by alchemists and others was vigorously pursued. In our generation, ageing and its diverse ramifications have been studied extensively, especially by experiments on animals. The results of observations have been discussed and speculated upon in numerous papers, reviews, books, symposia, and seminars.

The purpose of the present contribution is to emphasize afresh that some of the sequelae of ageing do lend themselves to effective manipulation and to favourable alteration, and that this should be recognized, even although the likelihood of the knowledge available becoming implemented on a large scale is believed to be virtually nil. In seeking to present this view within a short space, the aspects to be discussed will be limited to changes in relation to growth rate, weight, blood pressure, and atheroma. Of the large number of biochemical components that have been studied and could be deliberated upon, it will be possible to refer only to blood lipids and glucose tolerance. The parameters mentioned will be discussed in relation to (a) populations in the past, (b) primitive and emerging populations, and (c) present-day western populations. Next, the factors primarily responsible for the adverse changes that have taken place will be discussed as they occur in the three types of population cited. Finally, the question will be considered — in the middle-aged or elderly, among whom stigmata of ageing are obvious what changes *must* be made, by those who are

* From the C.S.I.R. Human Biochemistry Research Unit, South African Institute for Medical Research, Johannesburg, South Africa.

truly determined, to ameliorate further degeneration, and hence promote an increase in expectation of life?

While it is well understood that the parameters cited usually increase with age, frequently far more than is desirable, many hopefully think that since expectation of life has risen considerably within the last few generations, medical science and its application can be relied upon to facilitate still further increases. The first part of this belief is abundantly true. Over the second part, however, while there is euphoria on the one hand, there is complete scepticism on the other.

At the commencement, it is necessary to have a clear idea of the past and present situations regarding expectation of life.

Changes in expectation of life

Changes in expectation have been summarized recently by ROCHE [1]. He stated, "A baby born to any mother, during the reign of the Emperor Augustus, could expect to live for 23 years. There was almost certainly no gain during the Middle Ages, but life expectancy slowly increased during modern times, and by 1850 had reached 40 years. By 1900, another upward move had brought it to 47 years. Today, in most Western countries, life expectancy at birth has reached the impressive figure of 70 years." But he continued, "Our smug satisfaction with this achievement, however, needs correction. While in the last half century, medical science succeeded in pushing life expectancy at birth up by some 20 years, the life expectancy of a 65-year old during the same period has risen by less than one year. To put it bluntly, while we have almost eradicated infectious illnesses of childhood and adulthood, we have not succeeded in preventing degenerative processes and malignant growth, the two most common diseases of middle life and old age." In some populations, however, for example, Swiss males, JECKLIN [2] has shown that the gains in the elderly have been somewhat greater than those indicated by ROCHE [1]. Nevertheless, the meagre increases remain conspicuous especially if one accepts as valid the earliest of life tables, that of HALLEY [3] (the astronomer), for the population of Breslau in 1687.

As demonstrated in Table I, the most tremendous change responsible for increased expectation has been the enormous increase in the survival rate of the young. This is illustrated further in Table II.

By way of further illustration, in the middle of the 19th century, when the population of England and Wales was about 17 million, individual epidemics accounted for the following: In 1849, cholera caused 50000 deaths; in 1871 to 1872, smallpox accounted for 42000 deaths; and in 1873, scarlet fever was responsible for 30000 deaths [4]. Mortality from these diseases in most Western countries has now been almost wholly eliminated. It will be appreciated that even if still further reductions in mortality occur in the young (JECKLIN [2] thinks that further reductions are unlikely), such will have only a very slight effect on expectation of life of adults.

A point of major importance, probably insufficiently appreciated, is the far less satisfactory mortality position in men compared with women. This is demonstrable from South African data [6] (Table III).

Table I.
Expectation of life in Breslau in 1687, and of Swiss males from 1876—1880 to 1948—1953

Age	Breslau 1687	Swiss males 1876—1880	1929—1932	1942—1950	1948—1953
				Expectation of life	
Years	Years	Years	Years	Years	Years
0	33.5	40.6	59.3	64.0	66.4
20	33.61	38.8	45.4	48.8	50.2
40	21.78	24.8	28.6	31.0	31.9
60	12.09	12.2	13.9	15.1	15.7
80	5.74	4.1	4.6	4.9	5.2

Table II. *Changes in infantile mortality rate in England and Wales* [4, 5] *(per 1000 live births)*

Period	Infantile mortality rate
1838—1901	150
1910	110
1925	75
1955	25.4
1965	17.5

Table III. *Expectation of life at birth in South African populations in 1952*

Population	Males (years)	Females (years)
Whites	64.57	70.08
"Coloureds" (Eurafrican)	44.82	47.77
Asiatics (largely Indian)	48.51	54.75

Other evidence of this differential is provided by the proportions of the sexes seen at post-mortem. At an International Symposium on the "Etiology of Myocardial Infarction" held in Detroit in 1962, Thomas [7] stated, "Looking at total deaths in this country (U.S.A.), we find that in the age group of our autopsies — mostly middle-aged or older people — for the past ten years or so men have been dying off faster than women, at a rate of just below 3 : 2. If we go on at the rate we are going now, we will have a population of women entirely".

Chief causes of death in western populations

Any attempt to retard ageing and to significantly increase expectation of life thus necessitates reductions in the chief causes of deaths of adults. When vital statistics of different western countries (among whom expectation is at its highest) are examined, it can be seen that the proportions of deaths due to leading causes are much the same [8]. Coronary heart disease accounts for about a third, cancer a quarter or less, and "strokes", 10—15 per cent, of total mortality. Accordingly, any enquiry and discussion on ageing and of efforts to reduce its lethal sequelae, approximates to asking what can be done to reduce the high toll exacted by these diseases, especially by coronary heart disease. It must be made clear, however, that the prime motive by no means is to increase the percentage of centenarians in a population. At best, the over-riding objective is to reduce the number of deaths from the diseases mentioned. At second best, the cardinal aim is to seek to prolong life by delaying death from such causes until later age periods. This is particularly the case with coronary heart disease in which the increase in mortality appears to be involving those under 45 years of age at a faster rate than older sections of the population [9].

It is now proposed to discuss the subjects of growth rate, etc., referred to earlier, as seen in the contrasting types of population mentioned. The chief aim will be to seek to learn of the circumstances under which the minimum changes in these components, compatible with good health, occur.

Differences in sequelae of ageing seen in contrasting populations

Growth rate:

The growth of children in primitive and underprivileged communities almost invariably is slower than that of Western communities. With prosperity, increases in growth rate occur, just as they have done in Western populations over the past few generations, and the usual conclusion is reached over previous caloric, etc., insufficiency. But in what measure is this view valid? In the case of Bantu, as discussed elsewhere [10, 11], should we be gratified when their children attain the growth rate of the offspring of prosperous Bantu, or should we admit inferiority of health status until the growth rate is the same as that, say, of Iowa White children [12]? In this respect we have to ask ourselves, as Garrow [13] has done: "Is the normal growth for a North American child necessarily optimal? Are the children who are smaller than this necessarily malnourished?". Experimental studies on animals have amply demonstrated that slower growth makes for retarded senescence [14]. But does this apply to human beings? Roche [1] has related that a hundred years ago, English children attained maximum height at about 25 years. At present the figure is about 16 years. Among our rural Bantu, maximum height is reached at about 20 years. Does *their* slower growth make for delayed ageing? It is of interest to note that, allowing for differences in population numbers, in South Africa there are at least twenty times more Bantu over 100 years old than Whites [15]. While the ages of many of the former are uncertain, there is no doubt that, proportionally, far more Bantu than Whites do reach a great age. But to return to desirable rates of growth, we have to face the fact that (obvious stunting and obesity apart) too little is known about these rates to permit categorical assertions or recommendations. Knowledge will be forthcoming only by undertaking long-term studies on children in different socio-economic strata. In groups where the lower and upper quartiles, in terms of growth, display the same broad picture of clinical and subjective well-being, it would seem wholly unwarranted to insist on further acceleration of growth [10, 11]. To give further point to this view, consider the situation regarding skinfold thickness. Data in Table IV illustrate the problem in mind.

Table IV. *Skinfolds of males of 16—19 years*

Skinfold thickness (mm)	Rural South African Bantu	Urban South African Bantu	South African Whites (Johannesburg)	English Whites (Liverpool) [16]	U.S.A. Whites (Iowa) [17]
Triceps	6.9	7.2	7.6	7.5	13.9
Scapula	6.6	7.7	9.7	9.7	12.4

It will be observed that Iowa males have far greater skinfolds than the other groups, White and Non-White. But it would be preposterous to consider that such superiority indicates proportionally higher nutritional status. The growth rate "standards" now recommended and demanded of Western children have questionable physiological basis; as Cathcart [18] and other workers [19] have stressed, they may be far removed from the optimum. On account of these and other considerations, Roche [1] has stated, "If, as has been suggested, degenerative diseases occur at younger ages than in the past, this may be related to the acceleration of maturation that has been observed in some body systems."

Weight:

Certain primitive or less privileged populations after reaching adulthood gain little or no weight with age, e. g. indigent Indians [20], African Samburu [21], and Bushmen [22]. But with urbanization and westernization the situation changes [23, 24]. In Durban, in an investigation on groups of urban Bantu, average weights of males and females between the ages of 20 and 64 years were given as 142 and 158 pounds, respectively [25], corresponding figures for Zulu studied by us in rural areas were 133 and 131 pounds [23]. The relatively sudden change from inadequate nutrition to overnutrition which has occurred recently in other emerging countries, for example, Chile [26], has also resulted in obesity being perhaps the main nutritional problem of adults.

Average weights of children and adults are now greater than in past generations. A recent study has indicated that within the last century in England, average height at maturity has increased by about an inch per generation. But weight has increased much more proportionally than height, and the adult male population is becoming progressively more obese. Young and middle-aged men of the same height and age now weigh 15 lb. more than 30 years ago [27]. In this respect, it is illuminating that the average American white male and female is 19 and 15 lb., respectively, heavier than their British counterparts [28]. Commenting on this change, STAMLER [29] maintains that "excess weight and the common American pattern of gain in weight from young adulthood into middle age are highly prevalent and highly serious risk factors from premature hypertensive and atherosclerotic cardiovascular diseases. The problem is not the severe, marked, huge, circus type of obesity, but rather the 25 or 40 pounds put on gradually over the years — the moderate, creeping obesity so common among middle-aged American men." In one extensive study among insured persons, HUTCHINSON [30] reported that 20 and 23 per cent of the men and women, respectively, weighed 10 per cent or more than the average; moreover, 6 and 11 per cent weighed 20 per cent or more than average weight. It may be noted that the urban-rural differential described above in emerging populations, no longer prevails in present-day western populations; it was not apparent in the Health Examination Survey in U.S.A. in 1960—1962 [28].

What is the significance of overweight in relation to mortality? In some overweight groups, according to HUTCHINSON [29], the incidence of fatal heart disease is doubled, the incidence of vascular lesions of the central nervous system is significantly increased, the incidence of death from renal disease is two and one half times that expected, and the incidence of deaths attributed to diabetes is increased by three and one half times. In terms of life expectancy, in U.S.A., persons who are 25 per cent overweight at 40 years are believed to have a decreased expectancy of about 20 per cent [29]. Thus, at 40 years, the expectancy of males, assuming it to be 32 years (Table I), is shortened by severe obesity to $25^1/_2$ years, i. e. by $6^1/_2$ years.

Blood pressure:

Some primitive or underdeveloped populations show little or no rise in blood pressure with age, e. g. indigent Indians [20, 31], African Samburu [21], and Bushmen [22], certain Australasian [32] and South American populations [33], and Gilbertese [34]. Among rural Bantu, mean pressures for age appear to be only slightly less than those reported for White populations [23, 24]. With urbanization, however, blood pressure tends to rise; in some groups the elevation is enormous. In one investigation on Natal Bantu [25], between the ages of 45 and 64 years, proportions with diastolic pressure of 90 mm mercury or higher, in a comparison of rural and urban areas, rose from 26 to 44 per cent in the case of males, and from 36 to 59 per cent in the case of females. In Transvaal Bantu we have found the same trend, although to a less marked degree [24]. In West Africa [35], blood pressures of Africans are of much the same order as those of Whites; on the other hand, the pressures reported for American Negroes (whose forbears came from West Africa) are higher than those of U.S.A. Whites [36]. This phenomenon of rise in blood pressure with increasing westernization appears to be the usual response, and has been reported from diverse parts of the world, — Easter Island [37], India [20, 31], New Zealand [38], and Russia [39]. It is important to note that an urban-rural differential in blood pressure is no longer conspicuous in western countries, such as the United States [40].

Blood pressure has been reported to be higher with particular types of stress, for example, under conditions of industrial noise and tension [39]. Yet even in situations far removed from intensive urban life, differences have been noted in those pursuing contrasting occupations. Thus, in a population in the Faroe Islands, the blood pressure of the pastoral farming community was found to be significantly lower than that of the fishing section with their more rigorous existence [41].

Information is lacking on the blood pressures of Caucasian populations in the past. At present, in the United States, according to Master and associates [42], from ages 40 through 64 years, blood pressure rises such that 22.7 to 38.7, and 18.0 to 39.3 per cent, respectively, of men and women, have a diastolic pressure of 90 mm mercury or more. Page [43] has stated, "Even though it is often not thought of, the problem of the control of arterial hypertension is, next to that of atherosclerosis, civilized man's greatest cardiovascular problem". Hypertension is regarded by UNGERLEIDER [44] as "the most commonly encountered form of chronic disease in U.S. adults".

What is the handicap linked with hypertension? This may be illustrated by the example given recently by GILL [45], who referred to a 40-year old man with blood pressures 135/90 mm Hg. According to the 1959 Build and Blood Pressure Study of the Society of Actuaries [46], males aged 40 years with the above-mentioned pressures are exposed each year to a risk of death one and one half times as great as that of normal insured individuals. GILL indicates that the life expectancy of the man referred to is reduced by 4 years, i. e. from 32 to 28 years.

The reduced expectations just mentioned from overweight and from hypertension superficially may not seem inordinately large. GILL [45], however, has put the situation in perspective by referring to cancer; he stated that "if deaths ascribable to malignant neoplasms were entirely eliminated, it would increase the average span of insured males, aged 40 years, only slightly over 2 years. Compare this with the 4-year reduction caused by a modest blood pressure elevation", namely, that of 135/90 mm mercury cited.

The adverse influence of hypertension on the development of coronary heart disease has been evident in a number of careful prospective and other studies [47—50]. The bearing of hypertension on cerebral-vascular disease is adequately established. For example, in the prospective study of MORRIS et al. [49] on 687 London bus drivers, among the moiety with "normal" blood pressures, no cerebral vascular episode occurred in the 5 year observation period; yet, in the hypertensive group there were 10 cases.

Atheroma:

In contrast to changes in weight and blood pressure, the development of atheromatous lesions does not lend itself to precise measurement in the living. Numerous studies have shown that lesions are present to a much less severe degree in primitive communities compared with western populations (among whom advanced changes in young adults are common [51]), and that changes with age occur far more slowly [52]. In elderly urban Bantu, we have found that the calcium concentration of aorta is much the same as that of White subjects of 20—29 years [53]. Observations of a similar type have been made elsewhere [54]. Furthermore, in a recent study of aortic calcification in series of 100 each of aged rural Bantu men and women, obvious evidence of calcification was detected radiologically in 5 and 2 per cent of men and women [55]. In Whites, the proportions with such calcification found in one study in the United States were 37—66, and 46—60 per cent, respectively, in males and females, aged 65 years and over [56]. The foregoing studies relate to aorta. There is sufficient information, however, that similar, although not necessarily parallel, changes occur in the coronary vessels. The New Orleans workers, MCGILL et al. [52], maintain that the extent and severity of coronary atherosclerosis determine the risk of ischaemic heart disease in a population. While fatty streaks and possibly the development of fibrous plaques may be accepted as inevitable accompaniments of ageing, it is clear that the severe lesions of ulceration and calcification seen so often in the aorta and coronary vessels of Western adults are not physiological.

Serum lipids:

Among Western populations and the prosperous moiety of Non-White populations, serum cholesterol and other blood lipids rise with age [57, 58]. Yet only a slight increase, or even no increase, occurs among many underprivileged Non-White populations, for example, poor Indians [31], rural Japanese [59], and certain groups of South African Bantu [60, 61]. In the latter we have found that ultracentrifuge serum lipo-protein Sf. values, also Gofman's Atherogenic Index, reveal Bantu of 60 and more years to have data similar to Whites of 15—24 years [62]. However, in more privileged groups, the situation has now deteriorated. Serum lipid data on populations in the past are not known. Numerous prospective studies on Western populations have indicated a close correlation between the moiety with elevated cholesterol levels and their proneness to ischaemic heart disease [47—50, 63, 64]. It has been noted that serum cholesterol data on rural Bantu (and similar communities) are less than in urban groups [60]. An urban-rural differential in this component was no longer apparent in the United States Health Examination Survey [58].

Glucose tolerance abnormality and diabetes:

In western nations, glycosuria, glucose tolerance abnormality, and diabetes are common [65, 66]. But they are less common or even rare among certain communities, for example, Alaskan Eskimos [67], and the indigenous populations of Papua and New Guinea [68]. Among emerging populations such as New Zealand Maori, there is adequate evidence that diabetes is increasing [38, 69]. Information is accumulating that the same situation prevails with Bantu [70, 71]. We have found glucose load glycosuria to be rare in elderly rural Bantu males, 0.5 per cent, but to be much increased in prosperous urban Bantu of the same age range, 5.0 per cent [71]. In the Health Examination Survey [66] in U.S.A. the corresponding figure for males was 20—25 per cent, and in the Bedford [66] study in England, 37.5 per cent. The greater proneness of subjects with poor glucose tolerance to coronary and cerebral vascular disease has been referred to in a number of investigations [66, 72, 73].

It would now seem reasonable to reach the following conclusions. Rapid growth in the young is not essentially meritorious, and may be deleterious. Gain in weight and increase in blood pressure after reaching adulthood are neither physiological nor inevitable. The development of severe atherosclerosis, especially of severe calcification of arteries, need not occur. The marked rises in blood lipids and deterioration in glucose tolerance with age, — neither is irrevocably linked with ageing. The important point, which will be enlarged upon later, is that the environmental conditions which favour minimal changes in these components with age are not encountered in the West and can only be simulated with great difficulty.

It is now proposed to discuss the changes in environmental factors which are believed to be primarily responsible for the differences in the sequelae of ageing found in contrasting populations.

Changes in environmental factors associated with or responsible for differences in sequelae of ageing

Diet:

As described elsewhere [23], less than a hundred years ago, among Whites, the diet was bulky and thus militated against overeating. Nowadays, this is facilitated because most common foodstuffs are palatable, concentrated, and highly digestible [74]. In Britain a century ago, average daily consumption of bread made from whole grain or lightly milled flour was about 600 grammes *per diem;* moreover, among the under-privileged a large amount of oatmeal porridge was eaten [75, 76]. The consumption of bread now averages about 200 grammes *per diem* [77]. The current daily consumption of sugar in Britain is about 160 grammes, which contrasts with the figure of 60 grammes *per diem* consumed in Britain in 1881, and less, earlier in that century [77—80]. The present daily consumption of fat in Britain averages about 140 grammes; the figure was 80 grammes in 1881, and about 30 grammes in 1835 [77, 78]. Similar, although probably more marked, changes occurred in the United States. YUDKIN [80] believes that the vast increase in sugar consumption in the developed countries may well have contributed to the increased incidence not only of obesity but also of coronary thrombosis and diabetes. Briefly, the chief changes in dietary pattern that have taken place are increased calories, higher consumptions of fat and sugar, and lower consumptions of carbohydrate.

Among primitive and emerging populations, intakes of calories, animal protein, fatty foods and sugar, are lower, often much lower, than in the Western nations; intakes resemble those found in the latter at the turn of the century [24]. Yet among emerging countries, marked changes in diet, toward a Western pattern, are already occurring.

Other dietary changes, too, however, may be relevant. Thus, DAHL and associate workers [81] have suggested that the high salt content of Western infants' diet (from cow's milk and proprietary food-stuffs) may have a relationship to hypertension in the adult. One particular component of the diet to suffer considerable reduction is crude fibre. Initially, roughage was believed to be of great relevance to general health, partly because of its rôle in bowel motility. The salient questions which arise are — what is the significance to health when stools are hard or soft, large or small, formed or formless, eliminated regularly or infrequently, with ease or with pain [82]? In the early days, clinicians had no doubt that constipation was deleterious. Sir LAUDER BRUNTON [83] and many others discoursed expansively on the relevant toxaemias and other ill effects. For a period soon after the turn of the century, patients with "intractable constipation" were subjected to mutilating operations (severe at that time) whereby various lengths of the large gut were removed. Sir WILLAM MCEWEN [84], in his Huxley lecture in 1910, sarcastically stated: "There is at present openly expressed discontent about the alimentary tract. Some are persuaded that there is an intestinal whorl too much, and that this extra whorl requires to be short circuited". As late as 1929, an Annotation in the *Lancet* [85] indicated that "constipation is undoubtedly the cause of much ill-health". About that time, arising from careful studies of able gastroenterologists like ALVAREZ [86], it was claimed that the direct ill effects of constipation are largely psychogenic, and that the "well recognized train of symptoms: malaise, headache, hebetude, poor appetite, coated tongue and foul breath", associated with a loaded intestine, are mainly of nervous origin. On the other hand, there have been a number of investigations on animals which have associated a high roughage diet not only with improvements in health, fertility, and longevity [87], but with reduced atheromatous lesions [88, 89]. In man, long-term studies on Bantu and White prisoners by ANTONIS and BERSOHN [90] revealed that a rise in crude fibre intake increased excretions of steroids and bile acids; such may well influence the general picture of lipid metabolism of the body [60, 90, 91]. In a recent epidemiological study on Indian railway sweepers [92, 93], mortality from ischaemic heart disease was fifteen times higher in the south than in the north, although the fat intake was nine times higher in the north. Conditions of work, economic status, etc., were equal. The northerners, moreover, were heavier and smoked more. The higher prevalence in the south was thus exactly the opposite to that expected. The chief difference between the two groups was that the roughage content of the diet in the north was high and in the south low. It is, of course, tempting to accord aetiological importance to crude fibre in the given context. The findings at least suggest that the bearing of fibre on pattern of disease in populations with contrasting intakes should be investigated more intensively.

Physical activity:

What is the situation regarding activity in primitive and emerging population? Firstly, in respect of the young, — in a study in north-eastern Transvaal, observations were made on poorly-nourished Bantu children, severely infected with bilharzia and other helminths. It was found that in a race of 600 yards, the Bantu childrens' performances were equal to, and in the younger age groups superior to those of White children [94, 95]. In the same region, we have obtained ample evidence of good physical performances of 600 and 1200 yards races, and have confirmed earlier reports [96] of the superiority of Bantu over White children in Harvard Step Test scores [97]. It has been stated by RODAHL et al. [98] that "maximal oxygen uptake is undoubtedly the best indication of physical work capacity". In studies in Philadelphia on White boys of 10 years weighing about 77 lb., a mean figure of 1.13 litres oxygen per minute was found [98]. This is the same figure as that reported for German boys of the same age and weight at Freiburg [99]. Yet, in western Transvaal at an altitude of 4000 ft., in tests on poorly-nourished Bantu boys infected with vesical bilharzia, of the same weight although of course older, a virtually identical figure, 1.1—1.2 litres per minute was obtained [100]. Clearly, primitive children, even when handicapped in the respects indicated, have a high level of physical fitness. The important point, however, on which emphasis is laid, is that with urbanisation, as shown by SLOAN [101], this high level of fitness falls in Bantu children. Among Whites, too, there is evidence of deterioration. Thus, the maximal oxygen consumption data of the U.S. and German children cited above are far lower than the "standards" for Swedish children reported by ASTRAND [102] in 1952; it is now doubted if the latter are still valid for present-day Swedish children [98]. Regarding older children and young White adults, investigations on British students have shown that only one eighth take any noteworthy physical exercise over the weekend [103].

Among adults, a century or more ago, as many as 19 out of 20 men were employed, directly or indirectly, in agriculture; at present, in the United States, only 1 worker in 20 is so employed. In the process of time even in occupations that are normally associated with activity, the actual amount of physical work carried out is decreasing, on account of labour-saving devices. In the last war, the motor fitness of American recruits was described as "appalling" [104]. There is no doubt that the habitual "on the job" activity of Western populations has fallen considerably, and that still further decreases are likely to take place. PASSMORE [105] sardonically has written, "Americans are gluttons for sedentary work. At a recent medical conference in New York during January, a visitor could not but wonder that the lecture hall was packed with people from 9 a.m. to 6 p.m. for 6 days of the week, yet, when walking in snow covered Central Park before breakfast he was as lonely as on a Scottish moor." One outcome of decreasing activity is that appetite is no longer a reliable guide to nutritional need; eating to satiety often involves over-eating.

In relation to the bearing of physical activity on degenerative disease, numerous studies have correlated activity inversely with proneness to coronary heart disease. In Israel, for example, BRUNNER [106] has reported that myocardial infarction had a three-fold higher incidence in sedentary compared with active workers in collective settlements. FRANK et al. [107], from a study undertaken in New York, have reported a three-fold differential in early mortality subsequent to a coronary heart disease episode between least and most active men; furthermore, among least active smokers the differential was nine times that obtaining the most active non-smokers.

Cigarette smoking:

The unfavourable bearing of cigarette smoking on coronary atheroma, and on the incidence and prevalence of coronary heart disease, has been well demonstrated [108—110]. Among primitive communities, as in western populations in the past, smoking is uncommon, but as contact with Whites increases, the habit is becoming more widely practiced. At present the prevalence of smoking in urban Bantu is reported to be about half that of Whites [111]. An opinion of the bearing of smoking on future degenerative disease in the young has been given by HAY [112]. He stated "In 1964, there were in New Zealand some 436 432 White males under the age of 15 years. Assuming that two-thirds will become smokers and that present mortality rates in New Zealand continue for the next 60 or more years, and using the mortality ratios derived from the combined prospective studies, my colleagues have calculated the following impressive facts. When all these boys have ultimately died, the number of excess deaths from lung cancer attributable to smoking will be about 14000. For coronary disease the position may not be so clear but we have estimated that ultimately some 125000 boys will die from coronary disease and about 40000 of these deaths will probably be excess deaths due to smoking. These calculations are not very exact but they do give rough estimates. One must surely conclude that this constitutes a public health problem of major significance." The greater bearing of smoking on mortality from coronary heart disease compared with lung cancer is insufficiently appreciated.

Changes in the general "milieu" of living:

Before the industrial revolution, in some countries more so than in others, our forefathers in rural areas scarcely ever left the region in which they were born; and although often very poor, and having numerous anxieties, they pursued their labours in the tranquil atmosphere depicted in Gray's "Elegy in a Country Churchyard" [23]. Large families of eight or more children were usual. Nowadays, the moving and uprooting of families are commonplace, their size is much smaller, competition is severe, and the acquiring of money and of status symbols are the main goals of ambition.

Exposure to increasing westernization is occurring with emerging populations, certain of whom, like the Bantu, are being subjected to a rapidity of urbanization far greater than that which occurred in the past with Whites. There is the continuing sophistication of diet, and an increase in sedentary occupations. The regularity of kraal life in tribal communities, the production of large families — these are known to fewer Bantu as the trek to centres of population continues. Within the changing contexts of diet, activity, and stress, perhaps the most far-reaching hindrance to health is failure in adaptation. Scotch [113], in his thoughtful study of socio-cultural factors in the epidemiology of hypertension in the Zulu, has concluded that "the individuals most likely to be hypertensive were those who maintained traditional cultural practices and who were thus unable to adapt successfully to the demands of urban living".

In western populations, the differentials referred to which prevail between urban and rural emerging populations, in respect of weight, hypertension, serum cholesterol concentration and glucose tolerance, are no longer conspicuous. Nevertheless, it is noteworthy that differences in mortality from certain degenerative diseases between town and country still remain, and this fact is insufficiently appreciated. In his National Atlas of Disease Mortality in the United Kingdom, Howe [114] showed that mortality rates from coronary heart disease, from certain types of cancer, and from "strokes", were lower in rural areas compared with urban centres of population. For example, in respect of "strokes", in Londonderry County, rural and urban figures were 52 and 132 per cent of the standard mortality [114]. In the United States, Berkson and co-workers [115] have shown that mortality from all cardiovascular diseases is approximately twice as high in Chicago as it is in rural Illinois. This type of difference was also noted in a nation-wide survey in U.S.A. [116]. In Norway [117], it has been shown that six rural centres of population studied had mortality rates for arteriosclerotic and degenerative heart disease and malignant tumours only a third of the corresponding rates obtaining in Oslo for the period 1952—1961. To give a further example, it has been reported from Israel that there is a six-fold higher incidence of myocardial infarction in Tel-aviv compared with rural collective settlements [106]. The foregoing depict a remarkable situation, the validity, elucidation, and causes of which require much further study.

Apart from differences in mortality rates associated with region of abode, Russek [118] has drawn attention to widely different coronary heart disease prevalences occurring in different sections of the medical and legal professions, presumably arising from their being exposed to different intensities of stressful conditions. Furthermore, the different prevalences of this disease in population groups exhibiting contrasting behaviour patterns has been investigated intensively by the Los Angeles workers [119]. In addition, the bearing of cultural mobility on coronary heart disease has been studied by Syme et al. [120]; in their investigations in California, they found that men who had held 3 or more jobs in their lifetime and had held none for extended periods had an episode ratio 4 times higher than men who had held one or two jobs and who had held these jobs for extended periods of time.

The trend of alterations in context, attitudes, and demands of living, has engendered misgiving and dismay, and such have been expressed not just recently but in past generations. Thus, over a hundred and fifty years ago, Wordsworth wrote, "The world is too much with us; late and soon, getting and spending, we lay waste our powers". A century later, fifty years ago, Muller [121], with most remarkable prescience, wrote, "There can be no doubt that modern man wears himself out more rapidly than did his forbears. Competition is keener, work is more exacting, and technical advances make increasing demands. There is little, alas, that we can do to change this state of affairs. The railway, the motor car, the aeroplane, the telegraph and telephone have contributed only in appearance to ease of living. This armed peace exerts slower but more continuous pressure than many a previous war. Men are grinding each other gradually, instead of destroying each other suddenly. In spite of all humanitarian efforts these items are inflexible. If this trend continues, we may expect the speed of attrition to rise and the age limit for working capacity to fall. We must attempt to re-adjust the balance of our lives by creating rational, extra-professional activities, by attaching greater importance to recreation, and above all by developing sources of interest within ourselves which will compete at least in some measure with the greatly increasing interests which assail us from without. Concentration of effort instead of the all too common dispersion, turning our interests inwards instead of ever more outwards, simplification of our mode of living, especially of our food, instead of ever greater luxury, re-establishment of contact with Nature, which has been lost to a large extent, and continuous medical supervision — these might well be the most effective weapons for conducting this struggle against death." At present, half a century later, these words cannot be improved upon. At one recent Symposium on the subject, according to Dr. PAUL DUDLEY WHITE, it was concluded that "Stress is life: and you had better enjoy it".

It is, of course, plausible to lay heavy responsibility on changes in *milieu*, particularly stress, for much of the alterations that have occurred in the health patterns of the elderly. Stress, however, cannot be satisfactorily measured. While accepting as valid the foregoing items of evidence (e. g. differences in urban-rural mortalities, etc.), it would be prudent to remain cautious over attaching too great a weight to the influence of stress on ageing and degeneration. Undoubtedly, there are varieties of stress, some of which may well have a much more profound influence on metabolism than others. The anxieties of our ancestors in relation to poverty, disease, etc., must often have been severe; yet coronary heart disease was not a problem with the elderly. This currently applies to people such as Bantu, who, additionally, have fears and superstitions of which Whites have little conception. Among Whites there is no record that the particular stresses of war time increased the prevalence of coronary heart disease; the converse was rather the case. Furthermore among Whites pursuing mundane and competitionless occupations, myocardial infarction is very far from being rare. Notwithstanding, it would seem legitimate to conclude that in a western context, some individuals with certain temperaments and in certain vocational settings, are much more prone than others to the disease. No claim has been made regarding the bearing of stress on cancer, moreover, cerebral vascular disease appears to occur just as readily in Bantu as Whites.

What retarding measures are feasible?

Alterations in the total context:

What are the chances of extrication from this context or *milieu* of western life? It is considered that the changes in the sequelae of ageing described are implicit, inherent, and "built in" to present-day existence, and it is believed, moreover, that environmental conditions are propitious for still further deterioration. Modern diets tend to greater palatability, with the likelihood of greater intakes of calories, fat, sugar, and animal protein. Foods high in bulk-forming capacity are becoming decreasingly popular. More and more people have the means of running cars. Even among the South African Bantu, a greater proportion own cars than is the case in certain European countries. National fitness campaigns seem to make little headway with pupils who have left school, and scarcely touch the middle-aged. Despite enlightened warnings, decreases in the practice of smoking are slight. Finally, present-day man is likely to meet more, not less, vocational responsibility, competition, etc., in the future.

In terms of seeking *total* re-orientation, to what extent can changes be made? In practice, a White person does not become a Bantu just by lowering his intake of fat or his level of serum cholesterol [122, 123], nor a Masai simply by considerably increasing his habitual activity [124]. Nor upon request or with intention does he become relaxed and lessen his competitive or anxious personality merely by resolving that it shall be so. In terms of groups, there are those with low prevalence of coronary heart disease such as the elderly but very active Swiss mountain farm workers [125]. Can the relevant protecting features, including presumably their regular and tranquil manner of life, really be adopted? In the recent study in Norway [117] already cited, it was shown that certain farming communities, as compared with the population of Oslo, had far lower mortalities from arteriosclerotic and degenerative heart disease and also from cancer. But how can the sophisticated man of Oslo hope to take on the necessary protective features of the rural farm worker's life? Or how can the elderly in Bucharest incline toward the life led by Danube Delta fishermen [126]? Then there are Seventh-Day Adventists [127, 128]; does adoption only of their diet, and non-smoking habits, etc., confer the lower prevalence of coronary heart disease that they enjoy? What of the rôle of their religion and philosophy?

To those who attach considerable aetiological or aggravational importance to stress, and bearing in mind the observations of RUSSEK [118] and others [129], — consider first the medical profession. At middle life can the general practitioner change over and do the work of the more favourably placed consultant? Or the surgeon become pathologist or skin specialist? In the legal profession, can the advocate change to the more favourable attorneys' work? Can the director of companies reduce his responsibilities by directing one company instead of ten? Or a president step down to vice-presidentship or lower? Can the headmaster abdicate his responsibilities for less onerous duties, or the mine-captain, or the works foreman? or indeed, any one who feels the burden of stressful employment no matter how lowly the occupation? At the time of life when fears may begin to assail the individual that his way of life is more taxing than he would wish, it is deemed that it is virtually impossible for him to disentangle himself; he is tied, indeed, trussed, for reasons of prestige, financial obligations, retirement pension, and so forth. If he survives until retirement age he has a measure of choice of what to do, but what is the proportion of persons at that age who constructively change their manner of life?

Alterations in particular factors

Diet:

As already indicated, the pattern of diet and manner of life pursued in western countries in the past when degenerative disease, particularly coronary heart disease, was far less prevalent than at present, is similar in certain aspects to that now prevailing in some primitive and emerging populations. But this context also obtained in measure in certain European countries during the last war, when the staple cereal was of high extraction rate, consumptions of fat and sugar were reduced, and physical activity increased. Several studies showed that in the populations most affected, deaths from diabetes fell, the rate of development of atheroma decreased, and mortality from coronary heart disease became slightly reduced. Admittedly, there are limitations in the relevant evidence, which have been pointed out and discussed by many workers, such as KEYS [57]. Notwithstanding, it may be accepted that certain of the effects of ageing *were* retarded. This changed context, of course, was involuntarily imposed by war-time conditions for a limited period; moreover, the ageing sequelae referred to reverted to peace-time levels once dietary and other restrictions were lifted. But under other conditions of privation and change, for example, in prisons, there is some evidence that ageing effects are delayed. At Pretoria Gaol, ANTONIS and BERSOHN [131] have shown that by dietary manipulation the blood lipid picture of White prisoners in a few weeks can be changed to that of Bantu, and *vice versa*. In addition, certain studies, both in U.S. [132] and South Africa [123] have indicated that under prison conditions, mortality from coronary heart disease is less than in the general population.

One of the earliest serious attempts to combat overweight, hypertension, and hypercholesterolaemia, was that of STAMLER et al. [133] in Chicago in 1958, undertaken on high risk men of 40—59 years. The overall changes in daily nutrient and foodstuff intake involved less calories and reduced intakes of chiefly fat. As a result of these nutritional alterations, a highly significant overall decline in serum cholesterol was induced in the order of 14.7 per cent. Weight and blood pressure were significantly reduced. In a sizable number of men, these falls resulted in their attaining levels of serum cholesterol, weight and blood pressure below those set as criteria for the high risk designation.

Several prospective dietary investigations have been carried out on subjects with or without myocardial infarction. Eight of such major studies have been undertaken, according to HICKIE [134], with favourable results in six. Perhaps the best known and most rewarding is that being pursued by the New York Anti-Coronary Club. Volunteers of 40—59 years in whom was no obvious evidence of coronary disease, changed from a diet in which, briefly, the proportions of calories were derived as follows, — protein 18 per cent, carbohydrate, 42 per cent, and fat, 40 per cent, to a diet in which calories were supplied by protein, 19 per cent, carbohydrate, 48 per cent, and fat, 33 per cent. No changes were made in activity or smoking habits. After 7 years of observation there were one third of the number of new episodes of myocardial infarction in the experimental compared with the general population [135]. In Oslo, LEREN [136] has studied the effect of a plasma cholesterol lowering diet in 206 male survivors of myocardial infarction over a 5 year period, and compared results with 206 patients who continued on their habitual diet. The experimental diet reduced the incidence of relapses, especially in patients under 60 years. There were 43 new infarctions in the experimental group and 64 in the control group. The caloric intake of the experimental diet was 2400 calories of which 39 per cent were derived from fat (72 per cent of fat was soya bean oil), 15 per cent from protein, and 65 per cent from carbohydrate. Sugar intake was considerably reduced.

Weight:

DUBLIN and MARKS [137] have examined data in the Metropolitan Life study, also the data obtained in the Build and Blood Pressure Study [46] undertaken in 1959. They concluded that reduction of weight by overweight individuals conferred on them more favourable mortality rates, much the same as that of standard risks. The effect of weight reduction by "average" weight individuals, whether it confers on them the reduced risks associated with habitually underweight individuals, is not known with certainty.

Cigarette smoking:

Although heavy cigarette smokers have a death rate two to three times that of non-smokers, on reform this is reduced to normal or, at least, 1.5 times the normal risk [108, 109]. In a study on stress, tobacco, and coronary disease in North American professional groups, RUSSEK [138] reported that cigarette smoking was statistically correlated with the reported frequency of ischaemic heart disease in the groups studied; an unexpected finding was that the prevalence of the disease in ex-smokers became reduced to a level below that for non-smokers.

Blood pressure:

In the dietary treatment of hypertension, as UNGERLEIDER [44] has emphasized, the two chief aspects that lend themselves to change are weight and salt intake. The association of overweight and hypertension, and *vice versa*, has already been discussed. Although vigorous restriction of salt intake, involving lowering sodium intake to 200 milligrammes or less daily has been very successful as a sole measure in controlling hypertension, such restriction is not very suitable for long-term practice. Patients may fare very well during long periods of drastic sodium restriction while living in an institution, but results are far less gratifying on returning home. Nevertheless, with appropriate discipline, it can be done. A reduction in the prevalence of hypertension occurred in persons participating in the Anti-Coronary Club study [135]. A reduction has also been found to occur with sustained increase in exercise; in one investigation a mean fall from 155/95 to 133/85 has been reported [139]. BLACKBURN and PARLIN [140] have stated "The most pertinent question concerning the effect of modern anti-hypertensive therapy on mortality is of considerable interest to the insurance industry as well as to the general public health. There are no insurance mortality data available which permit investigation of this question." There is, however, evidence which indicates that modern anti-hypertensive treatment has prolonged life in persons with cerebral vascular disease and hypertensive heart disease. Thus, in U.S.A. from 1950 to 1960, death rate per 100 000 for "strokes" fell from 182.2 to 139.0 in males of 55—64 years; the figures for females were 156.9 to 103.0 [141].

Physical activity:

Knowledge is lacking of the beneficial effects of increased activity in the middle-aged. In a recent review by Katz [142] in which the bearing of increasing exercise on proneness to coronary heart disease was examined, available evidence was considered inconclusive. Frank et al. [107] in their study of survival after myocardial infarction in relation to activity and smoking habits concluded, "One cannot judge from the data presented whether the relatively inactive adult male who moderately increases his customary level of physical activity thereby acquires the advantage of the lower mortality from first infarction shown by the other (active) men. Nor is it possible to predict how soon such a postulated advantage might appear. The importance of obtaining answers to these questions is evident. Favourable answers would project the exciting possibility that moderate increases in the physical activities of the least active members of an adult male population without prior myocardial infarction might significantly reduce the incidence of, and the morbidity from this manifestation." Cumming [143], in a contribution on physical fitness and cardiovascular health, has made similar comments.

Stress:

In contrast to previous changes deemed feasible and advocated, it is not believed that in the great majority of people affected, the amelioration of stressful contexts is practicable. At middle age, the changing of a person's occupation, or a migration from a big city to a small town or village, is considered to be almost out of the question.

Comment

There is no doubt that the bulk of middle-aged western populations (in Australia, Hickie [134] mentions 40 per cent of males over 40 years), would benefit by favourable alterations in the parameters discussed. Weight could be reduced, blood pressure decreased in measure, the development of atheroma retarded, and biochemical components such as blood lipids and glucose tolerance changed to the good. The situations regarding coronary heart disease also diabetes could be improved; the same applies to "strokes" and hypertensive heart disease. On the other hand, benefits in respect of malignant growths, excluding cancers affected by cigarette smoking, may not be claimed. Quantitatively, what improvement could reasonably be expected? Hickie [134] has compiled figures indicating predicted coronary morbidity after a preventive programme. Expressing expected coronary morbidity as 100 units, he considers that appropriate and severe changes in diet could reduce the index to 50; ceasing to smoke could have the same effect. Increase in exercise could reduce the figure from 100 to 70; reduction in weight, 100 to 85, and reduction in blood pressure, 100 to 75. It might well be asked, should mortality from this disease be reduced by application of one or more of the measures indicated, is it likely that the total death rate would fall correspondingly, or would the people "protected" just die from other causes? In this connection it is interesting to note that Japanese males in California, aged 55—64 years, whose death rate from the disease in 1960 was 254.6, had a death rate from all causes of 1 111 per 100 000. The corresponding figures for U.S.A. males were 901.3 and 2225.2 [141]. Thus, while Japanese males had less than a quarter of the coronary mortality of U.S.A. males, their death rate, although not proportionately lower, was still much below that of U.S.A. males. On the other hand, looking elsewhere, present mortalities from coronary heart disease (420—422) and "strokes" (330—334) are about twice as high in Finland as in Sweden, in the 55—64 year age group, although mortality rate from all causes is slightly *lower* in Finland than in Sweden [8]. Clearly, in population groups embarking on preventive or remedial programmes, a satisfactory picture regarding falls in age specific mortality rates and gains in expectation of life will only emerge from observations undertaken in a long-term manner.

What are the chances of preventive measures being implemented on a *national* scale? Public Health authorities or other medical or health workers may be expected to go to great lengths to encourage people to eat frugally of diets of lesser sophistication, to stop smoking, and to take more exercise in their leisure time. But who will heed? The young regard the perils of middle-age as too far away to concern them. The middle-aged and over have minimal capacity for altering habits of a life time; moreover, many, with defeatism, accept that it is too late to change. In the view of the writer [123], "It would seem to be inescapable that most people prefer to continue to pursue their habitual way of life, which at least has not the physical rigour of the past and to accept the risks of degenerate disease which are implicit in the manner of life prevailing, risks which may well be increased by every milestone of socio-cultural-economic advancement — the rapid growth of the middle-class, the 'Affluent Society', the 'New Frontier', the 'Great Society'." The frame of mind prevailing is such that it cannot be frightened or stampeded into making radical changes. Should it be thought that the danger of the situation is being exaggerated, it may be well to cite the experience of South African Indians. With their rise in prosperity they have very greatly increased mortalities from coronary heart disease, cerebral vascular disease, hypertensive heart disease, and diabetes; the increases are such that already the population has an expectation of life at middle-age *less* than that in infection-ridden rural dwellers in India [144]. But to revert, a widespread alteration in diet and manner of life would seem feasible only if a measure of compulsion were employed. Even Hickie [134], in his detailed and enthusiastic contribution on the prevention of coronary heart disease, reluctantly concludes that for a programme to be really effective "coersion" will be needed. But it would be wholly wrong to say that beneficial changes *cannot* be made. Cassius said to Brutus, "The fault, dear Brutus, is not in our stars, but in ourselves that we are underlings." In a leading article in the *British Medical Journal* [145] on the inheritance of diabetes, it was stated, "It is gluttony more than genes which causes us to degenerate".

There is one very important point which must be kept clearly in mind in any contribution bearing on endeavours to increase expectation of life. In many western countries, the proportion of the population of 65 years and over already exceeds a tenth. This proportion, with implementation of recommendations discussed in this paper, could conceivably be augmented considerably. Unless the increase in expectation of life be matched by a corresponding increase in months or years of effective working capacity, the economic and sociological consequences in the extreme could be disastrous. To add five years to expectation of life would be in the nature of a Pyrrhic victory, if it had the effect merely of adding a proportional moiety to the ranks of the helpless and senile. Nor is this an idle fear. In 1846, it was accepted that "the frequency of mental illness is generally in direct proportion to civilization and the social collisions accompanying it" [146]. Dunlop [147] has recently written with grim humour that "There are lots of men who become mentally enfeebled old dotards at the age of 50 with characters set into a cast like plaster, never to soften again; creatures who move in determinate grooves, the iron yoke of conformity on their necks, the current slogans in their mouths, and the pain of a new idea agonizing to their brains". While this may seem unduly severe, the magnitude of the problem is well recognized [148, 149], and in the changing context that could arise, the problem could be of far greater moment.

Summary

(1) From Roman times until about the beginning of the nineteenth century, expectation of life was consistently low, about 25—30 years. Since then, it has lengthened enormously to about 70 years. Most of this increase is due to the near elimination of mortality from infectious diseases in the young. In the elderly, expectation of life has benefited by only a few years.

(2) Only slight further reductions in deaths among the young appear feasible. In the middle-aged and elderly, a significant increase in expectation of life cannot be accomplished apart from reducing or delaying mortalities from leading causes of death, coronary heart disease, cancer, and "strokes".

(3) To throw light on the practicability of increasing expectation of life of adults, a number of the sequelae of ageing have been discussed, namely, changes in growth rate, weight, blood pressure, atheroma, also serum lipids and glucose tolerance, in relation to (a) populations in the past, (b) primitive or emerging populations, and (c) present-day western populations. The conclusion has been reached that in virtually all the respects enumerated, the increases in levels of these health parameters which occur from adulthood onwards are not physiological.

(4) The factors primarily responsible for these adverse changes in western populations, namely, alterations in diet, activity, smoking, and stress, have been examined as they obtain in the three types of population cited. It has been concluded that all the adverse changes that have occurred are implicit and inherent in the mode of life prevailing.

(5) Arising from the foregoing, the question is posed, — in the middle-aged or elderly among whom stigmata of ageing are already very evident, what changes must be made, by those who are truly determined, to ameliorate further degeneration, to ward off mortality from the diseases mentioned, and hence to promote an increase in expectation of life?

(6) In answer, discussion of available information indicates the following:

(a) Changes in diet such as those made by subjects participating in the New York Anti-Coronary Club study, also the Oslo study, unquestionably were beneficial and resulted in reductions in weight, blood pressure, and in the incidence of myocardial infarction, compared with control populations. Adequate validation is urgently needed of these findings, which illustrate what *can* be accomplished, and whose measure of success conceivably could be enhanced by more stringent changes in diet.

(b) Evidence has demonstrated that sustained reduction in weight by the overweight in time confers on them the lower mortality risks linked with persons of average weight.

(c) A number of investigations have indicated that the stopping of smoking in time confers greatly reduced mortality, not only from cancer of the lung and similarly affected sites, but, in terms of numbers, more particularly from coronary heart disease.

(d) The extent of benefit to be derived from measures for reducing blood pressure, whether by decreasing salt intake or by the use of anti-hypertensive drugs, remains to be defined. Life, however, has been prolonged, and in U.S.A. mortality from "strokes" for example has fallen considerably in the 55—64 year age group.

(e) The extent of the benefit to be attained from increasing habitual activity in the middle-aged, whether during work or leisure time, unfortunately has not been satisfactorily demonstrated.

(f) Furthermore, the profit to be obtained by withdrawing from a more stressful to a less stressful context has not yet been effectively studied.

(7) The benefits described, in terms of falls in mortality, relate primarily to coronary heart disease. But they also apply to "strokes", hypertensive heart disease, and diabetes. Improvements in respect of cancer (excluding lung and similarly affected cancers) are not claimed.

(8) Despite the known favourable results from the changes advocated it is considered that in western populations there is not the intensity of will present to make changes of the magnitude needed to slow down the development of the sequelae of ageing. It is believed that environmental conditions favour further increases in mortality from degenerative diseases, especially coronary heart disease. Should this occur then a diminution of expectation of life is inevitable.

References

1. Roche, A. F.: Ageing in man. Med. J. Aust. **2**, 11 (1964).
2. Jecklin, H.: Extra mortality and expectation of life. Ann. Life Insur. Med. **2**, 1 (1967).
3. Halley, E.: Quoted from: H. Wiesler: The investigation of mortality. Ann. Life Insur. Med. **1**, 3 (1962).
4. Gale, A. H.: Epidemic diseases. Baltimore: Penguin Books Ltd. 1959.
5. Studies on medical and population subjects: No. 19. Regional and social factors in infant mortality. London: H.M.S.O. 1966.
6. South African life tables: Vol. VIII. Bureau of census and statistics. Pretoria: Government Printer UG/49/1960.
7. Thomas, W. A.: In: The etiology of myocardial infarction. Ed. T. N. James and J. W. Keys. Boston (Mass.): Little John and Co. 1963, p. 30.
8. Mortality statistics: Malignant neoplasms; all sites. Cardiovascular disease: 1955—1964 by sex and age. Epidemiol. Vital Statist. Reps. **20**, 401, 535 (1967).
9. Oliver, M. F., and C. H. Stuart-Harris: Present position concerning prevention of heart disease. Brit. med. J. **2**, 1203 (1965).
10. Walker, A. R. P.: Complexity of nutritional problems in developing countries. Bull. int. Acad. Path. **8**, 71 (1967).
11. — Growth rate, longevity, and sequelae of ageing. J. Trop. Paediat. **14**, 205 (1968).
12. Roderuck, C. E.: Nutrition and growth of Iowa school girls. Amer. J. clin. Nutr. **13**, 173 (1963).
13. Garrow, J. S.: Growth of children after malnutrition. Lancet **1**, 278 (1967).
14. Ciba foundation: Colloquia on ageing. Vol. 1. London 1955.
15. Population census, 8 May 1951: Vol. 5. All ages and races. Bureau of census and statistics: Pretoria: Government Printer U.G. 42/1958.
16. Tanner, J. M., and R. H. Whitehouse: Standards for sub-cutaneous fat in British children. Brit. Med. J. **I**, 446 (1962).
17. Hodges, R. E., and W. A. Krehl: Nutritional status of teenagers in Iowa. Amer. J. clin. Nutr. **17**, 200 (1965).
18. Cathcart, E. P.: The mystery of alimentation. Lancet **I**, 533 (1940).
19. Walker, A. R. P.: Optimal intakes of nutrients. Nutr. Rev. **23**, 321 (1965).
20. Padmavati, S., and S. Gupta: Blood pressure studies in rural and urban groups in Delhi. Circulation **19**, 395 (1959).
21. Shaper, A. G., A. W. Williams, and P. Spenser: Blood pressure and body build in an African tribe living on a diet of milk and meat. E. Afr. med. J. **38**, 569 (1961).
22. Kaminer, B., and W. P. Lutz: Blood pressure in Bushmen of the Kalahari Desert. Circulation **22**, 289 (1960).

23. Walker, A. R. P.: Overweight and hypertension in emerging populations. Editorial. Amer. Heart J. **68**, 581 (1964).
24. — Nutritional, biochemical, and other studies on South African populations. S. Afr. med. J. **40**, 814 (1966).
25. Abrahamson, J. H., B. Gampel, C. Slome, and N. Scotch: Sex variation in the nutritional state of urban Zulu adults. I. Weight, skinfold thickness, and skin and mucosal lesions. Amer. J. clin. Nutr. **9**, 217 (1961).
26. Valiente, S., A. Arteaga, and J. Santa-Maria: Obesity in a developing country, — Chile. Proc. 6th. International Congress on Nutrition, Edinburgh, 1963. Gen. Eds.: C. F. Mills and R. Passmore. Edinburgh: Livingstone 1964.
27. Khosla, T., and C. R. Lowe: Height and weight of British men. Lancet **I**, 742 (1968).
28. Weight, height and selected body dimensions, United States 1960—1962: U.S. Department of Health, Education and Welfare. National Centre for. Health Statistics. Series 11, No. 8 (1966).
29. Stamler, J.: The early detection of heart disease. Continued Education Ser. No. 97, p. 57. Univ. Michigan School of Public Health 1962.
30. Hutchinson, J. J.: Clinical implications of an extensive actuarial study of build and blood pressure. Ann. intern. Med. **54**, 90 (1961).
31. Srikantia, S. G., S. N. Jagganatham, and C. Gopalan: Serum cholesterol and blood pressure levels in some Indian population groups. Ind. J. med. Res. **49**, 99 (1961).
32. Whyte, H. M.: Body fat and blood pressure in New Guinea: reflections on essential hypertension. Aust. Ann. Med. **7**, 36 (1958).
33. Lowenstein, F. W.: Blood pressure in relation to age and sex in the tropics and semitropics: A review of the literature and investigation of two tribes of Brazil Indians. Lancet **I**, 389 (1961).
34. Maddocks, J., and R. R. H. Lovell: Body temperature in Pacific Islanders, and its relationship to blood pressure. Brit. med. J. **I**, 436 (1962).
35. Abrahams, D. G., C. A. Alele, and B. G. Barnard: The systemic blood pressure in a rural West African community. W. Afr. med. J. **9**, 45 (1960).
36. Moser, M.: Epidemiology of hypertension, with particular reference to racial susceptibility. Ann. N. Y. Acad. Sci. **84**, 989 (1960).
37. Cruz-Coke, R., R. Etcheverry, and R. Nagel: Influence of migration on blood pressure of Eastern Islanders. Lancet **I**, 697 (1964).
38. Prior, I. A. M., B. S. Rose, and F. Davidson: Metabolic maladies in the New Zealand Maoris. 6th International Congress on Nutrition, Edinburgh, 1963. Gen. Eds.: C. F. Mills and R. Passmore. Edinburgh: Livingstone 1964, p. 618.
39. Maisnikov, A. L.: Diagnostic and pathogenic borderlines between hypertensive disease and atherosclerosis. Amer. J. Cardiol. **5**, 692 (1960).
40. Blood pressure of adults by race and area. United States, 1960—1962. U.S. Department of Health, Education, and Welfare. National Centre for Health Statistics. Series 11, No. 5 (1966).
41. Lygonis, C.: Arterial pressure in a Faroese fishing community. Dan. med. Bull. **14**, 82 (1967).
42. Master, A. M., C. L. Garfield, and M. B. Walters: Normal blood pressure and hypertension. London: Kimpton 1952.
43. Page, I. H.: Persistence of normal blood pressure after discontinuing treatment in hypertensive patients. Circulation **25**, 433 (1962).
44. Ungerleider, H. E.: Anti-hypertensive therapy and its effect on risk evaluation. Ann. Life Insur. Med. **2**, 122 (1964).
45. Gill, A.: An actuarial view of mortality. N. Y. med. J. **63**, 1718 (1963).
46. Build and blood pressure study: Society of actuaries. Chicago 1959.
47. Stamler, J., H. J. Lindberg, D. M. Berkson, A. Shaffer, W. Miller, A. Poindexter, M. Colwell, and Y. Hall: Prevalence and incidence of coronary heart disease in strata of the labour force of a Chicago industrial corporation. J. chron. Dis. **11**, 405 (1960).
48. Dawber, T. R., W. B. Kannel, and P. M. McNamara: The prediction of coronary heart disease. Trans. Ass. Life Insur. med. Dir. Amer. **47**, 70 (1963).

49. Morris, J. N., A. Kagan, D. C. Pattison, M. J. Gardner, and P. A. B. Raffle: Incidence and prediction of ischaemic heart disease in London busmen. Lancet **II**, 553 (1966).
50. Keys, A., and H. Blackburn: Background of the patient with coronary heart disease. Progr. cardiovasc. Dis. **6**, 14 (1963).
51. Enos, W. F., J. C. Beyer, and R. H. Holmes: Pathogenesis of coronary disease in American soldiers killed in Korea. J. Amer. med. Ass. **158**, 912 (1955).
52. McGill, H. C., J. C. Geer, and J. P. Strong: Natural history of human atherosclerotic lesions. In: Atherosclerosis and its origin. Eds.: M. Sandler and G. H. Bourne. New York: Academic Press 1963, p. 39.
53. Andersson, M., A. R. P. Walker, J. Higginson, and W. Lutz: Chemical and pathological studies on aortic atherosclerosis. Arch. Path. **68**, 380 (1959).
54. Hirst, E. A., P. Piyartin, and I. Gore: A comparison of the aorta and coronary arteries. Atherosclerosis in Bang-Kok and Los Angeles. Amer. J. publ. Hlth **38**, 162 (1962).
55. Walker, A. R. P.: Studies of calcification of aorta assessed radiologically in aged South African Bantu subjects. Unpublished work (1968).
56. Bernstein, D. S., N. Sadowsky, D. M. Hegsted, C. D. Guri, and F. J. Stare: Prevalence of osteoporosis in high and low fluoride areas in North Dakota. J. Amer. med. Ass. **198**, 499 (1966).
57. Keys, A.: The rôle of diet in human atherosclerosis and its complications. In: Atherosclerosis and its origin. Eds. M. Sandler and G. H. Bourne. New York: Academic Press 1963, p. 263.
58. Serum cholesterol levels of adults. United States, 1960—1962. Department of Health, Education, and Welfare. National Center for Health Statistics. Series 11, No. 22 (1966).
59. Keys, A., N. Kimura, A. Kusukawa, B. Bronte-Stewart, N. Larsen, and M. H. Keys: Lessons from serum cholesterol studies in Japan, Hawaii and Los Angeles. Ann. intern. Med. **48**, 83 (1958).
60. Walker, A. R. P., and U. B. Arvidsson: Fat intake, serum cholesterol concentration, and atherosclerosis. Part 1. Low fat intake and the age trend of serum cholesterol concentration in the South African Bantu. J. clin. Invest. **33**, 1358 (1954).
61. Bersohn, I., and S. Wayburne: Serum cholesterol concentration in newborn African and European infants and their mothers. Amer. J. clin. Nutr. **4**, 117 (1956).
62. Joubert, F. J., A. van Bergen, I. Bersohn, A. R. P. Walker, and W. Lutz: Serum liproprotein concentrations (Sf. values) in South African Bantu and White subjects. S. Afr. J. Lab. clin. Med. **8**, 10 (1962).
63. Chapman, J. M., and F. J. Massay: The inter-relationship of serum cholesterol, hypertension, body weight and risk of coronary heart disease: Results during the first ten years follow-up in Los Angeles Heart Study. J. chron. Dis. **17**, 933 (1964).
64. Stamler, J., D. M. Berkson, H. A. Lindberg, Y. Hall, W. Miller, L. Majonnier, M. Levinson, D. B. Cohen, and Q. D. Young: Coronary risk factors. Med. clin. N. Amer. **50**, 229 (1966).
65. Keen, H.: The Bedford study. Proc. roy. Soc. Med. **57**, 200 (1964).
66. Glucose tolerance of adults: United States, 1960—1962. U.S. Department of Health, Education and Welfare. National Center for Health Statistics. Series 11, No. 2.
67. Scott, E. M., and I. V. Griffith: Diabetes mellitus in Eskimos. Metabolism **6**, 320 (1957).
68. Campbell, C. H.: Diabetes mellitus in the territory of Papua and New Guinea. Aust. Ann. Med. **2**, 607 (1963).
69. Prior, I. A., B. S. Rose, H. P. Harvey, and F. Davidson: Hyperuracaemia, gout, and diabetes abnormality in Polynesian people. Lancet **I**, 333 (1966).
70. Cleave, T. L., and G. D. Campbell: Diabetes, coronary thrombosis, and saccharine disease. Bristol: Wright 1966.
71. Walker, A. R. P., B. D. Richardson, and S. D. Mistry: Studies in glucose metabolism. Brit. med. J. **II**, 1394 (1964).

72. Epstein, F. H., L. D. Ostrander, B. C. Johnston, M. W. Payne, N. S. Hayner, J. B. Keller, and J. Francis: Epidemiological studies of cardiovascular disease in a total community-Tecumseh, Michigan. Ann. intern. Med. **62,** 1170 (1965).
73. Ostrander, L. D., T. Francis, N. S. Hayner, M. O. Kjeldsberg, and F. H. Epstein: Relationship of cardiocvascular disease to hyperglycaemia. Ann. intern. Med. **62,** 1188 (1965).
74. Walker, A. R. P.: The effect of recent changes of food habits on bowel motility. S. Afr. med. J. **21,** 590 (1947).
75. Brown bread versus white (Editorial): Brit. med. J. **II,** 752 (1937).
76. Smith, E.: Dietaries in the workhouses of England and Wales. Brit. med. J. **II,** 222 (1871).
77. Domestic food consumption and expenditure, 1961. Annual Report of the National Food Survey Committee: London H.M.S.O. 1963.
78. Orr, J. B.: Food, health and income. London: The Macmillan Co. 1936.
79. Drummond, J., and A. Wilbraham: The Englishman's Food. London: Jonathan Cape 1939.
80. Yudkin, J.: Changing food habits. Nature **200,** 728 (1963).
81. Dahl, L. K., M. Heine, and L. Tassinari: High salt content of Western infants diet: possible relationship to hypertension in the adult. Nature **198,** 1204 (1963).
82. Walker, A. R. P.: Crude fibre, bowel motility and pattern of diet. S. Afr. med. J. **35,** 114 (1961).
83. Brunton, T. L.: On constipation and diarrhoea. Lancet **I,** 1483 (1896).
84. McEwen, W.: The function of the caecum and appendix. Brit. med. J. **II,** 873 (1904).
85. Annotation: The nervous element in chronic constipation. Lancet **I,** 1368 (1929).
86. Alvarez, W. C.: Intestinal auto-intoxication. Physiol. Rev. **4,** 352 (1924).
87. Carlson, A. J., and F. Hoelzel: Effect of rich, bulky, and poor diets on fertility in rats. Fed. Proc. **9,** 354 (1950).
88. Coleman, D. L., and C. A. Baumann: Intestinal sterols. Arch. Biochem. **66,** 226 (1957).
89. Moore, J. H.: The effect of the type of roughage in the diet on plasma cholesterol levels and aortic atherosis in rabbits. Brit. J. Nutr. **21,** 207 (1967).
90. Antonis, A., and I. Bersohn: The influence of diet on fecal lipids in South African White and Bantu prisoners. Amer. J. clin. Nutr. **11,** 142 (1962).
91. Walker, A. R. P.: Effect of low fat intake and of crude fibre on the absorption of fat. Nature **164,** 825 (1949).
92. Malhotra, S. L.: Geographical aspects of acute myocardial infarction in India, with special reference to the pattern of diet and of eating. Brit. Heart J. **29,** 777 (1967).
93. — Serum lipids, dietary factors and ischemic heart disease. Amer. J. clin. Nutr. **20,** 462 (1967).
94. Botha, T. F., D. Clarke, and E. Jokl: Medical research in physical education. iv. Health and efficiency. S. Afr. med. J. **19,** 381 (1945).
95. Jokl, E.: Physical activity and body composition: fitness and fatness. Ann. N. Y. Acad. Sci. **110,** 778 (1963).
96. Le Riche, H., D. Riordon, P. Best, A. A. Kinnear, and A. R. P. Walker: The Diepkloof nutrition and health study on Bantu boys, South Africa. S. Afr. med. J. **26,** 207 and 233 (1952).
97. Walker, A. R. P.: Certain biochemical findings in man as they relate to diet. Ann. N. Y. Acad. Sci. **69,** 989 (1958).
98. Rhodahl, K., P. O. Astrand, N. C. Birkhead, T. Hettinger, B. Issekutz, D. M. Jones, and R. Weaver: Physical work capacity. Arch. environm. Hlth **2,** 499 (1961).
99. Reindell, H., K. Koning, H. Rosskamp, and J. Keul: Sport und Schreibtischherz. Arz. H. Fortb. **4** (1959).
100. Wyndham, C. H.: A study of the effects on the capacity for physical effort of bilharzia infection in African children up to the age of 16 years. Proc. Transv. Mine med. Offrs' Ass. 1969 (in press).
101. Sloan, A. C.: Physical fitness of Cape Town High School children. S. Afr. J. Lab. clin. Med. **12,** 46 and 52 (1966).

102. Astrand, P. O.: Experimental studies of physical working capacity in relation to sex and age. Copenhagen: Ejner Munksgaard Forlag 1952.
103. Covell, B., Nasr. El Din, and R. Passmore: Energy expenditure in young men during the weekend. Lancet **I**, 727 (1965).
104. Cureton, T. K.: Physical fitness workbook. St. Louis: Mosby 1947.
105. Passmore, R.: Energy, recreations, and the cardiac patient. Editorial. Amer. Heart J. **71**, 579 (1966).
106. Brunner, D.: In: The etiology of myocardial infarction. Eds. T. N. James and J. W. Keyes. Boston (Mass.): Little Brown Co. 1963.
107. Frank, C. W., E. Weinblatt, A. Shapiro, and R. V. Sager: Physical inactivity as a lethal factor in myocardial infarction among men. Circulation **34**, 1022 (1966).
108. Hammond, E. C., and D. Horn: Smoking and death rates—Report on fortyfour months follow-up of 187 783 men: Total mortality. J. Amer. med. Ass. **166**, 1159 (1958).
109. Doll, R., and A. B. Hill: Mortality in relation to smoking: Ten years observations of British doctors. Brit. med. J. **I**, 1461 (1964).
110. Auerbach, O., E. C. Hammond, and L. Garfinkel: Smoking in relation to atherosclerosis of the coronary arteries. New Engl. J,. Med. **273**, 755 (1966).
111. Higginson, J., and A. G. Oettle: Cancer incidence in the Bantu and "Cape Coloured" races of South Africa. Report of a Cancer survey in the Transvaal (1953—1955). J. nat. Cancer Inst. **24**, 589 (1960).
112. Hay, D. R.: An appraisal of the relation of smoking to health. N. Z. med. J. **66**, 362 (1967).
113. Scotch, N. A.: A preliminary report on the relation of socio-cultural factors to hypertension among the Zulu. Ann. N. Y. Acad. Sci. **84**, 1000 (1960).
114. Howe, G. M.: National atlas of disease mortality in the United Kingdom. London: Nelson 1963.
115. Berkson, D. M., J. Stamler, H. A. Lindberg, and Y. Hall: Socio-economic correlates of atherosclerotic and hypertensive diseases. Ann. N. Y. Acad. Sci. **84**, 835 (1960).
116. Enterline, P. E., A. E. Rikli, H. I. Sauer, and M. Hyman: Death rates for coronary heart disease in metropolitan and other areas. Publ. Hlth Rep. (Wash.) **75**, 759 (1960).
117. Jervell, A., K. Meyer, and K. Westlund: Coronary heart disease and serum cholesterol in males in different parts of Norway. Acta med. scand. **177**, 13 (1965).
118. Russek, H. I.: Stress, tobacco, and coronary heart disease in American physicians, dentists, and lawyers. Amer. J. med. Sci. **243**, 716 (1962).
119. Rosenman, R. H., M. Friedman, R. Straus, M. Wurm, R. Kositchek, W. Hahn, and N. T. Werthessen: A predictive study of coronary heart disease. J. Amer. med. Ass. **189**, 15 (1964).
120. Syme, S. L., N. O. Borhani, and R. W. Beuchley: Cultural mobility and coronary heart disease. Amer. J. Epidemiol. **82**, 209 (1965).
121. Muller, O.: Arterienverkalkung. Stuttgart: Strecker and Schreder 1909. Quoted from G. Schettler: Ethnological and clinical considerations on the relationship between body-weight and arteriosclerosis. Ann. Life Insur. Med. **1**, 100 (1962).
122. Walker, A. R. P.: Coronary heart disease: Limitations to the application to White populations of lessons learned from the underprivileged. Editorial. Circulation **29**, 1 (1964).
123. — Prevention of coronary heart disease. Editorial. Amer. Heart J. **72**, 721 (1966).
124. Mann, G. V., R. S. Shaffer, R. S. Anderson, and H. H. Sandstead: Cardiovascular disease in the Masai. J. Atheroscler. Res. **4**, 289 (1964).
125. Gsell, D., and J. Mayer: Low blood cholesterol associated with a high calorie, high unsaturated fat intake in a Swiss alpine village population. Amer. J. clin. Nutr. **10**, 471 (1962).
126. Steinbach, M.: The normal in cardiovascular disease. Lancet **II**, 1116 (1964).
127. Wynder, E. L., F. L. Lemon, and I. J. Bross: Cancer and coronary artery diseases among Seventh-Day Adventists. Cancer **12**, 1016 (1959).
128. Walden, R. T., L. E. Schaefer, F. R. Lemon, A. Sunshine, and E. L. Wynder: Effect of environment on the serum cholesterol-triglyceride distribution among Seventh-Day Adventists. Amer. J. Med. **36**, 269 (1964).

129. Morris, J. N., J. A. Heady, and R. G. Barley: Coronary heart disease in medical practitioners. Brit. med. J. **I**, 503 (1952).
130. Russek, H. I.: The rôle of heredity, diet, and emotional stress in coronary heart disease. J. Amer. med. Ass. **171**, 503 (1959).
131. Antons, A., and I. Bersohn: The influence of long-term high fat diets on the serum lipid patterns of White and Bantu subjects in a prison research study. S. Afr. med. J. **37**, 440 (1963).
132. Sprague, H. B.: The search for the "coronary" archtype and the Damocles test. Editorial. Amer. Heart J. **33**, 676 (1966).
133. Stamler, J.: Current status of the dietary prevention and treatment of atherosclerotic coronary heart disease. Progr. cardiovasc. Dis. **3**, 56 (1960).
134. Hickie, J. B.: The prevention of coronary heart disease. Med. J. Aust. **I**, 159 (1968).
135. Rinzler, S. H., M. Archer, and G. J. Christakis: Primary prevention of coronary heart disease by diet. Amer. Heart J. **73**, 287 (1967).
136. Leren, P.: The effect of a plasma cholesterol lowering diet in male survivors of myocardial infarction. A controlled clinical trial. Acta med. scand. Suppl. 466 (1966).
137. Dublin, L. I., and H. H. Marks: The inheritance of longevity: a study based upon life insurance records. Trans. Ass. Life Insur. med. Dir. Amer. **28**, 89 (1941).
138. Russek, H. I.: Stress, tobacco, and coronary disease in North American professional groups. J. Amer. med. Ass. **192**, 189 (1965).
139. Judd, J. L., and W. C. Day: A physical fitness programme for patients with hypertension. J. Amer. Geriat. Soc. **15**, 373 (1967).
140. Blackburn, H. W., and R. W. Parlin: Antecedents of disease: Insurance mortality experience. Ann. Life Insur. Med. **3**, 33 (1967).
141. Gordon, T.: Further mortality experience among Japanese Americans. Publ. Hlth Rep. (Wash.) **82**, 973 (1967).
142. Katz, L. H.: Physical fitness and coronary heart disease. Circulations **35**, 405 (1967).
143. Cumming, G. R.: Physical fitness and cardiovascular health. Circulation **37**, 4 (1968).
144. Walker, A. R. P.: Coronary heart disease and future expectation of life. Circulation **37**, 126 (1968).
145. Leading Article: Inheritance of diabetes mellitus. Brit. med. J. **I**, 940 (1965).
146. Panum, P. L.: Quoted from "Mental health in the Faroe Islands". J. Amer. med. Assoc. **194**, 898 (1965).
147. Dunlop, D.: Personal view. Brit. med. J. **I**, 573 (1968).
148. Lewis, A.: Medicine and affections of the mind. Brit. med. J. **II**, 1549 (1963).
149. Notes and news. Senile or psychiatric? Lancet **II**, 867 (1966).

Claims settlement problems in life assurance

W. G. Müller-Matheesen

Insurance companies not only examine applications, issue policies and accept money, but also make benefit payments. Concerning the last subject, we must bear in mind that over and above a very high percentage of purely routine payments there are still a number of problematic cases that are the subject of great controversy. Questions of medicine and law are likewise involved in this respect. The economic structure and the reputation of the insurance company are both at stake.

Due to the very special nature of this field, it might be useful to trace by means of a few examples the general as well as the imponderable features of these difficult cases. The following examples are cases which have occurred at our company during the past years.

Great difficulties are involved now, as in the past, in cases of suicide within the waiting period (here: 3 years). Raestrup tells us in this respect that in each case the beneficiaries had presented a medical attendant's certificate in which it had been certified that the insured, at the time of the act, was not in possession of his entire mental faculties; however, this was in fact true in only about 10% of the cases. We can confirm this by comparing Raestrup's findings with our own experience. It happens that general practitioners combine several contributing factors and also present irrelevant speculations regarding the cause of death as though they were facts, as if the persons at the insurance company who deal with these questions were medical laymen. The following case is comparatively harmless, but typical in the argumentation:

1956, amputation of the right thigh following a traffic accident. July 1963, insurance contract. Stump complications caused by decubital ulcers and suppurations, necessary incisions and fistulas. June 1966 — thus shortly before the expiry of the three-year period — suicide by hanging. The family doctor certified that the patient had been "temporarily without possession of his mental faculties due to the strain of his 10 years of suffering and committed suicide in a state of mental disturbance". We rejected this claim and have heard nothing more about the matter.

When rejecting such claims we usually try to explain to the relatives as clearly as possible our decision from the medical point of view in order to avoid litigation. Recently we have tried to achieve a compromise settlement when the relatives did not accept our decision as we do not wish to enter into court proceedings except for very clearcut cases. Our experiences with the courts and with the medical experts appointed by the courts for cases of suicide have been discouraging. Unfortunately in some instances we have observed some subtle emotional behavior of the gentlemen responsible which — though hardly noticeable or challengeable — nevertheless influenced the entire proceedings considerably. Doctors and lawyers have always felt themselves to be the protectors of the little man in this wicked world and have nominated themselves as social regulators who protect the individual against the mighty institutions. This attitude towards the ill and helpless is part of a doctor's professional ethics, and it happens frequently that he projects this feeling into other aspects of human life. His objectivity may vary with the conditions of the case. For instance, it is a widely known practice of certain doctors to attest certain facts on the request of the patients or relatives and to make out certificates that permit refund of medical expenses or material supplies to which the recipient is not entitled.

To come back to the expert opinion of psychiatrists in court, it appears as if psychiatry were heading in a direction in which the human being is merely a puppet influenced by both its heredity and its environment in varying proportions. In this sense the majority of suicides have been committed in the absence of free will. The judgment of crime and other subject matter is handled in a similar way. This may be interesting from the point of view of epistemology, but in practical life this attitude would make the functioning of our society impossible.

Another example concerning this matter: A 53-year old insurance agent took out a policy of DM 25 000 in 1964 and committed suicide by hanging in 1965. The attending neurologist had made out a certificate for the health insurance, only four weeks before the insured's death, stating that the patient had "a vegetative dystonia during a nervous exhaustion". After the death, the doctor made out a certificate for the relatives of the deceased in which he certified an "endogenic depression". In response to our reproaches he postulated that the certificate for the health insurance had been made out in a "very indulgent manner" in order "to comply with the wishes of the patient". His own therapeutic treatment, however, proved that the certificate had had rather the object of complying with "the wishes of others", for no neurologist sends his patient who is suffering from an endogenic depression to the mountains or the sea for "a change of environment". (Quotation from a written recommendation by the doctor which is also in our possession.) Such a therapy for the psychotic depressive person is not only useless but even dangerous due to the risk of suicide.

Before and during the legal process we succeeded in discovering the following facts: The relatives spoke of the "sensitiveness" of Mr. B. His study at the university was troubled by home-sickness. Although inclined toward philology, he started a study of medicine, from which he changed to law. He failed his first exam in law and never repeated it. During his military service he apparently suffered from a blackout that was interpreted as "a light case of nerves". A trivial car accident was over-emphasized. In his profession, Mr. B. proved to be a failure. The day before the suicide his principal had demanded harshly a better professional performance and had warned him that he would be dismissed if he did not improve. On the same day, Mr. B. tried to cut his arteries. The following day, he committed a successful suicide by hanging. On the basis of the biographical anamnesis and in conformity with the first certificate by the neurologist, we took Mr. B. as a complete failure figure and judged his depressive nature as reactive behavior.

Among other things I maintained at that time in a report for the court: "The real endogenic depression is a melancholy that attacks the sick without any reason and thus reveals the psychotic character. Contrary to this, reactive depression generally is due to comprehensible reasons that are accepted also by the normal individual with the difference that the consequences are not so severe for the well-adjusted personality. This, however, must not mislead us into believing that when reactive depression leads to suicide, free will is excluded. Mr. B.'s decision to commit suicide, a suicide based upon a rational weighing of his situation, is comprehensible and the motive which lay behind the act was directed by his free will. Due to his professional difficulties, Mr. B. was faced with no further prospects and therefore decided consciously to commit suicide. His recent professional experience gave him reason enough to commit suicide. The fact that the majority of people would not react the same way in similar situations does not prove that all suicides act psychotically. A psychasthenic or psychologically unstable person does not require such a strong pressure in situations of conflict as well-adjusted personalities to commit suicide. The frequency of suicides with people like Mr. B. is greater than for "normal" people, i. e. in situations on conflict they have more of a tendency to commit suicide than "normal" people who would require extraordinary pressure. In principle, any person is potentially capable of suicide. Unusual periods such as the last world war have proved this. The main difference lies in the degree of pressure needed to evoke such an act. The type of suicide just discussed has nothing to do with a "psychosis".

The verdict of the Regional Court of Flensburg stated plainly: "As a conclusion, on the basis of the argumentation, it is quite certain that the deceased had committed suicide in a state of a pathological mental disorder in the absence of free will. This was demonstrated convincingly by a specialist in the subject in his written report and during the trial of 18th May, 1967. According to his statements, on the basis of the information given by the relatives of the deceased and by the attending physician, it was perfectly certain that the deceased had suffered from an endogenic depression, i. e. an illness that excluded his free will."

We did not appeal against this judgment as there was little hope of finding an authority that would go against this first opinion without further medical evidence. Any further controversies of experts would remain more or less theoretical. It is characteristic that already in the first instance no regard at all was given to the very opportunistic diagnosis of the attending neurologist.

In the case of a young man of a very low intelligence level, there was a similar disaster. The police were watching this individual because of a car theft. At the approach of a patrol car — which was, by the way, not even looking for him at the time —, he fled into the woods nearby and hanged himself. Apart from the obvious motive, there was no apparent psychotic reaction in the behavior of the suicide although he was intellectually dull. In spite of the psychiatric testimony collected by the court, we won the case at the first stage of proceedings. However after the other party had appealed to the superior court, we had to accept defeat.

As a rarity, we also mention the suicide of a young man who, in front of his relatives, put a bread knife into his heart, just as in ancient times. We shall not, however, make further comments about this case.

The paragraph about suicide in the general insurance conditions should be changed, as the present wording is not suitable for practical use. Suggestions in this respect have already been published.

Great difficulties can arise in differentiating a suicide from an accident. A 47-year old woman insured herself in 1965. In 1967 — within the three-year period — she was found in a state of intoxication from illuminating gas. Later, she died at the hospital. The findings of the police left the question open as to whether this was a case of suicide or an accident. We accepted it as an accident as the intoxicated person was found lying in her drawing room which was separated from the kitchen by another room. Furthermore, the upper part of the kitchen window was open. The circumstances in an act of suicide would have been different. The sum insured was paid. Double indemnity benefits were not attached to the policy.

In the case of a 45-year old physician and university lecturer it was not necessary to investigate the suicide as the company was not liable because of false information given in the Personal Statement. Proposal 1965. Suicide by means of soporifics at a hotel in his home town in 1967. The personal history given in the Personal Statement did not disclose that he had had an encephalitis with cerebral convulsions, that he was addicted to alcohol and sleeping tablets, nor that he had been hospitalized in a neurological clinic for treatment in 1962 and 1964. Due to his not observing the obligation to give complete information, we refused to pay. The relatives of the deceased accepted our decision. No proceedings in court followed. If the question whether the person had died in the absence of free will at the moment of the act had arisen, this matter would have had a different outcome, although, here again, I cannot see without further evidence the absence of free will. It is quite likely that we would have lost a court case.

Recently the Americans have drawn our attention to cases where people for no apparent reason drive head-on into bridge pillars and are killed. They suspect that among these cases there is a large number of disguised suicides. I have also noted in our company cases of persons running their cars into a bridge pillar or a tree under excellent road conditions. However I was unable to find any indications pointing to suicide. Our cases at hand included more often problematic relationships with organic troubles or alcohol so that the question of payment of double indemnity benefits was of primary importance.

A 57-year old taxi driver took out an insurance policy in 1956 and drove into a pillar without applying the brakes of his car in 1965. The road at the site of the accident was straight and in good condition, 9 meters wide and almost dry. We discovered that the taxi driver was seen by his mother-in-law taking a Thomapyrin tablet early in the morning of that day. The mother-in-law said: "Generally he did not take tablets". According to his wife he had been very run down recently and she had told him to see a doctor. At 8.15 a.m. Mr. G. left his house and witnesses (who are known to us) saw him parking his car on the main road at the entrance of a turning to the right. He sat at the steering wheel. The witnesses wondered how a man could park a car at such a dangerous place. After a short while, he continued his drive, and the accident described above occurred. A lacerated wound under the chin with rupture of the base of the tongue was found. No autopsy was performed. We were informed of the accidental death only after the funeral.

We refused to pay double indemnity benefits since — on the basis of all the ascertained details — we could assume with a high degree of probability that the cause of death had been an infarction. All of the policyholder's actions point to a premonitory symptom of an internal emergency, and the type of injury indicated is not satisfactory as an explanation of his sudden death.

A 25-year old man insured himself in 1965. In 1966 he drove with a passenger into a tree on a straight, flat road with full visibility. Both occupants died. The surface of the road was rough and dry, the weather bright and sunny. There could have been no glaring light as the sun was shining from behind. At the time of the accident there were no other vehicles at the site. No alcohol was involved. Because of his age, an internal illness, in particular an infarction could be excluded. Suicide was also very unlikely as there was a passenger in the car. The double indemnity benefits were paid.

At this stage, I should like to draw your attention to the difficulties arising when alcohol is involved. A 26-year old man died as a consequence of a road accident in a heavy snowfall and slush. He crashed into an oncoming car. He had traffic accidents already in 1958 and 1965; the latter involved an alcohol blood content of 1.57‰. The third and fatal accident occurred in 1966. The alcohol content by the Widmark method was 3.01‰; by the ferment (ADH)-alcohol dehydrogenase method, however, it was only 0.38‰. The presence of ether and putrefactive substances was established by gas chromatography. Ether is shown by the Widmark method but not by the ADH method. Because of the presence of these impurities, the double indemnity benefits were paid as after the last accident, there was no proof of alcohol, in spite of his personal history. When determining the alcohol content of the blood, one must watch these things.

The relatives of the deceased subconsciously accept only reluctantly the fact that an internal disease may have caused the accident. Such cases are numerous among accidental death claims. Very varied situations may result from this fact. I should like to mention here an asphyxia by alimentary bolus in the case of a person who had had consumed alcohol.

One morning at 6 o'clock, the wife of a practicing physician saw her 60-year old husband get out of bed and fall in the bedroom. He tried to get relief from the heavy pains on the left side of his chest, but was not successful. Due to the increasing pains towards midday, he went to the hospital. A diagnosis of serial fractures of his left ribs was made. The following day he died of an alleged accident shock. Request for payment from the life and accident insurance was submitted together with the respective medical certificates. No autopsy was performed. We were informed of his death only after the funeral.

From the clinical point of view I had doubts whether rib fractures after a simple fall indoor would cause death by shock after 24 hours. On my request to see the patient's original records, including electrocardiograms and X-rays, only the latter were submitted and these showed that an infarction could be excluded from the electrocardiographic point of view. The chest X-ray did in fact show serial fractures of the left ribs. The medical report did not contain an enzyme diagnosis; the latter could have excluded a fresh infarction categorically. However a leucocytosis and a slight hyperglycemia were mentioned in the surgical report, the only document which was made available to us. On the basis of these data, a myocardial infarction, confirmed by the corresponding clinical picture (first attack in the early morning, fatal reinfarction the next morning), was almost certain. We wrote a second time to the hospital and drew the attention of the head physician to the fact that without carrying out an enzymatic diagnosis a new infarction could not be excluded with certainty and that we would therefore like to have the original ECG for a brief study. We did not get a reply from the hospital and we therefore informed the wife of the deceased that no payment of the double indemnity benefits would be made. Thereafter we have heard nothing further about this matter. Considering the very strange course of this matter, it must be suspected that there existed some arrangement between the physicians at the hospital and the widow for getting the double indemnity benefits. I shall refer again later to such cases.

An elderly chemist died suddenly, during a handball match. We succeeded in having an autopsy carried out by a third party which showed serious degenerative changes of the heart muscle with a recent thrombosis of a coronary vessel. We declined payment of the double indemnity benefits as the fall was caused by a circulatory collapse and the fall in itself would not have been fatal. This case was very clear. Another insurance company in this instance offered an ex gratia payment of 50% of the double indemnity benefits so that we had to follow suit for reasons of public relations. I should like to say a word about the suitability of this kind of procedure in such evident cases. At the very least, the various insurers involved should get in touch with each other. (After my lecture on this subject, I was told by a physician of the other party that they had been in a state of frustration over this matter. Apparently not only a lawyer, but also a physician had taken part in this handball game and the latter, after having studied the clinical picture, rejected heart infarction as the cause of death. In spite of the clear pathological-anatomical evidence, the insurer did not want to get involved in a court case due to the inevitable confrontation with a physician and a lawyer.)

A 65-year old man suffered an apoplectic seizure due to hypertension in 1956. In December 1967, after returning home with his wife late at night, he fell down the stairs and died. It was not known whether or not he had been under the influence of alcohol. Payment was declined since our enquiry with the attending physician confirmed our suspicion of a recurrent and fatal apoplexy. Whether the relatives of the deceased will accept this decision is still pending.

At this point, I should like to draw your attention to the statistical studies in forensic medicine which indicate that 2/3 of all fatal accidents in the home are influenced by alcohol. The percentage of alcohol influence in accidents caused by drivers is not quite as high, I believe; however, it is still significant enough that in all cases of fatal accident the determination of the percentage of alcohol in the blood should also be requested by the insurance company.

Endeavors to clear up completely accidental deaths with the help of medical techniques and investigations with relatives and witnesses is often a very tiresome but undoubtedly worthwhile matter, even if our goal is not avoidance of payment. These investigations cannot be made critically enough as the few cases illustrated in the report have shown. Very often it happens that the relatives, witnesses, and even the attending physicians, give consciously or unconsciously a very simple and conclusive version as to the cause of death which, however, may differ considerably from reality.

The farther away the site of the accident is, the more sceptical one must be. In cases of fatal accidents abroad, where high sums insured are involved, we always try to get an autopsy, no matter what facts have been given to us. In these cases it is advisable to come to an agreement with the other insurers as to the extent of the expenses to be paid and the final decision.

A 50-year old self-employed business-man, who was a diabetic, was reported to have died as a result of an accident during his vacation in Spain. His application dated back to October 1964. His death occurred in May 1967. He had taken out a policy of DM 36 000 with double indemnity benefits. It appeared that the real cause of death may not have been disclosed truthfully as the three-year waiting period for suicide had not yet lapsed. The death certificate given by the Spanish physician some time after the event showed death by drowning, but this could not be confirmed by the autopsy. There were no pathological or anatomical signs of drowning, and no evidence of plankton in the lungs. Our further investigations led us to postulate the following sequence of events: Standing on the cliffs, the insured was suddenly hit from behind by the waves and thrown into the sea. The same occurred to his wife, but she was able to rescue herself. The man must have died from a reflexive heart arrest due to his sudden fall into the water or during his efforts to rescue himself. We were about to refuse payment of the double indemnity benefits on the basis of the results of the autopsy, which excluded drowning. After learning the true facts of the accident, which were confirmed by witnesses, we paid without objection.

Myocardial infarction as the fatal result of certain chronic illnesses or conditions (such as hypertension, disorders of carbohydrate or fat metabolism, overweight, excessive consumption of cigarettes, etc.) very often leads to the annulment of the contract because of the failure of the insured to give complete information.

A 48-year old man: 1960 and 1961 attacks of gastric colic. 1961 medical treatment for disturbances of circulation. Application in January 1962. No negative indications whatsoever regarding health. February—April 1962 alleged influenza. May 1962 ECG with serious findings. Death by infarction in June 1962. According to the certificate by the physician the influenza had induced the heart disease and finally led to death. Rejection of payment. Dismissal of action by the district court of Giessen. One must consider this gastric colic as a remote projection of angina pectoris.

A 50-year old man: 1962—1966 medical treatment. 1964 fatty liver diagnosed by laparoscopy. At the same time diagnosis of coronary and peripheral circulatory disturbances of the arteries due to an excessive use of nicotine. Application in 1965. Concealment of all these health troubles. Death from infarction in 1966. Especially interesting is the argument of the relatives: "The agent of the insurance company told us that it was not necessary to furnish all this information. He said that they had it already in their file from another insurance company."

We fully realize that the insurance company in the case of medical investigations is at a certain disadvantage and dependent on the goodwill of the people involved. This holds true likewise when the application is made as well as when a death claim arises. Also the allocation of the onus of proof in litigations does not change the unfavorable position of the insurance company. We are therefore of the opinion that irregularities must be checked closely in every case. The idea of this is not so much to save the last cent but rather to convince the people concerned (insured and physicians) by our actions that experts are at work whose decisions are made impartially and to the best of their knowledge and belief. It is also to teach them that manipulations of any kind do not pay off. Here, as in the case of the confidential medical service under compulsory health insurance, knowledge of the mere existence of an examining board is certainly the most important and decisive deterrent.

I am opposed to exaggerated leniency, due to the fact that among the claims paid in life insurance, the number of those which could be contested if the real cause were known, is exceedingly high. In addition to this there is the fact that insurance fraud in this country is considered a gentleman's delict. An exaggerated and systematic leniency on the part of the insurer only encourages this growing trend.

I have noted — and would urge that others watch this — that where we had asked for a re-check of medical findings we obtained in the majority of cases surprisingly normal results which could hardly be correct. This occurs especially in blood pressure re-checks. Merely the fact that an examination has been requested is a signal to the insured that "something is going on", and arrangements with the family doctor are not just negative imputations on my part. One of the worst cases I recall is a case of hypertension with all its clinical consequences where I was more in favor to decline the risk than accept it on special terms. The decisive examination of the circulatory system at rest and after exercise showed fully normal readings of the blood pressure, a condition that does not even arise after optimal treatment of such a hypertension.

Even worse: I was officially called by the district management of an insurance company and asked to weigh the applicant "leniently". I was told that the family doctor, who had carried out the first medical examination, had acted in the same way and they did not want a discrepancy to arise between the two reports. My examination had been requested for an increase in sum insured under an existing policy. The insured was grossly obese. Due to this and to other unfavorable findings he found it difficult to get insurance cover. He nevertheless succeeded quite unjustifiably in obtaining a policy on the basis of the first medical examination.

In conclusion may I recall: In cases of evident insurance fraud, it is wrong to think (as policy-holders and courts often do) that it is not so abominable when insurance companies pay outside the strict contractual rules. Far too often insurance companies are considered rich and anonymous institutions and are expected to readily adapt their insurance conditions either freely or due to pressure. However, it must be noted that the insurance company is a "community" composed of little people of the same sort as the unentitled insured considers himself to be. Therefore it is the duty of the insurance companies to administer the capital of the policyholders as impartially as possible. Every system must devote certain resources to educational work. If we fail to do this, our system of private insurance cannot survive.

Author Index

Figures in *italics* are references to the literature. Figures in square brackets are the numbers under which the literature references are cited.

www.ingramcontent.com/pod-product-compliance
Ingram Content Group UK Ltd.
Pitfield, Milton Keynes, MK11 3LW, UK
UKHW051003220926
475831UK00003B/108
* 9 7 8 3 6 4 2 8 5 6 2 2 8 *